Ṭāhā Ḥusain's Education

From the Azhar to the Sorbonne

Ṭāhā Ḥusain's Education

From the Azhar to the Sorbonne

Abdelrashid Mahmoudi

CURZON

First Published in 1998
by Curzon Press
15 The Quadrant, Richmond
Surrey, TW9 1BP

Typeset in New Baskerville by LaserScript Ltd, Mitcham, Surrey
Printed and bound in Great Britain by
TJ International, Padstow, Cornwall

British Library Cataloguing in Publication Data
A catalogue record of this book is available from the British Library

Library of Congress Cataloguing in Publication Data
A catalogue record for this book has been requested

ISBN 0-7007-1027-2

Contents

Abbreviations Used in the Notes

EI²	*Encyclopaedia of Islam,* new edn.
H	*al-Hidāya*
"L'Histoire"	Louis Massignon, "L'histoire des doctrines philosophiques arabes à l'Université du Caire", *La Revue du Monde Musulman,* XXI (1912), pp. 149–157
J	*al-Jarīda*
Al-Madhāhib	David Santillana, *al-Madhāhib al-Yūnāniyya al-falsafiyya fi'l-'ālam al-Islāmī,* ed. Muḥammad Jalāl Sharaf (Beirut 1981)
MK	*Al-Majmū'a al-kāmila li-mu'allafāt al-Ductūr Ṭāhā Ḥusain,* [*The Complete works of Dr Ṭāhā Ḥusain*], Beirut: Dār al-Kitāb al-Lubnānī
Muḥāḍarāt	Louis Massignon, *Muḥāḍarāt fī tārīkh al-iṣṭilāḥāt al-falsafiyya al-'Arabiyya,* ed. Zaynab al-Khuḍayrī (Cairo 1983)
"Rapport"	Idem, "Rapport : Mission d'études sur le mouvement des idées philosophiques dans le pays de langue arabe" (manuscript, 1913)
Tārīkh	Carlo Nallino, *Tārīkh al-ādāb al-'Arabiyya min al-jāhiliyya ḥattā 'aṣr Banī Umayya,* ed. Maria Nallino (Cairo 1970)
"Una conferenza"	Ṭāhā Husein, "Una conferenza di Ṭāhā Husein su I. Guidi, C.A. Nallino, D. Santillana e altri orientalisti Italiani che insegnarono in Egitto", *Oriente Moderno,* XXVIII (1948), pp. 103–107

Preface and Acknowledgements

The present work, which is a revised version of a doctoral dissertation for the University of Manchester, grew out of an initial plan to study Ṭāhā Ḥusain's role as a cultural mediator between the East and the West with special reference to his French writings, which I had collected and translated into Arabic.[1] The plan was subsequently abandoned, but something of it has survived in this work, namely the idea of studying Ṭāhā Ḥusain's educational journey with an eye to his experience and treatment of the cultural encounter between the East and the West. Some of the writings in question have been used and commented upon in the present work. While they do not occupy a prominent place in the argument, they were the main factor behind the choice of this intercultural approach to the subject of Ṭāhā's education.

I wish to acknowledge with gratitude the help I received from Moënis Ṭāhā Ḥusain and the late Dr Muḥammad Ḥasan al-Zayyāt,[2] who made some of the above-mentioned texts available to me. My special thanks go to the former for his amiability and unfailing readiness to answer my queries concerning his father.

I am also grateful to Daniel Massignon and Christian Destrenau who made available to me the as yet unpublished report written by Louis Massignon on his course of lectures at the nascent Egyptian University in 1912–1913.

As the present work makes a point of focusing attention on Ṭāhā Ḥusain's early writings, still scattered in now defunct and rare periodicals, I would like to extend my thanks to all those staff members of the Egyptian National Library who, in spite of the difficult conditions under which they work, have done their very best to facilitate my task.

My warmest thanks must go to Professor C.E. Bosworth without whose support, both scholarly and moral, this project could not have been carried out. His continued encouragement and perceptive comments have been invaluable. I am also grateful to Dr J. R. Smart whose detailed observations have been extremely helpful in editing the text.

Finally, I wish to thank all my friends and colleagues at UNESCO, particularly Ann Cook, Elizabeth Worgaft and Steve Hewitt, who have always been willing to help me through the intricacies of English usage.

Abdelrashid Mahmoudi, Paris

Notes

1 See Ṭāhā Ḥusain, *Min al-shāṭi' al-ākhar* ["From the other Shore"], ed. and tr. Abdelrashid Elsadik Mahmoudi (Beirut 1990).
2 Ṭāhā Ḥusain's son-in-law and literary trustee until his death.

Introduction

At a time when interest in Ṭāhā Ḥusain should be at its highest, there is a scarcity of good books on this great Egyptian writer. In the English-speaking world, Cachia's *Taha Husayn, his place in the Egyptian literary renaissance* (1956) still stands as the main landmark in the field. Apart from scattered articles in learned journals and chapters or sections in general works of reference and Fedwa Malti-Douglas's recent study on Ṭāhā Ḥusain's autobiography,[1] there is, as far as I know, nothing to show that he attracts much attention.

In the Arab world, on the other hand, Ṭāhā Ḥusain has never ceased to arouse the interest of both scholars and popular writers, especially since his death in 1973. Books on him abound, but the problem here is one of quality, as very few of these works are worth reading. In this part of the world, Ṭāhā Ḥusain has fallen victim to polemicists and propagandists of all sorts who, whether they are detractors or adulators, never read him attentively, let alone objectively.

Generally speaking, most Arab readers assume that they know their Ṭāhā Ḥusain fairly well. At its best, his style, which is a unique blend of classical (almost Qur'ānic) and modern Arabic, flows smoothly, discursively and melodiously, with varying rhythms and cadences, moving easily from the intimate and evocative to the grand and oratorical. His Arab readers, or at least his admirers, can be so carried away and lulled into something similar to hypnotic acquiescence as to lose the faculty of judgement. They fail to see that under the smooth and (apparently) transparent surface, Ṭāhā's thought is riddled with all sorts of tension and ambivalence, if not outright inconsistency.

The present work proposes to uncover these turbulent depths. It sets out to trace Ṭāhā's educational itinerary from the village *kuttāb* (Qur'ānic school) to the Sorbonne, and is intended to be a contribution towards a fuller intellectual biography. But although limited in scope, it exceeds at several points the bounds of Ṭāhā's formal schooling and deals both with Ṭāhā's experience of life and his attempts, sometimes running into his maturity, to grapple with the antinomies of his modernism.

To achieve this end, it has been necessary to adopt a stringently historical methodology, where being historical means not only respect for chronological order but also critical analysis combined with sensitivity to change and development. Without such a methodology there is no hope of understanding Ṭāhā Ḥusain.

Much as I appreciate Jābir 'Uṣfūr's *al-Marāyā al-mutajāwira* (Cairo 1983) as the fullest and most important study on Ṭāhā Ḥusain's critical thought, I believe that the work's value is diminished by its structuralist methodology. Parting company with that author's tendency to believe that Ṭāhā's critical thought underwent no essential change, falling as it were within one eclectic formula, I intend to give a more vivid, more dynamic, and I hope, truer picture of Ṭāhā as an ever restless thinker who achieved stability rather late in life, and even then only relatively.

To speak of the methodology adopted in this work as being historical is also to imply that the study is conducted from a specific angle, namely the theme of the modern cultural encounter between Europe and the Arab world. This choice of angle does not need any special pleading; apart from the fact that the subject is highly topical, Ṭāhā's experience of that encounter constituted the major event in his intellectual life as a graduate of the Azhar, the nascent Egyptian University and the Sorbonne. It is true that many other Egyptians, both before and after him, have travelled the same journey from the village *kuttāb* to the Sorbonne, even passing through the same intermediate stages. But Ṭāhā's case remains both unique and highly informative, in that he experienced the encounter more intensely and drew the consequences most methodically in prolific and varied writings of high quality.

As Ṭāhā's educational journey has already been studied, either wholly[2] or partly and indirectly,[3] I should perhaps indicate why I think that the same ground needs to be covered again and why I hope that the present work can fill several gaps in our knowledge. Unlike all of my predecessors, I have adopted a dynamic approach to the subject, whereby the educational environments through which Ṭāhā passed are represented as fields of forces, with the protagonist himself entering the scene as a force in his own right.

While I have especially benefited from Miftah Tahar's work, I have endeavoured to avoid the pitfalls of a purely analytical study of influences, which would be content with detecting and listing Ṭāhā's borrowings from other authors. In pursuing such influences and sources farther and deeper, I have made a point of situating the enquiry in the concrete context concerned, whether at the Azhar or the Sorbonne. In each case, as I have just suggested, the context is considered as a field of forces, in which Ṭāhā is never a passive recipient carrying his *tabula rasa*, but an active agent. The forces involved are on the one hand the ambient climate of ideas (revolving around major issues and preoccupations) and interests and, on the other hand, Ṭāhā's own predispositions, commitments and aspirations. In each case there were choices to be made, but the principle of selection was partly determined by the man's attempt to realize himself.

It is only in this way, I think, that the study of influences can be most fruitful. To illustrate the point, consider the situation, which is frequent in Ṭāhā's case, where a variety of influences are at work. This is particularly true of Ṭāhā's early positivism developed in Egypt in the years 1911–1914, before he travelled abroad or mastered a foreign language. The same is also true of Ṭāhā's radical scepticism concerning the authenticity of pre-Islamic poetry, a point of view which he developed in 1926 but which has a long history going back to 1911. It is amazing how writers on these subjects tend on the whole to explain Ṭāhā's position with reference to one influence (e.g. Nallino for the first case and Descartes' methodical doubt for the second) or, when forced to admit a plurality of influences, are at a loss to determine the respective role or contribution of each. Such problems, I think, can only be solved when all the influences are studied as an interplay of forces within the proper fields thus defined.

In a work such as the present one, where the confluence of two cultures is the main point of focus, the study of influences is essential and must be as exhaustive as possible, but it must also be so refined as to determine precisely and fairly the contribution of each side. Ṭāhā's modernism, being the outcome of his experience of, and reaction to, that confluence, can neither be adequately understood nor evaluated without such a discriminating study.

Another aspect which differentiates the present work from its predecessors is the attempt to base the enquiry as far as possible on the primary sources. While I am aware that the quest for these sources still requires further efforts, I have tried to push the door wide open with regard to the most critical and formative periods in Ṭāhā's journey. The first such period is 1907/8–1914, when Ṭāhā, while still a student at the Azhar, was initiated into secular knowledge and modern forms of thought, thanks to his encounter with Aḥmad Luṭfī al-Sayyid and his enrolment at the Egyptian University. In this case I have made a point of exploiting, for the first time and as amply as possible, the courses of lectures given at the University, especially by Ṭāhā's orientalist teachers, as well as his own early writings, so far unknown or relatively neglected.

As for the second period, which extends from 1914 to 1919 and encompasses Ṭāhā's education in France, I have tried to make as many inroads as possible into the relevant literature, whether relating to the teachings of Ṭāhā's masters at the Sorbonne or to the then prevailing climate of ideas, preoccupations and interests. A massive literature is now available on the French academic world and intellectual life at the highly charged turn of the century. I have tried to the best of my ability to find my way through this intellectual maze, guided by what I took to be the predominant concerns of those involved.

The final outcome, I hope, will, besides being an account of Ṭāhā's education, open the way for a fruitful comparative study of Egyptian and French cultures at the turn of the century. One of the main themes in this domain is how Ṭāhā Ḥusain, and Egypt by extension, received positivism and the ensuing rise of social sciences at the time. The reason why I think that Ṭāhā's case is unique and yet exemplary is that among his contemporaries he was the most passionate about, and the most involved in, that reception. His is truly a test case for examining the question of orientalism, now highly topical, and the question of intercultural dialogue, or conflict, in general.

In trying to recapture his enthusiasm at the prospect of discovering new disciplines (literary study, the history of literature, history and, to a lesser extent, sociology), I have been influenced by Edmund Wilson's beautiful essay on Michelet's discovery of Vico.[4] Bearing in mind the impression left by that most stimulating piece of work which I read a long time ago, I have embarked upon the arduous task of unravelling the whole process through which Ṭāhā assimilated the new knowledge. I hope that I have in this way established Ṭāhā Ḥusain's role as the first modern Arab thinker to have raised the question concerning the methodology of history to something like its previous, long-forgotten, status in Ibn Khaldūn, and to have created a modern history of Arabic literature.

The plan according to which the present work has been conceived may be presented as follows. Chapter I provides a brief outline of Ṭāhā's educational journey, laying emphasis on his experience of blindness as a form of confinement calling necessarily for release or outward movement into the wider world. Chapter II deals with Ṭāhā's education at the Azhar, with the stress being laid on the conflict, not so eye-catching at first sight, but raging all the same, between a conservative current of opinion represented by the Azhari establishment and a reformist trend represented by Muḥammad 'Abduh and his followers. It is within this context that I have situated Ṭāhā's exasperation with, and rebelliousness against, Azhari scholasticism as well as his "discovery of literature".

Chapter III signals the most important turning-point in Ṭāhā's career as a whole, as it examines his encounter with Luṭfī al-Sayyid, as well as his education at the Egyptian University, with reference to the courses taught there. It is at this stage that he makes yet another "discovery", namely that of history. Chapter IV, which takes up the story, studies this discovery as it was worked out in Ṭāhā's early writings.

Chapter V pushes the enquiry into these writings still deeper, as it seeks to identify in his early positivism the seeds of an anticipatory thrust bypassing his foreign teachers and heading directly for the French sources of positivist thought.

Chapter VI inaugurates the study of the second major development in Ṭāhā's education, namely his education in France, first in Montpellier and then in Paris. After a brief prelude in the former city, Ṭāhā goes to the Sorbonne, where he witnesses the twilight of positivism, a stage at which the movement, having already passed its heyday and given birth to several social disciplines, entered a period of fatigue and disintegration. The time was ripe for eclecticism or attempts at synthesis and reconciliation.

Chapter VII seeks to show how Ṭāhā, having refused to take sides in the positivist crisis, developed a set of syntheses or reconciliations. By investigating these conciliatory efforts as they continued well after Ṭāhā's education in France, the chapter aims to establish how they became characteristic features of his mature thought.

Finally, the conclusion is an attempt to sum up the whole journey and to evaluate Ṭāhā's performance, with special reference to two interrelated aspects of his thought, namely his modernism and humanism.

In conclusion, I should perhaps explain why I speak of Ṭāhā's experience of the encounter with European culture in general rather than French culture in particular. While bearing in mind the primacy of French culture for Ṭāhā, and taking into account that his westward turn was focused on France, one must never lose sight of the wider perspective. His foreign teachers at the Egyptian University were not all French: they were for the most part Italian (Guidi, Nallino, Santillana and Miloni) and they included one German (Littmann). Moreover, Ṭāhā's education in France and his subsequent thought included a classical (Graeco-Roman) component which one cannot afford to neglect with regard to his modernism or his humanism – both being interconnected in his mind. For him, France was the twentieth-century Athens, epitomizing Europe and Mediterranean (originally Hellenic) culture.

Notes

1 Fedwa Malti-Douglas, *Blindness and autobiography. Al-Ayyām of Ṭāhā Ḥusayn* (Princeton 1988).
2 See Aḥmad 'Ulbī, *Ṭāhā Ḥusain, qiṣṣat mukāfiḥ 'anīd* (Beirut 1990).
3 Miftah Tahar, *Ṭāhā Ḥusayn, sa critique littéraire et ses sources françaises* (Tunis 1968).
4 See Edmund Wilson, *To the Finland station. A Study in the writing and acting of history* (New York 1947), ch. I.

CHAPTER I

A Passion for the World

We may begin our study of Ṭāhā Ḥusain with a brief outline of his educational journey as related mainly in his autobiography, *al-Ayyām* ("The Days").[1]

The educational opportunities available to young Ṭāhā, born in 1889 in a small village near the town of Maghāgha in Upper Egypt, to a family of modest means and many children,[2] and who lost his eyesight at an early age,[3] were severely limited. He went to the village *kuttāb* (Qur'ānic school), the curriculum of which consisted almost exclusively of learning the Qur'ān by heart; and he memorized the entire Book at the age of nine. His education could have ended there, and he would have earned his living as a reciter of the Qur'ān for the rest of his days. He was, however, lucky enough to be sent at the age of thirteen to Cairo to study at the ancient Islamic University of the Azhar. The most that his father could wish for him at the time was for him to obtain the final '*ālimiyya* degree and thus be qualified to teach at that venerable university – with all that this might confer on him in terms of financial security and prestige. In the event, Ṭāhā did not fulfil his father's hopes. He became disaffected with Azharite learning; and got into trouble with the authorities.In 1908, he enrolled at the then newly established Egyptian University and devoted himself more or less completely to these new studies. In 1912 he failed (or was failed) his *'ālimiyya* examination,[4] but two years later obtained the first doctorate to be awarded by the young University for his thesis on Abu'l-'Alā' al-Ma'arrī, and won a scholarship to study in France. In 1917, he obtained from the Sorbonne a *licence-ès-lettres*, followed in 1918 by the University Doctorate for his thesis on the social philosophy of Ibn Khaldūn, and in 1919 by a higher diploma in ancient history.

Thus far, we are still at some distance from Ṭāhā Ḥusain's emergence as a great writer and an international figure. But his progression from the village *kuttāb* to the Sorbonne is in itself impressive. It reflects his ability to bridge, if only partly at this stage, what André Gide aptly described as the "immense and apparently unbridgeable chasm" which separated "the dereliction" of Ṭāhā Ḥusain's beginnings from his glorious achievement.[5] Even this accomplishment would not have been possible without the driving force which carried him even further, namely his deep-rooted and persistent need for ever-widening horizons.

Unlike certain characters whom Diderot portrayed in his *Lettre sur les aveugles* and who were born blind, Ṭāhā Ḥusain had never been resigned to his infirmity; he had never found satisfaction in a world without light and colour. This may be due to the fact that he lost his eyesight when he was old enough to retain some memory, however dim, of the visible world,[6] and to appreciate the magnitude of his loss. He characterizes blindness in different ways (e.g. as an affliction and even as "a cunning devil"[7]). But the one image which stands out as the most important is that of blindness as a barrier. Specifically, his frustration with this handicap took the form of an acute awareness, from his early years onwards, that access to the world was barred to him, as if it were hidden behind a thick curtain, a veil or a closed door.

Ṭāhā's barrier was not, however, a mere impediment barring access to the world; he also felt it to be a positive threat endangering his very existence. Being blind involved him in all the dangers normally inherent in being totally dependent on other people, the worst of which is to be reduced to an object.[8] Worst of all, the protagonist of *al-Ayyām* was sometimes led to doubt not only the reality of the external world but also of his own existence.[9]

To overcome the barrier was, therefore, a matter of life and death. It was essential for him to gain a foothold in the world if he was not to lose himself. Thus acute awareness of an oppressive and dangerous barrier went hand in hand with the equally strong impulse to overcome it.

All this is implicit in the highly charged scene described at the very beginning of *al-Ayyām*. In this scene, which sets the tone for the whole book, Ṭāhā Ḥusain evokes the most important of his early memories. He writes, "if there has remained to him any clear, distinct memory of this time about which there is no cause to doubt, it is the memory of a fence which stood in front of him and was made of maize stems and which was only a few paces away from the door of the house.

"He remembers the fence as though he saw it only yesterday. He remembers that the stalks of which this fence was composed were taller than he was, and it was difficult for him to get to the other side of it.

"He also recalls that the stalks of this fence were close together, as if they were stuck together, so that he could not squeeze between them. He recollects too that the stalks of this fence stretched from his left to an ending he could not conjecture; and it stretched from his right to the end of the world in that direction. And the end of the world in this direction was near, for it reached as far as the canal, which fact he discovered when he got a little older."[10]

It is interesting to notice how the child manages after all to overcome his barrier. The rabbits, we are told, were able to traverse the fence by leaping over it or by squeezing between the stalks.[11] He, on the other hand, "used to lean against the maize fence pondering deep in thought, until he was recalled to his surroundings by the voice of a poet who was sitting some distance to his left, with his audience round him. Then the poet would begin to recite in a wonderfully sweet tone the doings of Abū Zayd, Khalīfa and Diyāb, and his hearers would remain silent except when ecstasy enlivened them or desire startled them. Then they would demand a repetition and argue and dispute. And so the poet would be silent until they ceased their clamour after a period which might be short or long. Then he would continue his sweet recitation in a monotone."[12]

The young Ṭāhā discovers, together with his barrier, his own way of breaking out of it. If he could not, in the fence scene, physically join the poet's audience, he would nevertheless become a member of the group by using his hearing, imagination and sense of beauty. This pattern of thought is recurrent throughout *al-Ayyām*. We are told, for instance, that the child used to abstain from all kinds of sports and games, and would rather withdraw to a corner and play with some iron rods or join his brothers and friends in their games "with his mind, not with his hands".[13] It was because of his reluctance to take part in games that the child, according to the author, became fond of listening to stories and legends.[14] In yet another situation, Ṭāhā's father would sit with his friends listening to one of them recite all sorts of stories and legends, while Ṭāhā "would sit at a respectful distance *where a dog might be made to crouch*, and although they were oblivious of his presence, he was in no way unmindful of what he heard, or even of the impression these stories made upon the audience".[15]

It is this early realization on the part of the child that the use of the mind could make up for his physical disadvantage, cancel the distance separating him from other people and thereby widen the frontiers of his world, which constituted the basis of the whole enterprise of Ṭāhā's education, if not the whole of his life journey. Once the discovery was made, his way out of confinement was opened up. Thus he took in all that his rural environment could provide, both in and out of the *kuttāb*, as oral knowledge, whether it be the Qur'ān, folk tales and poetry, magical incantations or the stylized lamentations of peasant women.[16]

That education is a means of gaining access to the world becomes even clearer in the second volume of *al-Ayyām*, which deals mainly with Ṭāhā's years of study at the Azhar. This course of education, described in detail, is firmly situated within the protagonist's experience of release from confinement. There is, therefore, an elaborate portrayal of the daily life of the young student, now a boy of thirteen, as it runs its normal course in three "phases".[17] The first phase covers the boy's life within his "immediate environment",[18] that is to say a region of space stretching from the boy's place in the room which he shares with his brother to cover the whole building. Then comes the second phase, which occurs as the boy walks from his lodgings to the Azhar. In the third and final phase, he enters the courtyard of the venerable University, and comes within reach of "the sea of learning".

The boy's life as a student at the Azhar takes the form of a journey in an ever-widening environment. At the beginning, there is the boy in the confined space allocated to him, often suffering loneliness and darkness. As he steps out early in the morning heading for the Azhar, he enjoys only a relative sense of release, as his route leads him through the dereliction and squalor of a lane infested by bats. "At last", writes the author of *al-Ayyām*, "he came to a spot where he had to turn a little to the left and then plunge into a lane as narrow and crooked and filthy as could be. Its atmosphere was foul with an abominable medley of smells, and from time to time weak, hollow voices which reflected its misery and wretchedness echoed back cries for charity to the footfalls of passers-by, begging at the sound of steps, as if life had only been perceptible through the ears. They were answered by other voices:

the thin, harsh, strangled cries of those winged creatures which love darkness and desolation and ruins. Often enough these noises were accompanied by the flutter of wings, which sometimes, to his horror, shaved past his ear or his face. Instinctively his hand would fly up for protection, and for some time afterwards his heart would be throbbing with apprehension."[19]

This harrowing ordeal over, the boy has to walk for a while until he finally reaches the Azhar. It is only in this third phase of his day that the boy finds rest and security.[20] As he enters the courtyard of the Azhar he is welcomed by a caressing fresh breeze as sweet and reassuring as his mother's kisses. His soul yearns for the learning which now seems so close at hand.[21] "His father and the learned friends who came to visit him", we are told, "had spoken of knowledge as a boundless ocean, and the child had never taken this expression for a figure of speech or metaphor, but as the simple truth. He had come to Cairo and to the Azhar with the intention of throwing himself into this ocean and drinking what he could of it, until the day he drowned."[22]

The journey, thus described, reproduces in an elaborate form the structure of the first fence scene, and for that matter, of almost the whole story of Ṭāhā's education as related in *al-Ayyām.* The agony of the initial confinement finds its happy *dénouement* in a move outward, taking in this case the form of a prolonged journey towards boundless knowledge. It is this drive outward which took Ṭāhā, at a later stage, to the Sorbonne and farther afield. The drive is at work all the time, because the crisis of solitude and belonging is recurrent. There will come a time when Azharite learning, initially pursued with almost ecstatic fervour, proves to be suffocating. There will even come a time when learning as such is seen as a barrier.

This latter crisis took place during Ṭāhā's stay in Paris as a student at the Sorbonne. It was here, where horizons had been immensely widened, and where he could quench his thirst for Western knowledge, that Ṭāhā experienced his worst doubts as to the value of learning in gaining access to the world. Falling under the spell of his "sweet-voiced" reader (who was to become his permanent companion and wife), the as yet mere possibility of love, remote as it was at the time, made him feel that his diligence in the pursuit of academic accomplishment had all been in vain, since it brought him no closer to things. It was then that he felt as a stranger wherever he was, whether in Egypt or in France,[23] and suffered the most drastic doubts as to the existence of external nature and his own existence.[24]

It was also during that period that he was most haunted by the "voice of Abu'l-'Alā'"[25], apparently urging steadfastness and perseverance in the pursuit of knowledge, and warning of dependence on other human beings.[26] In the event, Ṭāhā could not bring himself to accept his mentor's advice and opted, once and for all, for closer ties with the world.

Love played a crucial role in Ṭāhā Ḥusain's development. It brought him as close as he could be to nature. "She", he writes, "talked to me about people until I felt within myself that I saw them and knew them in their innermost selves. She gave me a feel for nature, too, as she talked, the feel one has who knows it intimately. She spoke of the sun, flooding the sky with light, and of night bringing over the earth the brooding dark, of the lamps of heaven shedding their bright beams over the land, of the mountains crowned with snowy whiteness, of the trees spreading a gracious shadow, of the rivers flowing, strong, and the gentle brooks threading their way down, and all the vast spectacle of beauty and splendour, of crudity and ugliness, in the world of men and things."[27]

It was also through love that Ṭāhā began to lose his shyness and natural aloofness, and thus enter, so to speak, human society.[28] Given this solid base, he could multiply his inroads into the world both as a man of learning and a man of action. Thenceforth, he could assume with relish and amazing ingenuity, his diverse roles as a university don and writer, as an administrator and politician, as a social and world figure, and as a traveller, theatre-goer and "sightseer".

He was as close as he could be to things, but that was still not enough for him to feel completely at home in the world. Nothing would have completely satisfied him short of knowing nature as it lies open to the eye and to free, unaided movement. Thus he continued to feel, from time to time, that the "closed door" was not as yet quite open, that there were some things still submerged in darkness.

Hence the occasional sombre moods and bouts of depression[29] and the recurrent sense of being the victim of a curse. As an illustration of this latter point, the reader may consider the concluding chapter of the first volume of *al-Ayyām*, where the author abruptly addresses his daughter, evoking the time when he told her the story of the old, self-mutilated Oedipus being led by Antigone.[30]

But it speaks for Ṭāhā's basic strength and integrity that he never gave in to despair, that, on the contrary, he found in the very precariousness of his existence a source of strong motivation. He was indeed a pessimistic person, as Moënis Ṭāhā Ḥusain is reported to have said,[31] but this pessimism did not prevent him from being an optimist in practice. Luckily for him, he was endowed with a pragmatic temperament. He was not a man to dwell on his sense of calamity; his brooding states were only preludes to tremendous outbursts of productive energy. It is interesting, in this connection, to see how he himself diagnosed feelings of boredom and pessimism as the outcome of too much introspection and self-analysis, and how he believed that activity was the only cure. "I do not think," he writes, "that one should think of oneself too much, for man does not deserve that much attention. I am rather inclined to believe that one should divert his attention from oneself by reading, conversation, work and the enjoyment of pleasures permitted by God and morality." [32]

Thanks to his positive attitude, Ṭāhā never succumbed to the temptation of a life of self-imposed solitude, as proposed by Abu'l-'Alā'. While always identifying with the poet-philosopher, the latter's proposal was no more than a theoretical possibility. In practice, Ṭāhā was always sociable and gregarious, deeply involved in the intellectual and political life of his country, and never averse to worldly ambitions or the trappings of fame and glory.

In the course of time, he learnt to treat Abu'l-'Alā' as an alter ego though representing only part of himself. He continued to cherish him and to see his point of view, but that was as far as he could go. This is obvious from *Ma' Abi'l-'Alā' fī sijnih* ["With Abi'l-'Alā' in his prison"] (1939), a work of Ṭāhā's maturity, in which he takes special care to sympathize with his old "companion" and to understand his work from within. It is remarkable how in this same work the roles are completely reversed; it is now Ṭāhā's turn to criticize his friend, of course in the mildest of terms, for the severity of his logic and perfectionism, and to council moderation and realism. In the final analysis, Abu'l-'Alā' must be one of those philosophers whom Ṭāhā had in mind when he wrote that they advocated pessimism because they studied themselves too much.[33]

Profoundly pessimistic and yet an optimist. The key to understanding this paradox is the idea already formulated,

9.50

namely that from an early age Ṭāhā's acute awareness of confinement went hand in hand with the equally strong impulse to break out of it. According to the author of *al-Ayyām*, the protagonist's experience of the barrier as both an obstacle and an inciting challenge predated and underlay all other experiences and forms of learning. Jacques Berque is right when he speaks in this connection of an "existential premise" or a kind of *cogito* underlying all of Ṭāhā's endeavours.[34]

Given this, we can easily see why Anouar Louca goes wrong in his views on the central role of the Qur'ān in Ṭāhā's humanism. "At the age of nine", he writes, "he [i.e. Ṭāhā] could recite the entire Qur'ān. Even if he had not assimilated its substance, he had mastered its form. He delighted in its sonorous eloquence, its diffuse wisdom. Certain expressions lingered in his mind, or came back when he was alone, suggesting ideas to him. At the age when most children are absorbed in their games, he had thus become the depository of the Book. His little world had miraculously been extended to include the whole of creation; going beyond the confines of his village and even the prospect of Cairo, it now embraced the whole human race, the good and the wicked, to all of whom the Qur'ān was addressed. All mankind was seen in relationship to God. This precocious awareness of what is universal was of course a crucial factor in the development of Ṭāhā Ḥusain. It provided the mental framework in which all the subsequent preoccupations and discoveries of the thinker would automatically find their place."[35]

It is surely far-fetched to claim that the Qur'ān, learnt by heart at the age of nine, could have helped Ṭāhā extend the frontiers of his world so as to include the whole of humanity. The claim cannot in any way be supported by anything that Ṭāhā Ḥusain says or implies. What he suggests, on the other hand, is, as we have already seen, that those frontiers began to stretch starting from that point at which he stood in front of the maize fence and as a result of that primordial experience already described.

It is this experience which may be said to anticipate from afar and very indirectly Ṭāhā's later humanism, being as it were an elementary kind of disposition in favour of expansion. But let us not anticipate, and instead allow the story to unfold gradually according to its own logic. At this stage, i.e. Ṭāhā's early childhood, the experience in question is of a basic kind. Stemming from Ṭāhā's natural disability, it is focused on the world in its sheer physical aspect and its spatial dimension. Given that source point in front of the fence, the world is an ever-widening circle. This is the structure chosen by Ṭāhā for his story, and we have no reason to doubt that his life proceeded quite differently in actual fact.

Ṭāhā's world-oriented outlook did not originally stem from any belief, conscious or unconscious, in any doctrine or theory.[36] It goes without saying that this experience was conditioned and aggravated by the social and cultural environment in which he lived. We may also assume that later belief in theories and doctrines played a part in consolidating, articulating and giving expression to that experience. But there can be no doubt either that Ṭāhā's early, elementary dispositions, i.e. his abhorrence of confinement and his longing for freedom, explain, at least partly, his receptivity to later and more rational options such as literary study (as distinct from Azhari scholasticism), historicism and humanism.

Notes

1 In three volumes all translated into English under the following titles: I *An Egyptian childhood,* tr. E.H. Paxton (London 1932); II *The Stream of days,* tr. Hilary Wayment (London 1943); III *A Passage to France,* tr. Kenneth Cragg (Leiden 1976). Ṭāhā Ḥusain wrote the whole story in the third person. However, the translator of the third volume took the liberty of making Ṭāhā Ḥusain speak in the first person.

2 "He was the seventh of the thirteen children of his father, and the fifth out of the eleven children of his father's second wife." Taha Hussein, *An Egyptian childhood,* (London 1981), p. 7.

3 There is no consensus as to the time at which this event took place. It must have occurred between the ages of three and six.

4 Ṭāhā Ḥusain, *A Passage to France,* pp. 11, 12, 13.

5 See André Gide's preface to the French translation of the first and second volumes of *al-Ayyām* as *Le livre des jours,* tr. Jean Lecerf and Gaston Wiet, (Paris 1947), p. 12. Note that Gide met Ṭāhā Ḥusain in 1946, and that he refers to the latter's achievement thus far.

6 Thus Ṭāhā Ḥusain wrote: "She [i.e. the woman he loved and who was to become his wife] made me sense that she was disclosing realities to me hitherto hidden yet not alien, as if I had known them long ago at the beginning and had forgotten them for ages and was now recollecting them again as a very old possession". Op. cit., p. 113.

7 Ibid., p. 93.

8 Ibid., p. 112.

9 Ibid.

10 *An Egyptian childhood,* p. 1.

11 Ibid., p. 2.
12 Ibid.
13 Ibid., p. 11.
14 Ibid.
15 Ibid. Italics are mine. The phrase underlined is an addition I make to translate the original's "*mazjar al-kalb*" which is missing in the English version. The translator's "at a respectful distance" is convenient, but it misses a point which the author took care to emphasize, adding a footnote to define "*mazjar al-kalb*".
16 Ibid., pp. 11–12.
17 Ṭāhā Ḥusain, *The Stream of days*, 2nd edn. (London 1948), pp. 1 ff.
18 Ibid., p. 5, 'immediate environment' is a more literal, and I think, a more accurate rendering of the original's "*bī'atihī 'l-qarība*", than the "immediate surroundings" of the English version.
19 Ibid., pp. 8–9. Translation slightly revised: where the translator uses "wrong" to render the original's "*ḍurr*", I use "wretchedness".
20 Ibid., p. 11.
21 Ibid., p. 12.
22 Ibid.
23 *A Passage to France*, p. 111.
24 Ibid., p. 112.
25 Ibid., pp. 84, 102 and 111.
26 That is how I reconstruct this part of the story, as Ṭāhā Ḥusain is never precise on the circumstances of his love affair. It was the view of Abu'l-'Alā', as reported by Ṭāhā Ḥusain, that blindness was "a reproach" (ibid., p. 98), "something to be ashamed of" (ibid., p. 94), that a blind man should not have too many ties with other fellow men" (ibid., p. 102).
27 *A Passage to France*, pp. 112–113.
28 According to Ṭāhā Ḥusain, he had, before this new departure in his life, seen himself in Abu'l-'Alā''s saying that he was born human but was by instinct a wild animal. *A Passage to France*, p. 111.
29 In her memoirs about her life with her husband, Suzanne Ṭāhā Ḥusain relates how he would at times lock himself up behind impenetrable silence as if he had fallen into a pit from which he could not be extracted. See her *Ma'ak* ("With you"), tr. Badr al-Dīn 'Arawdakī (Cairo 1979), p. 107. The original French has not been published.
30 *The Stream of days*, p. 77.
31 See Philippe Cardinal's preface to Ṭāhā Ḥusain's *Adib ou l'aventure occidentale*, tr. Amina and Moënis Taha Hussein, (Paris 1988), pp. 15–16.
32 "Fi 'l-ṭarīq" in *Min ba'īd*, in *MK*, vol. XII, 1974, pp. 107–115, pp. 114–115.
33 Ibid., p. 115.
34 Ṭāhā Ḥussein, *Au delà du Nil*, ed. Jacques Berque (Paris 1977), p. 13. For a development of Berque's insight into a full-fledged study of the Cartesian aspects of Ṭāhā Ḥusain's thought, see Abdelrashid Mahmoudi, "Ṭāhā Ḥusain wa-Descartes", *Fuṣūl*, vol. III (July/August/September 1983), pp. 104–113.

35 "Ṭāhā Ḥussein et l'Occident", *Cultures*, Vol. II, No. 2, 1975, pp. 118–142, p. 119.

36 For a stimulating study of this experience from a comparative point of view, see Muḥammad Ṣādiq al-Kāshif, *Ṭāhā Ḥusain baṣīran* ["Ṭāhā Ḥusain as a sighted man"] (Cairo 1986). For a more extensive enquiry into Ṭāhā Ḥusain's treatment of the problem of blindness, see Fedwa Malti-Douglas, *Blindness and autobiography* (Princeton 1988).

CHAPTER II

From Theology to Literature

In relating Ṭāhā Ḥusain's intellectual development into a cultural mediator between East and West, one can easily be tempted to stress the Western-oriented phases in his education at the old Egyptian University in Cairo (where he was first initiated into modern methods of research) and at the Sorbonne in Paris. The instruction that Ṭāhā had previously received at the Azhar would then be neglected, glossed over or dismissed as "traditional" or "scholastic".

To do this would be entirely wrong. It was precisely at the Azhar that Ṭāhā learnt to question the so-called "traditional" culture, and to discern beneath this layer of ossified tradition, the primary sources of Arab creativity. Ṭāhā's disaffection with Azhari scholasticism was only the prelude to that magnificent discovery, through which he found both his own cultural identity and his true vocation in life. Henceforth, he was to be a man of letters who ought, according to the classical Arabic ideal, to have a wide-ranging culture. Given that discovery, the search for a wider cultural horizon could now begin. In other words, Ṭāhā's mature humanism can only be understood as the conclusion of a process of development which began with a literary fundamentalism or neo-classicism first learnt during his years of study at the Azhar.

The Azhari period was anything but stagnant. Both in *al-Ayyām* and elsewhere, Ṭāhā is at pains to describe, in detail, the turbulence and agitation of that period. We have already seen with what initial enthusiasm verging on religious fervour, he started his first day at the Azhar. Several years afterwards – when his ties with the venerable institution had been completely broken – he would still invoke that occasion and the whole period with poignant nostalgia and exquisite tenderness.[1] He carried "within his soul" – as he put it – a lively picture of his study days at the venerable mosque, and of the place itself.[2] Although after his initial enthusiasm he was soon disappointed and bored, he strove for several years to maintain his weakened ties with the Azhar, moving restlessly from one course of study to another and from one teacher to another. His was the exasperation of the disillusioned lover trying to the very end to recover the first spell of passionate happiness. Boredom and disappointment were at any rate the healthy signs of a rebellious mind searching for a more satisfying form of knowledge. Also, on the positive side, there was something attractive about the Azhar at the time, namely the informal character of teaching and learning, and the liveliness of the place as a meeting point for scholars and worshippers.[3] Finally, there was the majestic presence of Muḥammad ʻAbduh, the marathonic lessons of al-Marṣafī and – sweetest of all – the discovery of literature.

Ṭāhā went to the Azhar (in 1902) at a crucial moment of its history, a time of high tension between the staunch supporters of the status quo and an equally persistent current of reform represented mainly by Muḥammad ʻAbduh. This period which ended with the Imām's resignation and his death a few months later in 1905, constitutes, as justly remarked by Ṭāhā Ḥusain, an important and as yet unstudied chapter in the history of modern Egypt.[4] While we cannot here do justice to this tumultuous and fertile period, we have to bear in mind the conflicting currents which were then at work. Without this vital background, Ṭāhā's disaffection with Azhari education and his final and unremediable break with the Azhar, would remain something of a mystery.

There he was, an exceptionally gifted student, strongly motivated and in many ways ideally suited to follow an Azhari career. Apart from his phenomenal memory, he had an aptitude for many of the virtues and trappings of the Azhari form of intellect such as its biting humour and the typical dialectical skill or "*fanqala*".[5] Some of these habits and characteristics remained with Ṭāhā Ḥusain for the rest of his life. Even at his most modernist, his writing echoed Azhari modes of thinking and expression in many ways. Those who read him in Arabic cannot fail to notice the "reciting" or "chanting" tone, or the deeply embedded manners and mannerisms of Azhari scholasticism. What then went wrong?

Instruction at the Azhar consisted of studying a set of basic texts (*mutūn*), which were in fact highly condensed abridgements of the main works in their respective subjects. These texts were to be learnt by heart and explained by the teacher through three levels of exegesis: commentary (*sharḥ*); glosses or marginalia (*ḥāshiya*) and supercommentary (*taqrīr*). Having commenced reading the basic text with the words "The author said God rest his soul", he would launch into a word-by-word explanation of the text, not just discussing the subject dealt with, but going into linguistic and rhetorical digressions, even in a lecture on Law. After explaining the text, the teacher would read the first commentary, followed by the gloss and finally by the supercommentary.[6]

Underlying this whole procedure was the assumption that the main facts concerning any subject had already been established at some time in the past, and that all that remained for the following generations was to memorize and comment upon such final "truths". The desire to impart as much received information as briefly as possible inevitably gave rise to such turgid and highly cryptic texts (very often in verse) as would require elaborate word-by-word exegesis. This understandable necessity, coupled with a perverse taste for far-fetched hypotheses and dialectical juggling, resulted in an endless mass of irrelevant detail. It was difficult, if not impossible, for students to perceive through this overgrowth what was really at issue, or to exercise any faculty other than sheer memory. On the collective level, entanglement in what was derivative and purely verbal, meant, among other things, the relegation of major and original works to oblivion. Thus a procedure whose sole *raison d'être* was the conservation of traditions, resulted in a grave form of collective amnesia concerning what was best in Islamic culture, namely the classical heritage.

The practice of substituting what is derivative for what is original was already under way at the time of Ibn Khaldūn, who criticized the then "recent scholars" who presented the methods and contents of the sciences in brief textbooks or statements overcharged with meaning.[7] Much more recent and therefore more pertinent to our subject, are the acute comments which Rifā'a Rāfi' al-Ṭahṭāwī (1801–1873) makes in a comparison he draws between French and Arabic textbooks. "Among the factors which help the French to make progress in science and the arts", he writes, "is the facility of their language A [French] textbook does not need to explain its words with reference to any extraneous terms drawn from another discipline. They [i.e. French authors] have no commentaries or glosses except very rarely. The most that they would do is to add some brief comments to supplement the basic texts by a footnote or some such device. So once a man starts reading a book on any given subject, he can devote his whole attention to grasping the problems at issue without quibbling over words."[8]

For al-Ṭahṭāwī, Arabic textbooks are quite different: "Anyone who wishes to read an Arabic book on any subject, has to apply to its text all the tools available in the language, examine it word by word as closely as possible, and find for each statement a far-fetched interpretation with no relation whatsoever to its obvious significance".[9]

Both Ibn Khaldūn and al-Ṭahṭāwī would have agreed, therefore, that Azhari textbooks were harmful to the extent that they divert the learner's attention from what is essential, making it difficult for him to grasp the problems at issue. This point cannot, however, be applied without reservation to the particular case in hand. The young Ṭāhā normally had no difficulty in spotting, through the mass of commentary, the point at issue. His was rather the problem of a supergifted student who could not put up with what seemed to be a semblance of learning or utterly irrelevant. Thus, in a lesson on tradition, he understood the teacher perfectly and found nothing to criticize except the cascade of names which the latter poured forth, giving source and authority. "He [i.e. Ṭāhā] longed for the shaykh to have done with all this and come down to the tradition itself."[10]

In another lesson on rhetoric, the teacher was dealing with a famous statement to the effect that "every word varies in meaning according to its context". "What a sea of ink", says the author of *al-Ayyām*, "has been wasted on this sentence, in abridgements and expansions, in commentaries and glosses, in criticisms and objections, while all the time it is a truth as clear as daylight The sheikh, like many an Azharite before him, embarked upon the analysis of this sentence and the sifting of all the rigmarole that has been talked about it."[11]

But even where the point at issue was far from trivial and the commentary was good, it was not always easy to quench the young man's thirst for knowledge or to satisfy his appetite for argumentation. Such was the case when, in a lesson on exegesis at which David Santillana was present,[12] the shaykh had to explain a certain Qur'ānic verse which seemed to imply predestination. The explanation was excellent, but the teacher embarked upon a refutation of fatalists. Seizing upon the difficulty, Ṭāhā persisted in raising one objection after another, demonstrating as much dialectical skill (in the characteristically Azhari fashion) as he could muster. Said the shaykh vehemently, "Are you a Muslim?" His exasperation was such that Santillana had to intervene lest the scene degenerate any further.[13]

The shaykh's retort should remind us, however, that Ṭāhā's dissatisfaction with Azhari education cannot be fully explained only with reference to the then prevalent methods of instruction. Given such an inquisitive mind, the very contents of Azhari education were also bound to prove unsatisfactory. Restrictive Azhari procedures were after all related to, and dependent on, a whole 'philosophy' of education and knowledge, which was permeated by all sorts of archaic inhibitions and prohibitions. The implicit assumption that there was nothing for modern generations to discover went hand in hand with an explicit dictum that all that was worth studying must, in one way or another, be subordinated to religious knowledge as defined by Muslim orthodoxy. We thus need to consider the Azhari syllabus at the turn of the century.

Under a reform introduced in 1872, the Azhari syllabus was divided into two categories comprising, all in all, eleven obligatory subjects. There were, on the one hand, subjects wanted *per se*, such as jurisprudence (*fiqh*) and Qur'ānic exegesis (*tafsīr*), and, on the other, instrumental subjects such as grammar, morphology and logic.[14] The former were to be studied for their own sake, whereas the latter were to be pursued only to the extent that they served as tools for studying subjects *per se*.[15] This list was widened under another reform which was introduced in 1896 at the instigation of Muḥammad 'Abduh. Twelve more subjects, partly modern ones, were added, but this enlargement, as may be seen from the two following tables,[16] did not modify in any substantial way the basic structure.

Obligatory subjects	Subjects giving priority[17]
I. Subjects required *per se*:	
1) Theology (*kalām* or *tawḥīd*)	1) Islamic history +
2) Religious ethics +[18]	2) Composition +
3) Jurisprudence (*fiqh*)	3) Oratory +
4) Principles of jurisprudence (*uṣūl al-fiqh*)	
5) Qur'ānic exegesis (*tafsīr*)	
6) Traditions of the Prophet (*ḥadīth*)	

II. Instrumental subjects:

1) Grammar (*naḥw*)
2) Morphology (*ṣarf*)
3) Semantics of syntax[19] (*ma'ānī*)
4) Science of figurative expression[19] (*bayān*)
5) Embellishment of speech (*badī'*)
6) Logic
7) Terminology of Prophetic tradition (*muṣṭalaḥ al-ḥadīth*) +
8) Arithmetic +
9) Algebra +
10) Prosody and rhyme +

1) Arabic language +
2) Arabic literature +
3) Geometry +
4) Geography +

The newly proposed subjects were thus listed in turn under the two traditional headings, and most of them were classified as instrumental and/or optional. None of them, except religious ethics, was admitted to the highest rank of being both obligatory and *per se* – this rank thus remaining exclusively restricted to religious disciplines. It is also significant that of the newly introduced subjects only Islamic history and the two minor arts of composition and oratory were accommodated under the second highest grade of being *per se* but optional, and that Arabic language, Arabic literature, geography and geometry were admitted only as instrumental and optional.

The distinction between subjects wanted *per se* and instrumental subjects has a long history, which does not concern us here except to the extent that it weighed upon Azhari education. It should thus be noted that the distinction reflects in a way the manner in which various fields of knowledge originated with the Qur'ān and the Prophet's traditions (the Sunna) as their axis. This remark applies to such an obviously instrumental subject as theology (*kalām*) as much as it applies to the study of pre-Islamic poetry.[20] However, it should also be noted that these origins did not prevent the disciplines in question from developing into the fully fledged and marvellously independent subjects they came to be at the peak of Islamic culture. Thus theology itself became, in the course of time, a highly sophisticated and philosophically inclined subject. The attempt to curb this development must have been a relatively late phenomenon, and it probably originated in al-Ghazālī's classification of sciences, in which he subordinated all forms of knowledge to religious control. It was probably this classification, as elaborated in his *Iḥyā' 'ulūm al-dīn*,[21] which, through simplification and ossification, was finally reduced to the Azhari syllabus at the turn of the century.

Every time the Azhar was faced with the need to change, the fully fledged system was invoked as the main line of resistance. Any proposal for the introduction of a new science had to be tested against the tremendous and well-designed apparatus of pigeon-holes and fine distinctions. As an illustration of how the Azhari establishment skilfully wielded this forbidding weapon, we may cite the famous *fatwā* of Shaykh Imbābī,[22] who was asked to pronounce on the appropriateness of introducing mathematical and natural sciences into the Azhar. Those who requested the *fatwā* were in favour of such a step, but they sought to lure Shaykh Imbābi into giving his formal approval. They presented him with the following well-ordered questions,[23] which, they no doubt thought, would inevitably lead to a positive conclusion. Is it not permissible for Muslims to study mathematical and natural sciences, given that they are necessary for the nation's strength and state of readiness? Is it not even necessary to study at least some of these sciences as a matter of collective duty, in the manner indicated by the Imām al-Ghazālī? And if such is the case, would it not be permissible to study these sciences on the same footing as grammar and other instrumental subjects being currently studied at the Azhar?

To this, the Grand Shaykh gave an elaborate reply, invoking in his turn the authority of al-Ghazālī. The mathematical sciences, he argued, are permissible since they touch in no way on religious matters. In fact, it is a collective duty to pursue these disciplines to the extent that such a study might entail a religious or worldly benefit. In this respect, the mathematical sciences do not differ from medicine. As for the natural sciences, which deal with the properties and transformations of matter, there is no harm in studying them as long as they are not in conflict with religious law (*sharī'a*). They are, however, unlawful when studied according to the manner of philosophers. There is no reason why mathematics, physics and chemistry should not (within these limits) be studied as instrumental sciences.[24]

Notwithstanding this array of arguments in favour of the mathematical and natural sciences, the proposal for their introduction into the Azhar syllabus was not put into effect.

Shaykh Imbābī, as it has been justly remarked, eluded this practical problem, treating the whole affair as a purely theoretical exercise.[25] He did not feel hard pressed to change the status quo, as these disciplines did not, in the final analysis, matter – given the Azhar's own habits of thought. They were all considered to be inferior to religious disciplines; they carried the stigma of being related to philosophy (and hence to potential heresy); and they did not have such an evidently practical utility as medicine.[26]

To argue that the mathematical and natural sciences might be treated as instrumental subjects, anomalous as it was, could not have furthered their case, as these latter subjects were themselves held in contempt. For, as Ṭāhā Ḥusain put it, why should anyone care for merely instrumental sciences? Would it not be better to turn one's attention to subjects which should be pursued for their own sake?[27]

That Ṭāhā Ḥusain should have devoted most of his attention to what was merely instrumental, thus abandoning "respectable" Azhari subjects for literature, was partly due to non-literary reasons. For him, the study of literature constituted a release from the oppressive dominance of religious subjects. The first step on the way to "freedom" was taken under the influence of an Azharite and an outstanding theologian for that matter, namely the Imām Muḥammad 'Abduh (1849–1905).

An Azharite who had himself undergone twice in his life the trauma of Azhari education,[28] Muḥammad 'Abduh was the driving force behind the first serious attempt in modern times to reform the ancient University-Mosque. The 1896 reform, of which he was the architect, was wide-ranging,[29] involving, among other things, two aspects of particular relevance, namely the widening of the syllabus as outlined above and the reform of teaching methods through a ban on glosses and supercommentaries in the first four years of study, attention being confined to the basic texts and simple explanatory comments.[30] Of these two moderate reforms, the former was never implemented. Resistance to the latter resulted, as has already been shown, in the downgrading of most of the newly proposed subjects, especially secular ones. There can be no doubt, therefore, that the reformed syllabus was the outcome of tough negotiations which took into account the views and sensitivities of Azhari conservatives. In spite of his prestige and his shrewdness, Muḥammad 'Abduh had to pay a heavy price in order to have modern subjects grudgingly admitted. The question of whether he was outmanoeuvred will be examined below. It is necessary now to consider the influence he exerted through his ideas and teaching, especially as they affected the student Ṭāhā Ḥusain.

Important as it is, this subject has never been adequately studied. Pierre Cachia warned rightly against minimizing the influence exerted by Muḥammad 'Abduh on Ṭāhā Ḥusain. He pointed out that although Ṭāhā did not become an intimate of the Imām, and attended only two of his lectures, he was familiar with 'Abduh's ideas partly through his brother and his close friends, who were adherents of the great reformer, partly through reading.[31] This line of thought, thus far couched in general terms, needs, however, to be amplified and substantiated.

It would seem that 'Abduh's influence reached its zenith during Ṭāhā's first years of study, ending with the Imām's departure and death in 1905. It was roughly around that time that 'Abduh gathered, both within and outside the Azhar, a strong current of opinion clamouring for reform. It was also around that time that the conflict with the conservatives reached its peak. Young Ṭāhā did not, in a sense, need to come into contact with 'Abduh, as the latter's ideas were already in the air. It was in fact under that climate of conflict that some of Ṭāhā's basic positions on religion, literature and reform took shape.

Ṭāhā watched the agitation from such close quarters that he could provide, in *al-Ayyām* and elsewhere, very useful information on the ideas and activities of 'Abduh's young followers. They were, as he put it, those who were most influenced by the Imām, the most biased in favour of his positions and the most infatuated by his views.[32] There was among them a group of students who used to hold regular meetings at which they debated questions of social and political reform. These were in fact among the brightest young men in Egypt[33] into whose heart the Imām had "kindled the spark of revolution" after several years of Azhari stagnation.[34]

Ṭāhā did not, however, remain a mere witness. He was finally caught up in the battle and he came to be considered a follower of 'Abduh.[35] It is therefore necessary to consider those of 'Abduh's views which must have inflamed those young men, and Ṭāhā in particular. The strongest and most direct impact must have been exercised by 'Abduh's work on Islam as a religion of science and civilization. It was in this polemical work that he openly and most virulently attacked Azhari conservatives. He castigated the *fuqahā'* (specialists of religious law) for their ossified conservatism, narrow and rigid literalism and abject servility towards the texts of their recent predecessors. This servility, he argued, had led to the replacement of the great classics of their ancient ancestors (*al-salaf*) by abridged manuals, and the loss of independent judgement.[36] Such direct attacks which 'Abduh also made in his lectures at the Azhar and discussions at home, must have fed, and given expression to, his students' daily dissatisfaction and imbued some of them with the spirit of rebellion.

These polemics were in turn underlined by a positive theological and historical conception which had a more decisive and more lasting effect. Without belittling the contribution of his immediate predecessors,[37] 'Abduh, we may say, was the first to formulate the problem of reform and revival in an effective manner. Believing that progress could be achieved only gradually, and mainly through education, he offered the kind of thinking which in his view would set the process in motion. He redefined the Islamic heritage, otherwise received as an undifferentiated and overwhelming mass. As he attacked his fellow shaykhs for their servility vis-à-vis their immediate predecessors, their blind faith in authority (*taqlīd*), their neglect of the original sources of Islam and the great classics of the past, there emerged a clear distinction between the fundamentals of Islam as laid down by the early pioneers (*al-salaf*) and the accretions and distortions of later generations, that is between the basic sources and later traditions. Having made this fundamentalist distinction, 'Abduh would give it such an ingenious turn as to defeat fundamentalist reaction, arguing as he did that the original Islam was in perfect harmony with modern science and technological progress. According to him, there was no contradiction and no irreducible distinction between religion (so interpreted) and the use of reason.

One cannot but admire 'Abduh's historical acumen. Speaking primarily as a theologian within an Islamic context, he confronted his profoundly religious audience with the hard core of their history, with, that is, the original starting point for all enquiry in Islam, namely the fact of the revelation as embodied in the Qur'ān. Given this return to the sources, for which he had the backing of al-Ghazālī's impeccable authority, he undermined the whole edifice of Azhari dogmatism in one stroke. "It [i.e. Islam]", he wrote, "was the first religion to address the rational mind, summoning it to look into the whole material universe, giving it free rein to range at will through its secrets, saving only therein the maintenance of the faith."[38] Islam, according to him, granted to reason and will the honour of independence.[39] Thus, for the first time in modern Islamic thought, the door was flung wide open to the work of reason whether in the form of *ijtihād* (independent religious thinking) or, more generally, that of rational or scientific enquiry.

Such were the ideas which must have inflamed 'Abduh's followers, including the student Ṭāhā. We have in this connection a most precious document which the latter wrote in French many years later on, and which has remained unknown ever since its publication.[40] Giving an account of the two lectures of 'Abduh which he had attended, Ṭāhā Ḥusain wrote the following. " Nothing can efface from my mind the memory of that voice, the gentleness with which he recited passages from the Holy Book, the sincerity of his interpretation, or the strength of his conviction that nothing he said was in contradiction with the discoveries of modern science, or at variance with the demands of Western civilization. He was listened to with a passionate interest and admiration which verged on religious ecstasy. His lecture would be discussed throughout the evening and again the next day enthusiastically by his followers and with tenacious, if fearful, hatred by his opponents."[41]

The lecture in question would seem to have been part of the Imām's course on exegesis.[42] As it was thoroughly discussed a few hours after its delivery in Ṭāhā's presence, there can be hardly any doubt as to the faithfulness of his memory. The idea which struck him most was the one which he chose to underline, namely the perfect compatibility between the revealed text on the one hand and modern science and civilization on the other. The establishment of this compatibility, we are told, was based on an interpretation of the sacred texts aimed at reconciling Qur'ānic statements with the findings of modern science.[43]

A further aspect of 'Abduh's influence can be deduced from Ṭāhā Ḥusain's account of the Imām's method. According to him, the content of 'Abduh's teaching did not depart in the slightest from the traditions that had been laid down. "He used the most ancient and the most venerated of the classics as the basis of his teaching. The method was on the other hand quite new, representing a complete break with the Azharite scholastic tradition. He was deliberately and sometimes exaggeratedly negligent as regards everything connected with words, and extremely meticulous as regards everything connected with ideas. He took a close interest in anything which stimulated thought and reflection. He questioned his pupils and encouraged them to ask him questions, and then tried to make them answer, discussed their replies and in so doing opened up new horizons for them. He instilled in them an appreciation of reading and discussion; he made them love freedom of thought and taught them to express their opinions."[44]

Ṭāhā Ḥusain's remarks, based as they were on first-hand experience, may help us understand 'Abduh's strong impact. His ideas on the continuing relevance of Islam, considered in their context, were not simply agreeable to hear; they must also have struck his audience as a revelation. They brought to life, as he quoted chapter and verse, a glorious past long buried under a suffocating overgrowth of verbal knowledge. The mere perception of this past as a relatively articulated history, must have been a refreshing breath of fresh air. Though lacking in novelty, 'Abduh's ideas were by no means familiar. They derived their strength from the fact that they drew attention to what was so close and yet so long-forgotten.

'Abduh's method, as described by Ṭāhā Ḥusain, must have played a considerable part in this respect. Referring directly to primary sources, giving pride of place to ideas (rather than words), and engaging his audience in a free discussion of the matter at hand, must have had a liberating effect. This, according to Ṭāhā Ḥusain, is 'Abduh's lasting legacy. "There is no doubt", he says, "that it was Shaykh Muḥammad 'Abduh who gave Egypt its intellectual freedom.".[45]

We should, however, try to clarify the limits of this freedom – at least in Ṭāhā's case. There are indications in *al-Ayyām* to suggest that the young Azharite, under the influence of 'Abduh, became something of a "free thinker". Thus, back at home during summer vacations, he began to shock people there with his "heretical views". "They knew that he disparaged most of their learning, scoffed at the miracles of the saints and disapproved of making saints and prophets intermediaries between man and God."[46] In another incident, this time at the Azhar, the boy made a shocking comment on an episode related by al-Mubarrad in his *al-Kāmil*. "The *fuqahā'* accused al-Ḥajjāj of heresy because he said of worshippers who walked around the tomb and pulpit of the

Prophet, "What they revere is nothing but decayed bones and a few sticks". Said the boy, "al-Ḥajjāj may have been ill-mannered and thoughtless, but what he said did not amount to heresy".[47]

It was because of such incidents that the boy got into trouble with the Azhar authorities.[48] It would be mistaken, however, to argue that Ṭāhā was at that time "flirting with atheism", as Zakī Mubārak claims.[49] The truth of the matter was that Ṭāhā was simply advocating some of 'Abduh's fundamentalist and Mu'tazilite ideas. Following the Imām, he was for strict adherence to the fundamental principles of Islam as laid down in the Qur'ān and the Sunna and approved by human reason – the rest being no more than distortion and innovation (*bid'a*).

We should also stress the importance of 'Abduh's enlightened fundamentalism for Ṭāhā's developing interest in literature. 'Abduh's concern with the revival of Arabic classics, and more generally with the reform of Arabic,[50] must have contributed to Ṭāhā's hatred of, and final break with, conventional Azhari subjects and textbooks. Having started, with the help of his brother, to read some of the literary works recommended by the Imām, he learnt later on to find and read primary sources on his own at the National Library.[51] Then a decisive step was taken on the path to literature when Ṭāhā started attending the lessons of Shaykh Sayyid 'Alī al-Marṣafī – protégé of the Imām, to whom he had assigned the task of teaching the merely instrumental and optional subject of literature. It was through al-Marṣafī that 'Abduh's fundamentalism acquired a literary character.

The reader of the second volume of *al-Ayyām* cannot fail to notice the importance attached to Ṭāhā's discovery of literature. Coming almost at the end of the book, after a lengthy description of the squalor in which Azhari students lived, and of Ṭāhā's exasperation with the Azhar, chapter XIX, which is devoted to the discovery of literature, marks a turning point in the life of the protagonist, and brings this part of the story to a happy ending. At the centre of this scene of light and hope, there stands the towering figure of al-Marṣafī, described in passages which must count among Ṭāhā Ḥusain's finest prose.

Shaykh Sayyid 'Alī al-Marṣafī (c. 1862–1931) is depicted as a powerful but lonely figure swimming against the current and surrounded by enemies, against whom he lashes out mercilessly. His greatness is matched only by his human frailty. There is even what might be described as a tragic dimension to his story. His erudition, rigour and harshness are superbly counterbalanced by his humane and endearing qualities: his fatherly love for favourite students, his dignity and steadfastness in the face of stark poverty and his loving care for his mother rendered helpless by old age.[52]

The wondrous thing about this Azharite of the purest breed is that he survived his traditional training to become, unaided, the undisputed authority of his generation on Arabic language and literature.[53] No less remarkable is the manner in which he used literature, considered as a criticism of taste, as a means of liberation.

He based his teaching on a number of classical works, including al-Mubarrad's *al-Kāmil* and Abū Tammām's *al-Ḥamāsa.* The very use of these works, long-forgotten by Azharites, was in itself innovative. Written according to a broad definition of literature,[54] they are monumental treasuries of Arabic lore, whether in verse or in prose, in all fields of knowledge, and thus provide a kaleidoscopic view of Arab history and creativity. In contrast to Azhari manuals, these works ranged freely over many subjects without inhibition or mystification.

Al-Marṣafī's teaching consisted in commenting on these works. Many were the Azharites who flocked to his courses only to discover that they could not continue. The whole exercise seemed so alien and so demanding, and yet without great value – given the subject's low status in the curriculum. The Shaykh did not proceed exactly as they had expected, as he did not use *al-Ḥamāsa* as his text (*matn*) accompanied by the normal apparatus of commentary.[55] In addition, his mockery of Azhari doctors and textbooks, though amusing, was too harsh for them to tolerate.[56] For his part, al-Marṣafī found that such students were ill-equipped for literary studies, which, in his view, called for taste rather than dialectical skill.[57] He preferred to have a narrow circle of students who could not only endure his rigorous scrutiny of ancient texts but also appreciate their beauty.

Like 'Abduh, al-Marṣafī was in favour of a return to the sources, except that the latter's fundamentalism was of a literary kind. His heroes were not the early Muslims but the desert-dwelling Arabs of the *jāhiliyya* (pre-Islamic period), whose literary models had survived the rise of Islam and continued to be followed under the Umayyads.[58] Thus poetry was the better the closer it was to pre-Islamic bedouin ideals: straightforwardness, vigour, firmness of style and such complete command of the language as would resist the tyranny of poetic licence.[59] It was only natural that al-Marṣafī had an aversion for later city-dwelling poets, such as Muslim ibn al-Walīd, Abū Tammām, al-Mutanabbī and Abu'l-'Alā' al-Ma'arrī, who strained after their meanings, were fond of stylistic embellishments (*badī'*) and had a penchant for Greek philosophy and logic.[60] Their poetry, according to al-Marṣafī, was ornate, contrived and adulterated.

Since al-Marṣafī left no theoretical statement on his critical practice, Ṭāhā Ḥusain's succinct account of his master's methodology is of capital importance.[61] "I know of nothing in the world", he wrote, "which can exert so strong an influence for freedom, especially on the young, as literature, and above all literature as Shaykh Marṣafī taught it when he was explaining *al-Ḥamāsa* and later the *al-Kāmil* to his class. What then did this study consist in? Unfettered criticism of the poet, anthologist and commentator, not to mention the various philologists. Then the testing and exercise of taste through enquiry into the hidden constituents of beauty in literature, in prose and poetry, in general drift and detailed meaning, in rhyme and rhythm, and in the combination of individual words. Then assessment of contemporary taste as it was accepted in the students' immediate environment, and the constant contrast between the gross taste and jaded wits of the Azhar and the delicacy and penetration of the ancients. The final result of all this was to break the chains of the Azhar once and for all, to arouse utter disgust – as a rule entirely justified, but not always – with the taste, scholarship, conversation and general behaviour of the shaykhs."[62]

We should not be surprised if this description of al-Marṣafī's method reads like a manifesto, gradually mounting in tone until the final crescendo with the victorious onslaught on Azhari taste and sensibility. Al-Marṣafī's accomplishment amounted in fact to a critical "revolution" whose implications need to be described. The breakthrough consisted mainly in the firm establishment of literary texts as aesthetic phenomena, i.e. as objects of taste and value judgement. It is within this context that we should understand al-Marṣafī's aversion to questions of grammar and morphology,[63] his concern for "language and criticism" or more precisely for "ways and means of achieving eloquence in speech".[64] Instead of the then normal practice of indulging in an endless maze of grammatical analyses and thereby losing sight of what was specifically literary, al-Marṣafī made a point of highlighting such qualities as constituted and explained the "beauty" of the texts. His linguistic and critical scrutiny, as opposed to grammatical analysis, was stylistic or rhetorical in nature.

The extensive process of criticism – bearing on the poet, the anthologist and the commentator – aimed mainly at placing the text concerned under the most favourable conditions of reception. The text was corrected (whenever found to contain faults or to be corrupt) and put back within its natural context, whether literary or historical. In so doing, al-Marṣafī showed concern for the text's integrity and unity,[65] and provided ample information on its author.[66] Once this work of erudition was accomplished, the students were invited to consider the text's aesthetic qualities. At this point, so it seems, the master's stylistic analyses went hand in hand with a more active role on the part of the students. Like Muḥammad 'Abduh's, al-Marṣafī's teaching took at times a Socratic form, when students were encouraged to participate and judge for themselves.[67] Given this complicity between teacher and student through the shared experience of beauty, the former was able to launch his final devastating attack.

Those who attended al-Marṣafī's lessons and could put up with the ordeal,[68] were meant to feel liberated. According to Ṭāhā Ḥusain, al-Marṣafī's criticism was "unfettered" (lit: "free"); the aim of the whole process was to break the chains of the Azhar. There is an indissoluble link between literature, especially of the type taught by al-Marṣafī, and freedom. In fact, we cannot hope to understand the master's role in Ṭāhā's intellectual development until we have analysed the complex concept of freedom so used. Thus al-Marṣafī is said to be free insofar as he was a man of letters. Though solemn, as befits a great scholar when in society or with his class at the Azhar, he would, once alone with his best friends, act as a man of letters speaking freely on all matters. In so doing, he followed the example of ancient authors who, according to him, were free and spoke their minds fearlessly.[69] To be free in this sense implies the possession of such moral and intellectual qualities as courage, breadth of culture, versatility and fluency.

It would, however, be inaccurate to say that al-Marṣafī was "free" only when in the company of close friends. In fact, he achieved his highest form of freedom while teaching; for it was within this context that the man of letters became a critic. Having done away with the tyranny of verbal analysis (in the Azhari fashion) and having done his share of linguistic and scholarly work, he would at last finds himself face to face with his proper materials, namely texts as mere objects for taste, and he would be called upon to pass judgement. As these texts manifested their aesthetic qualities, the critic was thereby established as a truly independent subject – responsive and active.

A further strand in the complex concept of literary freedom as used by Ṭāhā Ḥusain is to be found in the long and magisterial introduction to his book on pre-Islamic literature (1927). There he calls for a certain kind of freedom to be enjoyed not by the man of letters, but by literature itself. For literature to be free in this sense is for it to be studied not as an instrument but as an end in itself. During the age of intellectual stagnation, so the argument goes, literature, like all disciplines related to the study of Arabic, were treated as a means to an extraneous end. Thus Arabic came to be held as something sacred and to be debased at the same time. Sacred because it was the language of the Qur'ān and Islam, and yet debased since it was not studied for its own sake but only as a subsidiary subject inferior to jurisprudence (*fiqh*) and theology (*tawḥīd*).[70]

At the time he called for freedom in this sense Ṭāhā Ḥusain had left both the Azhar and al-Marṣafī well behind, having adopted a modern historical outlook on literature. But the kind of freedom he claimed for literature at the time had already been achieved, at least in part, by his Azhari master.

The exclusively literary character of al-Marṣafī's endeavour must have helped to establish literature as an independent subject. It was he who first studied literary texts solely as objects of beauty, or sheer enjoyment and disinterested appreciation. While Muḥammad 'Abduh acted primarily as a theologian and a religious reformer, al-Marṣafī broke out of the theological frame of reference completely. While the former helped his audience to look beyond the Azhari system, the latter provided a concrete example of thinking independently of both the Azhar and religion. To the question of whether Muḥammad 'Abduh was not outmanoeuvred by his conservative adversaries in negotiating the reformed Azhari syllabus, the answer must, therefore, be in the negative. The heavy price he had to pay in order to create a loophole for modern subjects in the Azhar curriculum was not in vain. The man who was entrusted with teaching literature played in fact the part of a Trojan horse within the Azhari fortress.[71]

It could even be argued that al-Marṣafī was a precursor as far as the historical approach was concerned; for his critical practice, though mainly linguistic, involved a rudimentary form of historical awareness. In his work as editor and commentator of classical anthologies, he drew on his wide-ranging knowledge of the Arab past, and he rearranged his materials in historical order.[72] Again, al-Marṣafī's classicism, like 'Abduh's fundamentalism, must have paved the way for a truly historical approach, inasmuch as it distinguished within an otherwise undifferentiated past, between an early "golden age" and a later time of decadence.

Even after he had outgrown al-Marṣafī, Ṭāhā Ḥusain retained the essential lessons of his Azhari master. He was to widen his interests and preferences beyond the classical period, accommodating, and sometimes glorifying, the very poets and innovators whom al-Marṣafī had denigrated. All literary figures and phenomena were to be set within the all-embracing medium of history, and systematically studied insofar as they related to their societies. And yet, al-Marṣafī's linguistic or stylistic criticism was never abandoned. Even his predilection for eloquence and his aversion to poetic licence[73] were retained. To use a Hegelian term, al-Marṣafī's contribution was sublated, i.e. left behind and yet maintained in Ṭāhā Ḥusain's final synthesis. Once this synthesis had been established, literary criticism was to become forever after partly stylistic and partly historical.

Such was the importance of 'Abduh's and al-Marṣafī's influence on Ṭāhā that it would be true to say that he outgrew the Azhar while he was still a student there. It was through these two shaykhs that he became aware of the primary sources of Arab and Islamic culture. Having learnt this basic lesson about his own cultural identity, he was ready to progress towards his later modernism and humanism. This is all the more true in view of the fact that this return to the sources also involved a return to certain values and ideals, e.g. reason and the need to accommodate modern progress (in 'Abduh's case); freedom and breadth of culture (in al-Marṣafī's case); a return which was a prerequisite to any attempt to come to terms with other traditions.

In this respect, it would seem at first sight that Muḥammad 'Abduh was the more accommodating of the two. He affirmed most explicitly that true Islam was perfectly compatible with rationalism and Western scientific and technological achievements. And yet it was precisely on account of his assumption of religion as a basic point of reference, that his system was found by Ṭāhā to be restrictive and outmoded. Writing in 1934, Ṭāhā argued that 'Abduh's innovation was too timid; and his views on science and religion no longer corresponded to the progress achieved by peoples of the East on their way to total freedom. Very few Muslims would now wish to reconcile their faith with modern knowledge. They were simply plunging headlong into European civilization. 'Abduh's attempt to find in the sacred texts the rationale for science was harmful to both sides: it did violence to the texts in question and it impeded scientific progress.[74]

It was in fact the intransigent and rather parochial al-Marṣafī who had the stronger and more lasting effect, given that his views on, and practice of, literary freedom instilled the necessary open-mindedness for the reception and integration of foreign influences. So, while both Muḥammad 'Abduh and al-Marṣafī helped Ṭāhā to discover what he later called "the living ancient tradition",[75] it was chiefly the latter who gave that tradition its literary character, and thus shaped Ṭāhā's, essentially literary, sensitivity to foreign cultures. That much was implied by Ṭāhā Ḥusain when he stated that he owed his whole intellectual life to two great teachers, namely al-Marṣafī and Carlo Alfonso Nallino, and that everything he had learnt ever after, whether in Egypt or abroad, was based on their teachings.[76]

All these lessons would, however, have had little effect if it had not been for a certain receptivity on the part of Ṭāhā. Pierre Cachia aptly suggested that in discovering literature, Ṭāhā began to discover himself.[77] How was it that the young man's identity was fulfilled through literature? Here, I think, we need to evoke yet another connotation of literary freedom, which was peculiar to Ṭāhā's own experience of confinement, and was, therefore, so basic that it was never formulated straightforwardly. Literature had in his case a liberating effect inasmuch as it broke the barriers between the self and the world. As far as he was concerned, literature was essentially a kind of audible discourse (speech) which, by virtue of its sonorous and other aesthetic qualities, managed to come across, thus creating a bond between speaker and listener and reinserting both into the world of men. Such was the power of the spoken word that it penetrated the darkness of sightlessness and thereby established a higher community of feeling and communication.

Such ideas permeate Ṭāhā Ḥusain's thoughts to such an extent that it is hard to choose among the numerous possible illustrations. We may, however, begin with considering how a man of letters is supposed to long for an audience. Al-Marṣafī, as we have seen, was free and at his best when he spoke about literature with close friends. In fact, the most distinctive characteristic of a man of letters, according to Ṭāhā Ḥusain, is his lust for communication. This is made abundantly clear in the novel *Adīb*[78] ["A Man of letters"] whose protagonist is meant to exemplify, in an extreme and tragic form, what it is to be a man of letters. He is thus shown to be relentlessly driven, as if by an inner demon, to seek communication. His loneliness is matched only by his endless discourses.

No less remarkable is Ṭāhā Ḥusain's assumption about the readiness of his fellow men to respond to the literary message and the ease with which a community of feeling between artist and audience could be established. The nearest he ever came to a straightforward expression of that assumption was perhaps when he tried, in an article on the writer in the world today, to elucidate the social character of literature. It is significant that he chose for that purpose the model of a singer. "At some point in the existence of a community", he wrote, "a man began to sing. The others listened, liked his song, and wanted to hear it again. He, for his part, was glad to have an audience, and did not wait to be asked twice. A relationship was thus established between the singer and those around him, and a social institution was born."[79]

The desire to participate in such a superior form of community is implicit in Ṭāhā Ḥusain's consistent discursiveness. His works, even when they are scholarly, assume the form of a discourse, if not that of a straightforward dialogue. The existence of an interlocutor is always assumed or clearly stated. Sometimes, the reader himself is made to play this role.

Ṭāhā's receptivity to the spoken word had been developed well before his arrival at the Azhar. Early on, as a child in his village in Upper Egypt, he had already experienced the enchantment of literature as he listened to itinerant bards. When, after a period of loneliness in Cairo and despair at the Azhar, he listened to 'Abduh – whose gentle voice was unforgettable – and to al-Marṣafī – whose diction was also superb[80] – the words of the two shaykhs fell on fertile soil. What the latter, in particular, said or implied about (literary) freedom corresponded to, and was corroborated by, what Ṭāhā knew through experience. Thus Ṭāhā fulfilled himself in literature and the seeds of his later humanism were sown. For the liberation he achieved through literature meant breadth of culture, a return to classical sources and integration into a higher community.

Notes

1 See *Fi'l-ṣayf*, (Beirut 1981), pp. 30 ff. See also *Aḥādīth*, in *MK*, vol. XII, 1974, p. 708 ff.
2 Ibid., p. 709.
3 Ibid., p. 708.
4 Op. cit., p. 43.
5 "*Fanqala*": apparently coined by derivation from the expression "*fa-naqūlu*" ("then we would say") to stand for the Azhari form of dialectic involving objection and counter-objection. "If you say so and so, then we would say such and such"). See Sayf al-Naṣr al-Ṭalkhāwī, *Shaykh udabā' Miṣr Sayyid Ibn 'Alī al-Marṣafī*, (Cairo 1984), p. 48. See also Ṭāhā Hussein, *The Stream of days*, 2nd edn. (London 1948), p. 92.
6 Ibrahim Salama, *L'Enseignement Islamique en Egypte* (Cairo 1939), p. 273.
7 Ibn Khaldūn, *The Muqaddima. An Introduction to history*, tr. Franz Rosenthal (London 1986), vol. III, p. 415.
8 *Takhlīṣ al-ibrīz fī talkhīṣ Bārīz*, ed. Maḥmūd Fahmī Ḥijāzī (Cairo 1974), p. 297.
9 Ibid.
10 *The Stream of days*, p. 15.
11 Ibid., pp. 53–54.
12 Ṭāhā was accompanied to the lesson in question by Santillana under whom he studied at the nascent Egyptian University – without as yet breaking all ties with the Azhar.
13 Ṭāhā Ḥusain, *A Passage to France*, (Leiden 1976), pp. 36–37.
14 Ibrahim Salama, op. cit., p. 240.
15 For a definition of these two categories of disciplines, see Ibn Khaldūn, op. cit., p. 420.
16 Reproduced, with minor adaptations, from Ibrahim Salama, op. cit., pp. 269–270.
17 Subjects giving priority: these were optional, but those who chose to study them were given preferential treatment with regard to employment and salaries. See 'Abd al-Muta'āl al-Ṣa'īdī, *Tārikh al-iṣlāḥ fi'l-Azhar wa-ṣafaḥāt min al-jihād fi'l-iṣlāḥ* (Cairo n.d.), p. 59.
18 The sign + marks subjects introduced under the 1896 reform.
19 According to the translation proposed by B. Reinert, *EI*[2] art. "al-Ma'ānī wa'l-Bayān".
20 Pre-Islamic poetry used to be studied for the evidence it might provide with regard to interpreting the Qur'ān and demonstrating the purity of its Arabic.

21 *Iḥyā' 'ulūm al-dīn,* ed. Badawī Ṭabāna (Cairo 1957), vol. I, p. 14 ff.
22 Rector of the Azhar from 1886 to 1895. See J. Jomier, *EI*[2] art. "al-Azhar". 5. List of Rectors. The *fatwā* was issued in 1305/1888. See 'Abd al-Muta'āl al-Ṣa'īdī, op. cit., p. 39.
23 Proceeding from what is most general to what is most specific. See Ibid., p. 40.
24 Ibid., pp. 40,41, 42.
25 Ibid., pp. 42–43.
26 Knowledge of arithmetic was, however, recognized to be necessary for the division of heritages and such practical matters. Ibid., p. 16.
27 *Fi 'l-adab al-jāhilī,* in *MK,* vol. V, 1973, p. 59.
28 The first crisis took place when 'Abduh, as a boy, studied at al-Aḥmadī Mosque (in Ṭanṭa) where the instruction was modelled on the Azhar. The second crisis occurred three years after he went to the Azhar in 1866. See 'Uthmān Amīn, *Rā'id al-fikr al-Miṣrī al-Imām Muḥammad 'Abduh* (Cairo 1965), pp. 34 and 35.
29 For a fairly detailed account of this reform, see 'Abd al-Muta'āl al-Ṣa'īdī, op. cit., pp. 270–271.
30 Ibid., pp. 58–59. See also Ibrahim Salama, op. cit., pp. 270–271.
31 Pierre Cachia, *Taha Husayn, his place in the Egyptian literary renaissance* (London 1956), p. 50.
32 *Fi'l-ṣayf,* p. 43.
33 "Muṣṭafā 'Abd al-Rāziq kamā 'araftuh", in *Kutub wa-mu'allifūn,* in *MK,* vol. XVI, 1981, p. 44.
34 Ibid.
35 *The Stream of days,* p. 89. See also idem, "Muḥammad 'Abduh", *al-Wādī,* 11 July 1934.
36 Muḥammad 'Abduh, *al-Islām dīn al-'ilm wa'l-madaniyya,* ed. 'Āṭif al-'Irāqī, (Cairo 1987), pp. 145, 151 and 171. See also J. Schacht, *EI*[2], art. "Muḥammad 'Abduh".
37 Such as Ḥasan al-'Aṭṭār, Ḥusain al-Marṣafī and Rifā'a al-Ṭahtāwī. See Gilbert Delanoue, *Moralistes et politiques musulmans dans l'Egypte du XIXe siècle* (Paris-Cairo 1982), vol. II.
38 Muḥammad 'Abduh, *The Theology of Unity* (English version of *Risālat al-tawḥīd*), tr. Isḥāq Mus'ad and Kenneth Cragg (London 1966), p. 152.
39 Ibid.
40 See Taha Hussein, "La grande figure du Cheikh Mohamed Abdo", *Effort,* June 1934, pp. 3–5. *Effort* was an Egyptian francophone magazine of which little is known, save that it was sponsored by a group of French-speaking intellectuals called *les Essayistes.*
41 Ibid., p. 4.
42 At this time 'Abduh lectured also on rhetoric and logic.
43 Taha Hussein, op. cit., p. 5.
44 Ibid., p.4.
45 Ibid.
46 *The Stream of days,* p. 89. See also idem, "Muḥammad 'Abduh", *al-Wādī,* 11 July 1934.
47 Op. cit., p. 121. I have made some changes in Hilary Wayment's translation.

48 Ibid., p. 121 ff.
49 Zakī Mubārak, *al-Badā'i'* (Cairo 1935), p. 71.
50 This was one of 'Abduh's fundamental aims as stated in his fragment of autobiography. See Muḥammad Rashīd Riḍā, *Tārīkh al-Ustādh al-Imām al-Ṣhaykh Muḥammad 'Abduh* (Cairo 1931), vol. I, p. 11. For an English translation of that statement, see Albert Hourani, *Arabic thought in the liberal age, 1798–1939* (Cambridge 1984), p. 141.
51 *The Stream of days*, p. 117.
52 Ibid., pp. 118–119.
53 Zakī Mubārak, op. cit., p. 68. See also Ṭāhā Ḥusain, *Tajdīd dhikrā Abi'l-'Alā'*, in *MK*, vol. X, 1974, p. 9.
54 "(Philologists) who wanted to define this discipline said: 'Literature is expert knowledge of the poetry and history of the Arabs as well as the possession of some knowledge regarding every science'" Ibn Khaldūn, op. cit., p. 340.
55 In his course on *al-Ḥamāsa,* al-Marṣafī used in fact al-Tibrīzi's commentary on this work, but he did so in his own critical way. See Ṭāhā Ḥusain, op. cit., pp. 10–11. Typically Azharite students, like Ṭāhā's elder brother and his friends, "regarded *al-Ḥamāsa* as text (*matn*), with al-Tibrīzī's work as its primary commentary, and were sorry to find that the commentary had not in its turn been glossed". *The Stream of days*, p. 115.
56 Ibid.
57 Ibid.
58 Ṭāhā Ḥusain, op. cit., pp. 9–10.
59 Ibid., p. 10.
60 Ibid.
61 This account will be supplemented in what follows with further information derived from Zakī Mubārak, op. cit., and Sayf al-Naṣr al-Ṭalkhāwī, op. cit.
62 *The Stream of days*, pp. 117–118. Translation revised.
63 Ṭāhā Ḥusain, op. cit., p. 10.
64 Ibid., p. 9.
65 Sayf al-Naṣr al-Ṭalkhāwī, op. cit., Ch. 4.
66 Ibid., p. 141 ff.
67 See Zakī Mubārak, op. cit., p. 66.
68 Zakī Mubārak relates (ibid., p. 73) that such lessons lasted for three hours.
69 *The Stream of days*, p. 118.
70 *Fi'l-adab al-jāhilī*, in *MK*, vol. V, p. 58.
71 For a list of his students who became distinguished men of letters, see Muḥammad Kāmil al-Faqī, *al-Azhar wa-atharuh fi'l-nahḍa al-adabiyya al-ḥadītha* (Cairo 1965), pp. 404–405.
72 Sayf al-Naṣr al-Ṭalkhāwī, op. cit., p. 147.
73 See for instance how Ṭāhā Ḥusain took to task the poets Aḥmad Shawqī and Ḥāfiẓ Ibrāhīm for yielding to the tyranny of poetic licence, in his *Ḥāfiẓ wa-Shawqī*, in *MK*, vol. XII, 1974, pp. 448 ff.
74 "La grande figure du Cheikh Mohamed Abdo", *Effort*, June 1934, p. 5.

75 *Adabunā al-ḥadīth mā lahū wa-mā 'alayh*, in *MK*, vol. XVI, 1981, p. 356. Notice how Ṭāhā Ḥusain, following 'Abduh, contrasts the so-called "living tradition" with the "obsolete" and "loathsome" later tradition which dates from the Ottoman era. Ibid., p. 356.
76 Preface to Nallino's *Tārīkh* (Cairo 1970), pp. 8–9.
77 Cachia, op. cit., p. 51.
78 First published in 1939, it relates the largely true story of a fellow student both at the old Egyptian University and at the Sorbonne.
79 "The Writer in the world today", in *The Artist in modern society; essays and statements collected by Unesco* (International Conference of Artists, Venice, 22–28 September 1952) (Paris: UNESCO 1952), pp. 69–83, p. 81. The text, originally in French, was Ṭāhā's contribution to the above-mentioned conference. Translation slightly revised.
80 Zakī Mubārak, op. cit., p. 66.

CHAPTER III

The Discovery of History

We saw in the preceding chapter how Ṭāhā, while still a student at the Azhar and under the influence of Muḥammad ʻAbduh and al-Marṣafī, was able to break out of the straitjacket of Azhari traditional education. Both teachers called for a return to a supposedly original and unadulterated source beyond the accumulated layers of scholastic learning. For the one, the primary holy texts of Islam were to serve as a criterion for the accommodation of science and modern civilization. For the other, ancient literature, especially pre-Islamic poetry, was an ideal to be pursued by a modern literary revival. In what follows, we shall deal with a further stage in Ṭāhā's intellectual development, in which he was able to dispense with ʻAbduh's fundamentalism and al-Marṣafī's neo-classicism and assume a modernist point of view. For reasons which will subsequently become clear, this stage, which coincided roughly with Ṭāhā's years of study at the nascent Egyptian University and his early writings, has been largely neglected. It is no exaggeration, however, to say that the period in question was the most crucial in Ṭāhā's education. It was at that time that he was initiated by both Aḥmad Luṭfī al-Sayyid and his university teachers into Western modes of thought and scientific methods of research. It was then that he experienced, for the first time and as never before or afterwards, the intoxication and fermentation arising from the encounter between the two cultures. During the same period, he made his second major discovery, namely that of history. This discovery which was no less important and no less liberating than the earlier discovery of literature, was to take him out of the realm of texts into the open world of events. Henceforth, he was to view everything, including of course East-West relations, within an overtly historical frame of reference. As he was then to begin his career as a writer and to recast his thought in the historical mould, we may say that the Ṭāhā we know was born at that time. We may therefore proceed to consider the kind of history that he was taught at the nascent Egyptian University, leaving for the next chapter the task of accounting for Ṭāhā's early, but highly formative, historical thought.

The Teacher of the Generation

The transition from the Azhar to the university was neither smooth nor clear-cut. It stretched over a fairly long and troubled period during which Ṭāhā remained for a while astride the two "worlds", attending only two Azhari courses[1] in the morning and going to the university in the afternoon;[2] the final rupture with the Azhar did not take place until Ṭāhā failed, or was failed, his final *'ālimiyya* examination. It was only then that Ṭāhā devoted himself to his new schooling. But before reaching this point of no-return, we may consider, again, the beginnings of this process of alienation. Let us recall how Ṭāhā, while still a student at the Azhar, felt mortified when he realized, on the death of 'Abduh in 1905, that the Imām had been betrayed by his Azhari followers. He "noticed ... something ... which increased his aversion to the Azhar and his contempt for both sheikhs and students. He found that the men who mourned sincerely for the Imām did not wear turbans, but tarbouches, and he conceived a secret inclination towards them and a desire to make some acquaintance with their society".[3]

Ṭāhā's secret wish began to be fulfilled, and in a grand manner for that matter, when he was offered the opportunity, in 1907, to meet Aḥmad Luṭfī al-Sayyid (1872–1963),[4] then editor-in-chief of *al-Jarīda*,[5] with a view to publishing an article against the Azhar and its Rector.[6] Instead of publishing the piece, presumably because it was too harsh, Luṭfī successfully interceded on behalf of the rebellious author.[7] From that point onward, Ṭāhā was irresistibly drawn into Luṭfī's circle of followers, who generally belonged to the higher strata of society.[8] He was left in no doubt that he was welcome in that privileged society,[9] and thus began Ṭāhā's access to the world of secular knowledge and to a privileged place, maintained and consolidated ever after, among the intellectual and political elite of the country.

Ṭāhā became in due course Luṭfī's favourite disciple and protégé. There was a time when he paid daily visits to the director of *al-Jarīda* in his office, and there he met Luṭfī's distinguished friends and followers. As the organ of the Umma party,[10] *al-Jarīda* was in fact something of a school or an anticipation of the Faculty of Arts to be,[11] in which Luṭfī set out to teach his heterogeneous audience what they had not learnt at their respective schools.[12] Thus it was at *al-Jarīda*'s "school" that they heard for the first time such names as Montesquieu, Voltaire, Rousseau, Diderot, Kant, Auguste Comte, J.S. Mill, Jules Simon and Herbert Spencer. Similarly, but perhaps less often, they heard references to Descartes, Leibniz, Malebranche and Spinoza.[13]

While Luṭfī was considered as the advocate of philosophy in the East, and in particular the philosophy of Aristotle and political philosophy, the manner in which Ṭāhā Ḥusain lists the above-mentioned names suggests that Luṭfī's preferences in modern philosophy were for the philosophers of the French Enlightenment, and for critical philosophy, positivism and utilitarianism – as distinct from the rationalist tradition of thought. Luṭfī could, again, amaze the Azharis among his audience with his knowledge in the domain of Islamic thought.[14] Being familiar in a fashion with Aristotle the logician and metaphysician, they were exhilarated to discover, through Luṭfī, the Stagirite's ethics and politics.[15] They were, to use Ṭāhā Ḥusain's own words, infatuated with such terms as democracy, aristocracy and oligarchy.[16]

Rightly named "the teacher of the generation", Luṭfī owed his influence to his *practical* bent of mind,[17] his sense of the relevant and his vision. Never writing systematically, he preferred to be discursive without, however, losing sight of a set of orientations to which he adhered with remarkable single-mindedness. His immediate task, as far as *al-Jarīda* was concerned, was to achieve reform by imparting information and ideas relating to political, social and pedagogical matters. On a much broader scale, he sought to achieve a "balanced blend" (*mizāj mu'tadil*) of Islamic and foreign cultures.[18] To do this, he assumed, it was necessary to recapture the expansive thrust of Islamic thought in its heyday, and cast the net widely so as to encompass the bases of Western culture in the Greek heritage.[19]

Luṭfī's teachings were in many ways a most appropriate prelude to, and consolidation of, Ṭāhā's university education. Let us first consider Luṭfī's receptive attitude to Western culture. The idea of "the balanced blend", already implicit in his mixed culture, is sometimes expressed in an emphatic, and perhaps defiant, manner. He calls explicitly for learning from the West, for taking

Europe as a guide.[20] In an article entitled *Taqlīd* ["Imitation"], Luṭfī would go so far as to affirm the need to imitate European civilization,[21] especially in useful matters.[22] A copy, he would argue, might be just as good as the original.[23] To those who accused Western civilization of materialism and colonialism, and feared that its wholehearted acceptance might lead to a loss of identity, he would sometimes give a pragmatic answer. Egyptians, so the argument went, had to import the products of Western civilization if they were to acquire the necessary "means of power" and to participate in "modern life".[24] Continued adherence to inherited customs and attitudes would be wrong once it had been shown that they impeded development.[25] In abandoning such traditions, Egyptians need not be unduly worried about their own identity. The imported products would be adapted in due course to Egyptian tastes and would carry an Egyptian "stamp".[26] This had happened in the past when the Greek and Persian heritages were received and "Islamicized" by the Arabs, and there was no reason why it should not happen again.[27]

At other times Luṭfī would not leave the matter entirely to the work of time, and would call for an effort to be made with a view to "Egyptianizing" cultural imports. Thus, to counteract Western materialism he would recommend falling back on the simple tenets of faith as expressed by early Muslim generations,[28] learning to appreciate ancient Egyptian monuments,[29] or adhering to certain traditional and typically Egyptian values such as solidarity, hospitality and sociability.[30] In either case, however, the process of imposing the Egyptian "stamp" was to take place without reference to Islam as a codified body of doctrine or holy texts.[31] Unlike 'Abduh and Jamāl al-Dīn al-Afghānī, Luṭfī based his main argument for accommodating Western culture on the need to keep up with the times or to achieve progress. He would attach no condition but the imposition of a loosely defined, and essentially accommodating, Egyptian character. As opposed to 'Abduh's fundamentalism (i.e. the introduction of modern forms of progress only insofar as they are adaptable to Islam), Luṭfī's "balanced blend" was meant to be definitely modernist.

The break with 'Abduh's fundamentalism is even more obvious when we take into account Luṭfī's views on Egyptian nationalism, where he develops an evidently secular conception of Egyptian identity. The basic point of reference in this case is territorial, namely the land of Egypt itself – the specific entity that it constitutes geographically and historically.[32] In this respect, Luṭfī's brand of nationalism seems to be an important exception to Vatikiotis' statement that Arab societies did not experience a movement for the secularization of political identity.[33] Egypt, for Luṭfī, is a nation in its own right; in fact its claim to uniqueness is stronger than that of any other nation.[34] The constituents of this nationhood are, as he put it, localized factors (*'awāmil mawḍi'iyya*) relating to the land itself and its inhabitants, e.g. geography, genealogy and common interests.[35] Given this down-to-earth approach, Luṭfī would declare, unceremoniously, that pan-Islamism and even Arab unity were no more than fantasies and illusions.[36] To claim that the land of Islam was a homeland for all Muslims could only serve the interests of a strong race or a colonialist power bent on conquering other countries in the name of religion.[37] Now that oriental countries could no longer play such a role, having fallen victim to Western colonialism, the most they could do was to reassert their independence.[38]

That Luṭfī's teachings were most favourable to Ṭāhā's schooling at the nascent Egyptian University can again be seen when we consider Luṭfī's views on education and its role, aims and methods. Being a staunch reformist, Luṭfī abhorred violence and all precipitate action. For him, Egypt's independence was to be achieved peacefully and gradually, mainly through institutional change,[39] and patient educational and intellectual work.

Neither "eye-catching" nor immediately rewarding, this kind of work was, according to Luṭfī, bound to be unpopular with the masses and the hot-headed young,[40] but it had the merit of being unobjectionable to the ruling powers and also of being indispensable.[41] Bearing in mind that he believed in the necessity of acquiring the "means of power", we need to stress that the "power" he had in mind was not primarily technological. For Egyptians, he would say, the only kind of power that mattered was moral (*ma'nawiyya*)[42] and the only form of freedom that was both easily attainable and absolutely indispensable was intellectual (lit: "scientific") freedom.[43]

As far as the aims of education were concerned, Luṭfī was critical of the policy, prevalent at the time, of producing candidates for work in the civil service or, as it were, cogs in the government wheel.[44] The Egyptian educational system should rather aim to bring the learners' faculties to their perfection, and more generally to consolidate such public and civil virtues as would promote homogeneity and national unity.[45] To achieve these aims, the emphasis should be shifted from purely practical subjects to such disciplines, so far neglected, as would contribute to the education of writers, political leaders and philosophers, namely the moral, social and pedagogical sciences.[46]

In other words, a reformed educational system should have as its immediate aim the training of an elite or intelligentsia, who would be able to extend the process of education beyond schools to society at large.[47] Armed with critical thinking, writers for instance could play a leading role in reforming relations within the family and in cultivating such public virtues as justice, courage, generosity and sociability.[48] It was only through such a combination of educational reform and extended intellectual effort that natural disparities between individuals could be reduced and national unity could be consolidated.[49]

With such aims in mind, it was natural for Luṭfī to condemn traditional methods of teaching and learning, and to criticize the reliance on memorization in Qur'ānic schools.[50] Given that the primary aim of education was the training of citizens, including a leading intellectual elite, we can understand perfectly Luṭfī's suggestion that a teacher should turn away from textbooks and address himself to the student, "communicating with his mind and thereby bringing its faculties to their perfection and preparing them for the fulfilment of their duty in [social] life".[51] Nor can we be left in any doubt that Luṭfī was guided in his teaching practice at *al-Jarīda*'s "school" by this precept of attending to the minds of his followers. Thus, according to Ṭāhā Ḥusain, Luṭfī would engage in dialogue with his students in the manner of Socrates with Athenian youth, lecture them or have lectures given to them (in evening classes); or, a particularly "modern" method, assign to those among them who knew a foreign language (i.e. English or French) the task of translating selected texts into Arabic.[52]

The Egyptian National University

When the university – commonly known as *al-Jāmi'a al-Ahliyya* to distinguish it from the later state university – finally opened its doors on 21 December 1908, Ṭāhā was thus prepared in a way to receive the kind of education it was to provide. In fact, some of the ideals and values that the university stood for had already been in the air through the influence of several pioneers other than Luṭfī, among whom were such prominent figures as Muḥammad 'Abduh, Muṣṭafā Kāmil, Qāsim Amīn and Sa'd Zaghlūl.[53] There was near unanimity among them in condemning the narrowly utilitarian character of the existing educational system. Thus 'Abduh is reported to have deplored the total neglect of the social sciences, philosophy, the fine arts and Arabic and foreign literature.[54] Thus again Qāsim Amīn called for the kind of education that would aim at disinterested research solely motivated by love of truth and the desire to explore the realm of the unknown.[55] The Egyptian University, he contended, should initiate a linguistic and literary revolution.[56]

Opposition to the utilitarian character of the existing educational system must, again, be seen in the context of rising Egyptian nationalism and the independence movement. Unlike the British occupation authorities, who were more in favour of the promotion of basic education,[57] the advocates of the university project sought thereby to assert Egypt's will to freedom and revival. Speaking at the inaugural ceremony, 'Abd al-Khāliq Tharwat pointed out that it was high time for Egypt to educate the young who would, through the pursuit of knowledge for its own sake, secure for their country its rightful place in the community of civilized nations.[58] This call in turn presupposed a certain vision of Egypt's role in history as the birthplace of civilization and a principal refuge for culture. Such assumptions were made explicit in another speech delivered on the same occasion by Aḥmad Zakī Bek.[59] Having recalled the glowing periods in Egyptian history under the Pharaohs, the Ptolemies and the Fatimids, he also reminded his audience of the spread of Islamic culture to Mediterranean and European countries. The fact that Europe had gradually become the main source of knowledge was, he maintained, a natural development in harmony with the movement of history. It was in the nature of things that civilization should migrate from one region of the world to another, that the leading role should be taken up by one country after another. If it was Egypt's destiny to wither and wane for centuries, the time was at last ripe for her to arise from her slumbers and make up for past losses. It was high time for Egypt to seek knowledge in Europe with a view to becoming a centre of learning again.[60]

To those who supported the university project, Egyptian independence and revival were, therefore, inseparable from receptiveness to the West and the ambition of establishing a fertile cultural exchange with Europe. Thus the university was meant to be a meeting point of various cultures. It was also meant to be democratic and secular.[61]

Implementation of the project was a national affair.[62] As the university was born in the midst of such high hopes, its inauguration was the occasion for a great deal of rejoicing. According to a foreign writer, "an interesting assortment of people came to hear the lectures: pashas well beyond the prime of life, driven to the main gate in splendid carriages, young civil servants in beautifully tailored suits, looking like advertisements for the "high life", earnest counsellors from the native law courts; students from al-Azhar University in their long flowing robes and immaculate white turbans, even more reflective in their measured gait; scattered-brained young Europeans, always smiling in a country where it never rains."[63]

The nascent university was, however, of modest size and scope, as it was no more than an embryonic Faculty of Arts.[64] Following a debate on the sort of subjects to be taught, it was decided that the university should start with the Arts.[65] This choice, dictated in the main by practical reasons, was justified by pointing out the human needs that the study of such disciplines might satisfy. It was argued, for instance, that the study of history and literature was both useful and enjoyable. The former discipline, it was maintained, should promote the faculty of thought, comparison and judgement, while the latter was most suited to teach the best achievements of the human mind.[66] In fact one cannot help the feeling that the decision to give precedence to the Arts had the approval of the majority or at least the more powerful elements among the university's supporters, and corresponded in particular with the wishes of Muḥammad ʻAbduh and his followers.[67] While the value of natural sciences and their applications was not to be denied, it was apparently assumed that the immediate national interests were better served by literary, historical and social studies.[68] A full explanation of this bias cannot be attempted here, but it seems to have responded to a deep-rooted preoccupation, since the very beginnings of the Nahḍa movement, with the problem of identity vis-à-vis the West. The generally felt need to pursue knowledge for its own sake was thus subordinated to, or equated with, the still deeper and more powerful impulse to understand the decline of Islamic civilization and the corresponding rise of European nations. It was for reasons such as these that the university, according to Aḥmad Zakī, thought fit "to begin with the beginning, taking the decision to teach the study of Islamic and ancient civilizations in addition to the study of Arabic geography, historiography and literature *insofar as they related to Western nations*".[69] In speaking thus, Aḥmad Zakī apparently was expressing the prevailing point of view.

It is also in this context that we can fully understand the predominantly historical character of the curriculum provided by the new university. Starting with a course on the history of literature, the programme was soon enlarged to cover the following subjects:[70] Islamic civilization;[71] ancient civilization (in Egypt and the Orient) before the rise of Islam;[72] geographical and linguistic sciences;[73] history of French literature; and history of English literature.[74] As from the academic year 1910–1911, the hitherto informal programme was further expanded and organized. Thus a Faculty of the Arts and Philosophy was officially set up and the curriculum was so designed as to include eight subjects:[75] Arabic literature;[76] history of Arabic literature;[76] philology of the Semitic languages (with special reference to Arabic);[77] ancient Oriental history;[78] history of the Islamic peoples (with special reference to Egypt);[79] and Arab and moral philosophy[80].

The fact that this historical emphasis might have echoed certain trends and traditions which were dominant at the turn of the century in European academic and orientalist circles need not imply that it was not also, and perhaps more importantly, a response to indigenous impulses. The orientialists and the Nahḍa thinkers shared an interest in the vicissitudes of Islamic history and the rise and fall of Islamic power. The mounting historical spirit on the one side was matched by an acute historical awareness on the other.

The idea that the university should be secular, democratic and open to different cultural traditions, was reflected in many ways. Thus a decision was taken to the effect that students and graduates from the Azhar and Dar al-'Ulūm could apply to enter it.[81] Again, the teaching staff was partly Egyptian, partly European, as a number of eminent orientalists were invited to lecture, in Arabic, on such subjects for which no Egyptian teaching staff was available.[82] Ignazio Guidi[83] was the first to arrive; he was followed a year later by Carlo Alfonso Nallino.[84] Then came David

Santillana,[85] Gerardo Miloni,[86] Enno Littmann, Louis Massignon[87] and Gaston Wiet.[88]

In view of the desire to open the doors so widely as to accommodate the ancient and the modern, the Eastern and Western, it is not surprising that life at the newly established university was, as Ṭāhā Ḥusain put it, a continual celebration. He, the young Azhari that he was at the time, had, however, his own "feast" within the general effervescence. Everything connected with the new "world" of learning was for him a source of wonder as well as a confirmation of his release from the Azhar.[89] Thus his new teachers, whether Egyptians or Europeans, dealt with the subject at hand directly and straightforwardly without reference to an authoritative text (*matn*) and without the whole paraphernalia of Azhari exegesis.[90] It was also wonderful to listen to those foreign teachers as they lectured on Arab and Islamic subjects using literary Arabic.[91] It looked as if he had at last found himself – at that crossroads of languages, traditions and civilizations – within reach of the "balanced harmony" envisaged by Luṭfī al-Sayyid. The author of *al-Ayyām* relates how his Egyptian teachers gave him "a new awareness of life, a new zeal for it, and a new awareness of the old and the new together".[92] They strengthened in him, we are again told, his Arab Egyptian personality amid all the wide learning provided by the orientalists and enabled him to cling to a strong element of authentic Eastern culture and to hold together in a balanced harmony the learning of both East and West.[93]

Most fascinating of all and most vital, as if implicating the young man's whole being, was the study of history. "It had amazed me to hear the two names [Ramses and Akhenaton] and to hear tell of that kind of history. It had convinced me that I was ordained by God to lead a lost and futile life. But now, here I was in a university classroom listening to Professor Aḥmad Kamāl ... talking about ancient civilization, referring to Ramses and Akhenaton and other Pharaohs and endeavouring to expound his point of view as to the connection between ancient Egyptian and Semitic languages, including Arabic."[94]

The "discovery" of history was in point of fact Ṭāhā's major achievement during the period under consideration. Of the kind of history that was "discovered", we may say straightaway that it was wide in scope, tending to be universal and comparative, i.e. establishing links and parallels between different civilizations and languages. It was through this subject, thus far generally characterized, that the young Azhari was, so he felt, to find his salvation. To know more about this vital subject we may first consider, rather selectively, the historical instruction provided at the time by three of Ṭāhā's European teachers, namely Nallino, Santillana and Massignon.

Carlo Alfonso Nallino (1872–1938)

None of the orientalists who taught Ṭāhā in this period had as decisive an influence on his development as Nallino. Having first given a course on the history of Arab astronomy,[95] he started lecturing for two more academic years on the history of Arabic literature.[96] That was, according to Ṭāhā Ḥusain, a turning point in the history of modern Egyptian thought and culture.[97] It was mainly from Nallino that Ṭāhā and a handful of other young Egyptian scholars learnt the modern methods of historical enquiry as applied to the study of Arabic literature.[98] Without this beneficial influence, the subject would have remained deprived of the critical method just as it had been a thousand years earlier.[99]

As far as Ṭāhā in particular was concerned, Nallino's lectures came to complement, the teachings of his Azhari master, al-Marṣafī. As he was to put it later, he owed to these two teachers the bases of all of his subsequent work.[100] More on this later, but we can say straightaway that, in complementing al-Marṣafī's lessons, Nallino's contribution was undoubtedly decisive in shaping the young man's literary destiny. The kind of history which was to become ever after closest to his mind and heart, was literary history – understood as a combination of al-Marṣafī's textual analysis and Nallino's critical methodology.

According to Ṭāhā Ḥusain, Nallino was the first to teach him and his fellow students ancient Arabic literature in a systematic fashion.[101] This meant, as he goes on to explain, that they were made aware for the first time of the following facts:

- that Arabic poetry differed, not only according to its traditionally recognized subjects (*al-funūn al-taqlīdiyya*),[102] but also according to its themes (*mawḍū'āt*), the conditions surrounding its production and the factors influencing both its authors and audiences;

- that politics had subtle and profound effects on the rise of new genres of Arabic poetry. Thus, for instance, Nallino's students were made aware for the first time of the difference between ancient traditional *nasīb* on the one hand and the two other kinds of love poetry which arose in the Arab Peninsula under the influence of the Islamic social system, namely the sensuous (*muḥaqqiq*) *ghazal* in Hijazi cities and the chaste (*'udhrī naqī*) *ghazal* among desert dwellers;
- that it is possible to study ancient Arabic literature comparatively, taking into account ancient world literatures; human life being [basically] the same (lit: "similar") in spite of its diverse states and circumstances; and
- that literature is a mirror of life at the time of its production, being a reflection (lit: "echo") of that life and one of its driving forces.[103]

Given this account of the essentials of Nallino's contribution, we may now turn to certain aspects with a view to underlining the historical character of his teachings. Nallino extolled the study of history and underlined its importance for progress. His remarks to this effect must have been all the more effective in that they bore on the immediate interests of his (literary-minded) audience. They were thus told that knowledge of the history and literature of a given language was essential to the revival, advancement and unity of the nation concerned.[104] Such a nation might suffer defeat in war, but could survive and hope for better days only if it held to its literature and retained its scientific and literary legacy.[105] Such remarks could not have fallen on more attentive ears. They carried a message of consolation and hope.

Stressing the need for a critical approach to history, Nallino showed, again, his acute awareness of what was topical. It was necessary, he maintained, to examine the opinions of one's predecessors and to scrutinize and test their experience.[106] Still more to the point, he affirmed that a review of the history of oriental nations would show that their scientific and political decline had begun just at the time when their thinkers had abandoned the way of independent enquiry (*ijtihād*), thereby acquiescing and sinking into conformism (*taqlīd*). Instead of writing fully fledged and creative studies, they were content to compile summaries, expositions, commentaries, notes and reports.[107]

As against this traditional and specifically Azhari view of learning, Nallino presented to his audience a different conception of the process of enquiry as an ever-renewed quest to comprehend reality and fathom the mysteries of the immense universe. Given the limits of the human mind, one could only hope to add one's modest contribution to those of one's predecessors.[108]

A further, and most novel step, was taken when Nallino proceeded to criticize the Arab historical tradition. It was at this stage that he made his major theoretical contribution, emphasizing as he did the need to base historical investigation on precisely that reality which constituted the ultimate object of the quest for knowledge. Historical methods of enquiry, the utility of which had been proven in the West, were, he affirmed, unknown to Arab scholars – apart from very brief and scattered fragments lacking precision and critical rigour.[109] This, in his view, was due to the fact that the Arabs, as compared with the ancient Greeks or Romans or the modern Europeans, had an imperfect command of history as a discipline, confining themselves as they did to narrative or chronological exposition of events and never seeking to bring out their causal interconnections. They did not extend their vision beyond the sequence of apparent occurrences to their deeper and hidden causes in the life of society.[110]

As far as the history of literature was concerned, Arab scholars were, according to Nallino, content to compile biographies of individual authors according to different classes (*ṭabaqāt*), or in alphabetical order. No attempt was made to investigate the origins and development of literary genres, the influence exerted by men of letters on one another, or the social factors underlying changes of taste and attitude.[111] Language, Nallino contended, was a living organism subject to growth, renewal and decay; words often change their significance as a result of change in the social and political conditions of the nation concerned, or in its state of intellectual progress.[112]

Identifying the deeper level of fact underlying literary texts as a given social entity (*al-hay'a al-ijtimā'iyya*)[113] or the life of a given society,[114] Nallino would argue, for instance, that the poetry of any given nation was a valuable historical document which mirrorred that nation's feelings, passions, morals and customs.[115] In fact, the literary mirror was at times a truer guide to historical reality than works based on official records or partisan documents.[116]

It should be noted, however, that Nallino's conception of historical reality was far from structured; the ultimate facts to which historical explanation had to refer could be political, religious, intellectual and/or strictly social. To illustrate Nallino's standpoint we may consider the explanation he offered for the emergence and flowering of a new kind of love poetry, namely the chaste *ghazal*, in Mecca and Medina, under the Umayyads.[117] Towards the end of the reign of the fourth caliph, 'Alī Ibn Abī Ṭālib, he argues, most of the men who had a role to play in politics or war had left the Arabian Peninsula, leaving behind those among *al-Muhājirūn* (those of the Prophet's companions and followers who migrated to Medina) and *al-Anṣār* (the Prophet's supporters in Medina) who were dedicated to a life of piety, devotion and asceticism. It was as though worldly affairs were the concern of Syria, while occupation with religion fell to Medina. At the same time, the two holy cities of Islam witnessed an economic boom as a result of the influx of pilgrims and the expansion of trade relations. With such an increase in wealth and affluence, there developed a passion for the pleasures and luxuries of life. Young people from aristocratic families, who could not occupy themselves in Hijazi cities with political affairs[118] nor with the as yet undeveloped rational sciences, became permissive and indulged in a life of refinement, courting and listening to singing. This latter favourite pastime was encouraged by the arrival of female slaves who sang in Greek and Persian – until the appearance at a later stage of singing in Arabic.[119]

From this argument, thus far loosely stated, we can see that Nallino ascribed the literary phenomenon under consideration to a set of political, economic and strictly social factors which he did not care to analyse or organize in a hierarchical order.[120] It was as if he assumed that historical explanation would ultimately invoke a multiplicity of factors woven into an open-textured social life. In contrast to the Marxist point of view, the factors in question did not fall within an articulate structure having economics as their foundation. As far as he was concerned, political conditions, questions relating to social psychology (e.g. tastes, attitudes and manners) and intellectual and religious affairs, mattered just as much, if not more than, economic factors.

It is true that one is reminded of the Marxist position when one considers the framework within which Nallino sets the whole of literary history, namely the contrast and interaction between two ways of life, or between nomadism and city-dwelling. There, it might be suggested, Nallino presupposes a distinction between two modes of life involving two different types of relation to nature, work, or economic life. Nallino would not, however, carry the analysis quite so far, preferring, so it seems, to maintain the above-mentioned distinction at face value, or at the level at which it was gleaned from Ibn Khaldūn.[121] Transition from the more primitive to the more sophisticated way of life is supposed to carry with it not only an economic transformation but also, and equally important, changes in the scale of values, interests, beliefs and manners. What mattered most was not so much the type of economic activity involved, but the increase in wealth and the concomitant leisure, love of luxury, pleasure-seeking, and elegance of manners and conversation.

Given the assumption that there is a deeper level of social fact underlying the "visible" events of history as well as literary texts and phenomena, Nallino drew two major critical conclusions, which were to have far-reaching consequences in Ṭāhā Ḥusain's thought. The first conclusion related to the question of periodization. For Nallino, periodization, whether in literary or political history, is inevitably artificial. As social changes take place slowly and imperceptibly, it is not possible to demarcate epochs within hard and fast boundaries. What looks at first sight like a sudden upheaval may turn out on closer inspection to be the outcome of long-standing and slow-working factors.[122] Furthermore, social changes in any given nation do not necessarily follow one and the same pattern in all regions. This is particularly true if, as was the case in the Arab empire, the regions in question were geographically scattered and the absence of printing impeded the spread of ideas.[123] It obviously follows from this that the literary historian has to seek his explanatory causes beyond the prominent and well-defined events and dates of literary and political history, and take into account regional variations.

The second major consequence concerned the question of the authenticity of ancient, and particularly, pre-Islamic poetry. Having raised a series of problems regarding this poetry, Nallino formulates the main questions as follows. "Were these [pre-Islamic] poems cast in one and the same language? How was this language formed? In what fashion was pre-Islamic poetry transmitted to us? Should we have confidence in the credibility of transmission, and rely on the stories related to explain the ancient verses?"[124] This problem, which had been familiar to classical Arab scholars, was given a new urgency when revived by Nallino. Earlier doubts had long been dead and buried; and modern Arab scholars at the time of Nallino took it for granted that the bulk of ancient poetry was authentic. The problem was, again, the more pressing in view of this new method of Nallino's, which involved a searching examination of the social, religious, and linguistic history of the Arabs prior to Islam. Thus Nallino cast doubts on the authenticity of some of the poems attributed to Labīd on the grounds that they reflected Islamic concepts and beliefs.[125] He also denied the authenticity of the whole corpus of poetry attributed to the Tabābi'a (ancient kings of the Yemen), arguing that the language used did not concord with newly discovered inscriptions. "The discrepancy between the poetic traditions attributed to the Tabābi'a and the authentic Ḥimyarite inscriptions", he wrote, "is the best proof that these traditions are made up (*mukhtalaqa*)."[126] Extending his criticism to ancient transmitters, Nallino took the famous Ḥammād to task for his fabrications and dealt, more generally, with the deeper motives and factors behind literary forgeries. Chief among these motives and factors were popular credulity with regard to wondrous reports, cupidity and greed on the part of transmitters, chauvinistic tendencies and tribal self-glorification.[127] All this was in fact the very stuff from which Ṭāhā was to make his controversial theory on the spurious character of most of pre-Islamic poetry. But more on that below.

David Santillana (1855–1931)

Santillana's lectures on the Greek philosophical doctrines in the Islamic world[128] adopted an explicit historical line. Hence he provided an overt defence of the study of history. To the sceptic who raises the question, "Why study obsolete histories, monuments in ruin, ancient myths and illusions?", Santillana would give the following, many-sided answer. Generally speaking, a nation setting out on the way of progress has to seek its own traditions and revive its ancient monuments. With regard to philosophy in particular – a subject where the major questions never change – knowledge of ancient ideas is indispensable to an understanding of philosophical doctrines, including contemporary ones. This is all the more true of Islamic philosophy. An Egyptian cannot afford to ignore the doctrines of Greek philosophers since "the Islamic sciences were based right from the beginning on Greek sciences, ideas and illusions".[129]

This answer, which bases the case for history on the debt of Islamic culture to Greek thought, sets the tone for the whole enquiry. The author thus proceeds to show the Greek elements in Islamic thought. His approach is selective in that it concentrates on those Greek elements with which the Arabs are supposed to be most familiar. The teachings of such philosophers as Empedocles, Pythagoras and Socrates are, therefore, ignored, while Democritus, Plato, Aristotle, the Stoics and the Neo-Platonists are given prominence.[130]

These restrictions, which could have been accepted as mere procedural matters dictated by methodology or convenience, were, however, coupled with a dangerously reductionist tendency. Adopting an overtly critical approach in the name of scientific rigour, Santillana sought to remove the confusions, distortions and legendary accretions to which Greek ideas were subjected by Arab doxographers.[131] Thus, for instance, he derides the attribution of Qur'ānic virtues to Aristotle.[132] Concerning the famous story about al-Ma'mūn's vision,[133] and its use to explain his decision to have the Stagirite's works translated into Arabic, Santillana would contend that all that pertained to the realm of legend. "A nation's life and progress …", he judiciously says, "have nothing to do with a caliph's vision – even if it did occur".[134] Transformations of that kind, he maintains, have remote causes which have to be deduced by whoever seeks historical truth.[135] It is unfortunate, however, that this tough-minded approach turns out to be excessive – amounting in practice to throwing out the baby with the bath water. For Santillana is not content to remove doxographic legends, distortions and illusions; he also treats Islamic efforts in philosophy as being … accretions. His attempt to detect the authentic Greek elements in Islamic thought degenerates into the famous view, originally put forward by Renan, that Islamic philosophies are no more than belated reflections, adaptations or distortions of Greek originals. Santillana's endeavours were thus no more than an unmasking of those originals supposedly hidden beneath Arabic names or Islamic moulds. The obsession with influences turns, in other words, into a destructive weapon, since it disregards the social and intellectual context in which Islamic philosophical doctrines were developed, and the preoccupations and strivings of their authors. For instance, Santillana claims that there is no more to the controversy between the Ash'arites and the Mu'tazilites over whether essences are immanent or have a separate existence,[136] than the dispute between Plato and Aristotle over the status of universals. Both the specific problem(s) faced by the two Muslim schools of theology and the manner in which they used Greek elements, if such elements were in fact used, are completely ignored.

There can be no doubt, however, that Santillana's ideas had a lasting effect on Ṭāhā and his fellow students at the Egyptian University. They were made aware for the first time of the heavy debt that Islamic thought owed to Greece. None of them, we are told, knew, for example, that Ibn Sīnā had "borrowed" his philosophy from the Greeks.[137] This, as well as other evidence, suggests that Ṭāhā was impressed, if not convinced, by Santillana's views on Islamic philosophy's lack of originality.[138] We can be sure at any rate that Santillana's emphasis of the Greek influence contributed to Ṭāhā's future views on the role of Greek elements in Arab literary life under the Abbasids and on Mediterranean culture. Again, it could be argued that Santillana's tough-minded attitude towards received opinions, and his denunciation of the legendary character of certain doxographical traditions, must have helped to shape Ṭāhā Ḥusain's own critical and largely sceptical attitude as a historian.

Louis Massignon (1883–1962)

Like Santillana, Massignon defines his historical position in opposition to Arab traditional authorities. Thus he begins his lectures on the history of Arabic philosophical terms[139] with a criticism of biographers and apologists, such as al-Qifṭī and Ibn al-Nadīm, who reviewed philosophical figures and doctrines in chronological and geographical order.[140] Undoubtedly useful from a documentary point of view, this method is said to be defective as far as didactic purposes are concerned. Being dry and lifeless, the material thus provided is bound to tire his listeners and lead others to an attitude of disillusioned scepticism.[141] Massignon himself would favour another approach, taking as his fixed point of reference abstract terms expressing general ideas[142] and tracing the successive definitions (or, as we may say nowadays, the conceptual transformations) that each such term underwent in the course of its circulation.[143] This apparently "lexical"[144] approach is in fact a history of the different "values" attached to the "basic currency" of philosophy as it was exchanged between East and West. For instance, having considered the term *'illa* ("cause") according to its original acceptation in ordinary (classical) Arabic and its definition as fixed by Arab grammarians, Massignon would expound the technical meanings that the term acquired, first under the impact of Greek thought (hence the concept of *aitia*), and later on as it was introduced into, and adapted by, European philosophers in medieval and modern times.[145] Similar treatment is accorded to other philosophical terms in a systematic fashion, beginning with what is most abstract and ending with what is highest in being: first, terms pertaining to logic considered as an instrument of all thinking or organon, (universals, categories, propositions, syllogisms and logistic), then terms relating to number, matter, life, society and God.[146]

It might be said, therefore, that Massignon's "lexicon" is embedded in, and suggestive of, a lively and more balanced vision of Islamic thought. Unlike Santillana, Massignon conceives of the relations between Europe and Islam as a kind of two-way "traffic" or "commerce". Having been formed, under the influence of Greek thought, out of indigenous rudimentary, but seminal, materials, Islamic philosophy, so the argument went, was later transferred, as a Hellenized product, to Europe, where it took root and had various ramifications.[147]

Massignon's insight that Islamic thought grew out of Arabic as a language rich in potentialities, and, in general, that sophisticated philosophical concepts were refinements of the materials of ordinary language, is ingenious and would certainly appeal not only to Muslims but also to Aristotle, al-Fārābi[148] and contemporary linguistic philosophers. It is therefore a pity that Massignon's erudition militates, in a way, against his historical ambitions. More often than not the discussion is reduced to a mere listing of definitions as given by different philosophies or schools of thought. With regard to a concept like that of *al-ruḥ* (spirit), for instance, Massignon is content to point out how, starting from an original point of departure in ordinary discourse (namely, "the soft emission of breath"), the term was given divergent meanings by the *fuqahā'* (specialists of religious law), the *mutakallimūn* (practitioners of dogmatic theology) and the ṣūfis.[149] Within the limits of such a review, no reference is made to the dilemmas and controversies that were involved or the conflicting pressures that were exerted so as to give the term concerned its novel and divergent functions.

It is only towards the end of Massignon's course that his deeper vision begins to be revealed. In lecture XXXI, he discusses and rejects Renan's racialist views on Semitic languages. It would seem therefore that Massignon's lexicon is really an elaborate attempt to refute Renan by showing how a certain Semitic language, in this case Arabic, was sufficiently resourceful to satisfy the needs of rational thought over centuries. In lecture XXXVI, this perspective is further confirmed as Massignon upholds the cause of literary Arabic (*al-fuṣḥā*) against those who advocate the use of colloquial Arabic (*al-dārija*) and as he warns against the dangers of dialectal chauvinism (*al-shuʿūbiyya*) for the unity of the nation.[150] In the last lecture but one, the point is more or less clinched as Massignon deals with the past, present and future roles of Arabic as an instrument of thought and action.[151] It then transpires that Arabic has had all along a mission to assume in universal culture. Just as it had served in the past as a meeting point for diverse cultures, it could once again, given renewed efforts, fulfil its international role. Massignon could even see over the horizon certain signs of a forthcoming renaissance.[152] It is obvious that nothing could have corresponded more to the dreams of the Nahḍa thinkers and the supporters of the Egyptian University than this elevated view of Arabic as outlined by the French orientalist.

Having thus outlined some of the views held by Ṭāhā's orientalist teachers at the Egyptian University, we ought to emphasize, in conclusion, that those views, novel as they were, corresponded to certain assumptions, expectations and tendencies that were already at work in the indigenous environment. We have seen in the course of this chapter how the views in question were anticipated and corroborated, in more than one way, by the ideas of Luṭfī al-Sayyid and other Egyptian intellectuals and reformers. Ṭāhā, and in fact Egypt in general, were well-prepared to receive the orientalists' message. Even the idea of a new brand of critical history fell on fertile indigenous soil to the extent that there was an acute historical awareness and a deeply felt need to review the past and define Egypt's identity and role in the region and the world. Thus Massignon's views on East-West exchange and the revival of Arabic as well as Santillana's ideas on the Greek influence on Islamic thought were most relevant.

It is obvious that those European masters were well aware of such indigenous needs and preoccupations, and that they made a special effort to meet them. For instance, they were familiar with the classical sources of Arabic culture, long neglected by the Azhar and much cherished by the Nahḍa leaders. Ṭāhā, as a disciple of al-Marṣafī, must have been delighted to see his European teachers resuscitate those venerable works, extracting from them the necessary materials of their history, just as he was impressed by their attachment to the classical language at a time of linguistic decadence.[153] It must have been wonderful to see Massignon defend literary Arabic against dialectal chauvinism or Nallino go out of his way to uphold the classical purity of Arabic, denouncing as he did the harmful effects of excessive foreign influence. "It led people", he said, "to be complacent with regard to their language, and introduced into some modern works and certain magazines and journals such preposterous barbarisms (*'ujma*) and such ugly constructions . . ."[154]

There are, again, several indications to suggest that these scholars were aware of, and sympathetic to, Egyptian political and cultural aspirations. We have already considered Massignon's views on the continuous role of Arabic in universal culture. We may now add that Nallino was more specific and more emphatic in this respect. He pointed out that his country had always had peaceful and amicable relations with Egypt and that no Italian ship had ever approached Egyptian ports in hostile action,[155] and expressed his satisfaction that some Italians had been invited to "take part in this scientific revival".[156] In addition, he deplored the current deterioration of literary Arabic and its diminishing influence in Algeria under French rule.[157]

We may, finally, take note of the courtesy shown by these orientalists towards their hosts, and their awareness of the consequent limits of their competence. In this way, Nallino was careful to pay tribute to "the many distinguished scholars, whether past or present, Eastern or Western" who were the target of his criticism,[158] and to define the limits of his competence as a foreigner teaching Arabic literature to an Arab audience. It was not for him, he said, to compete with the natives in their knowledge of the language; his mission was confined to the application to Arabic literature of the historical methods of research which had proved their utility in the study of European literature.[159]

Similarly, we may consider how Massignon, having argued that Arabic, like all languages, had its own specific and unique character,[160] hastens to add that it was not for him, the foreigner that he was, to define the character in question for those who possess that "creative gift" by right of birth.[161] His, as he put it, was the role of "him who carries the *fānūs* (lantern); he takes the lead in order to light the road to be walked. It is not for him, said Dante, to walk in the light; it is not for him either to enter Paradise; it is enough for him to have lit the way at night up till the door."[162]

It is only in the light of such considerations that we can understand why these orientalists struck Ṭāhā as being men of integrity and pure motives,[163] and why he was readily receptive to their influence and keen on establishing with them lifelong relations of friendship and collaboration. They used, we are told, to invite him to their hotel and make themselves accessible in conversation.[164] Paying Guidi a weekly visit, Ṭāhā used to give him copies of his publications as a present.[165] One of the "unforgettable" occasions for Ṭāhā was when he arranged for Santillana to accompany him to a lesson at the Azhar.[166] With Nallino, he used to frequent the old districts of Cairo hunting for ancient documents and manuscripts.

There is no doubt that the blind, but gifted, Azhari aroused the admiration and paternal feelings of his European masters.[167] Starting in 1915, the year in which his first doctoral thesis was published, he never missed an opportunity to pay them tribute.[168] It is important to emphasize these "special" relations, for it was through them that Ṭāhā had a rich extra-curricular source of knowledge. Such relations between these orientalists and the young rebellious Azhari, should, again, serve as an excellent illustration of the encounter between East and West with all that it involves in terms of complexity and ambiguity. Leaving for the moment the lessons to be learnt through reflection on this example, we may now turn to the study of Ṭāhā's early writings, where he sets out to assimilate the teachings of his foreign masters and to develop his own view of history. This is the subject of the following chapter.

Notes

1 One of which was al-Marṣafī's course on literature; the other was on rhetoric (*balāgha*).
2 Ṭāhā Ḥussein, *The Stream of days* (London 1948), p. 133.
3 Idem, *A Passage to France* (Leiden 1976).
4 Ibid., pp. 124–125. Ṭāhā Ḥusain does not specify when exactly he met Luṭfī for the first time. We can, however, infer the date from his statement elsewhere that he was eighteen at the time. See his obituary of Luṭfī entitled "al-Marḥūm al-Ustādh Aḥmad Luṭfī al-Sayyid" in *Majallat Majma' al-Lugha al-'Arabiyya*, XVIII (1965), pp. 113–166, p. 113.
5 Being the organ of the Umma party (of which Luṭfī was the secretary), this daily appeared from March 1907 until November 1915.
6 *The Stream of days*, p. 124. As Ṭāhā and two of his fellow students were denounced for expressing allegedly heretical views and making insulting comments about their sheikhs, the Rector had their names erased from the Azhar's register. Ibid., p. 122.
7 Ibid., p. 125.
8 "... In this society he [i.e. Ṭāhā] met the wealthiest and most influential of men, while he himself was a poor man from a middle class family ... and this gave him to think seriously about the fearful gulf which separates the rich and the well-to-do from the struggling poor." Ibid., p. 125. On some of the distinguished men that Ṭāhā met in Luṭfī's circle, see ibid.
9 Ṭāhā Ḥusain relates how on taking leave from Luṭfī he was asked to repeat the visit whenever he liked. Ṭāhā was about to kiss Luṭfī's hand according to the Azhari custom of greeting one's sheikhs, when the latter prevented him from doing so and kissed him on his forehead. See "al-Marḥūm al-Ustādh Aḥmad Luṭfī al-Sayyid", p. 113.
10 Founded on 20 September 1907, the party drew its members from among big landowners and eminent intellectuals. As education in secular schools was provided against high fees, the two categories of members were interconnected, the latter group being necessarily affiliated to the former. In contradistinction from the National Party (*al-Ḥizb al-Waṭanī*) led by Muṣṭafā Kāmil, the Umma was elitist, secular (rejecting all forms of pan-Islamism including allegiance to the Ottoman caliphate) and moderate towards the British occupation. This moderation, inherited from 'Abduh, implied readiness to seek independence and constitutional reform gradually and through negotiation. Elected as the party's secretary, Luṭfī was in fact the Umma's ideologue. See Yūnān Labīb Rizq, *al-Aḥzāb al-siyāsiyya fī Miṣr* (Cairo 1984), Ch. 3. Cf. P.J. Vatikiotis, *The History of modern Egypt from Muhammad Ali to Mubarak* (London 1991), pp. 226 and 227. See also Afaf Lutfi al-Sayyid, *Egypt and Cromer. A Study in Anglo-Egyptian relations* (London 1968), pp. 168–169.
11 See Ṭāhā Ḥusain, "*Kitāb al-Siyāsa* li'-Arisṭuṭālīs, tarjamat Aḥmad Luṭfī al-Sayyid" (review of Luṭfī's translation of Aristotle's *Politics*) in *Kutub wa-mu'allifūn,* in *MK*, vol. XVI, 1981, pp. 334–335.

12 Ibid. Cf. C. Wendell, *EI*[2] art. "Luṭfī al-Sayyid".
13 Ṭāhā Ḥusain, *op. cit.*, p. 334. According to Jamal Mohammed Ahmed, *The Intellectual origins of Egyptian nationalism*, reprint (Oxford 1968), p. 90, Luṭfī was also familiar with Durkheim's thought.
14 Ṭāhā Ḥusain, op. cit., p. 335.
15 Ibid., pp. 335–336.
16 Ibid., p. 336.
17 Where "practical" means being primarily interested in practical philosophy, i.e. ethics and politics, as distinct from logic and metaphysics.
18 Ṭāhā Ḥusain, op. cit., p. 337.
19 Ibid.
20 Charles Wendell, *The Evolution of the Egyptian national image from its origins to Aḥmad Luṭfī al-Sayyid* (Berkeley, Los Angeles, London 1972), p. 223.
21 Aḥmad Luṭfī al-Sayyid, *Ta'ammulāt*, ed. Ismā'īl Maẓhar (Cairo 1946), pp. 79–80.
22 Ibid., p. 80.
23 *Al-Muntakhabāt* I, ed. Ismā'il Maẓhar (Cairo 1937), p. 168.
24 Op. cit., pp. 73–74 and 79.
25 Ibid., p. 75. Notice that Luṭfī directs his criticism not to the early or original Islamic traditions but to the legacy of the near past (*afkār salafinā al-ṣāliḥ fī hādhā 'l-māḍī al-qarīb*).
26 Ibid., p. 80.
27 Ibid.
28 Ibid., p. 75.
29 Ibid., pp. 23–24.
30 Ibid., p. 75.
31 Cf. Albert Hourani, *Arabic thought in the liberal age, 1798–1939* (Cambridge 1984), p. 172.
32 Aḥmad Luṭfī al-Sayyid, op. cit., p. 61.
33 P.J. Vatikiotis, *EI*[2] art. "Ḳawmiyya".
34 Aḥmad Luṭfī al-Sayyid, op. cit., p. 61.
35 Ibid., p. 62. See also *al-Muntakhabāt* I, p. 170–171.
36 Op. cit., pp. 72 and 99.
37 Ibid., p. 68.
38 Ibid., pp. 68–69.
39 Ibid., p. 48.
40 Ibid., pp. 52 and 53.
41 Ibid., p. 59.
42 Ibid.
43 Ibid.
44 Aḥmad Luṭfī al-Sayyid, *Ṣafaḥāt maṭwiyya min tārīkh al-ḥaraka al-istiqlāliyya fī Miṣr*, ed. Ismā'īl Maẓhar (Cairo 1946), p. 20. See also pp. 119 and 130.
45 Ibid., pp. 114, 117 and 119.
46 Ibid., p. 20.
47 Ibid., p. 21.
48 Ibid.

49 Ibid.
50 Ibid., p. 20. See also pp. 115 and 116.
51 Ibid., p. 119.
52 Ṭāhā Ḥusain, op. cit., p. 334.
53 According to some writers, the first to call for the establishment of an Egyptian university was the Lebanese-born and editor-in-chief of *al-Hilāl,* Jurjī Zaydān. The idea was then taken up by Muṣṭafā Kāmil, Muḥammad 'Abduh and his followers. See 'Abd al-Mun'im al-Dusūqī al-Jamī'ī, *al-Jāmi'a al-Miṣriyya wa'l-mujtama', 1908–1940* (Cairo 1983), pp. 10 and 11. Cf. Sāmiya Ḥasan Ibrāhīm, *al-Jāmi'a al-Ahliyya bayn al-nash'a wa'l-taṭawwur* (Cairo 1985), p. 13.
54 From a letter written (in French) by 'Abduh and published by De Guerville in his *La Nouvelle Egypte* (Paris 1905), pp. 201–208; as cited by 'Uthmān Amīn, *Rā'id al-fikr al-Miṣrī al-Imām Muḥammad 'Abduh,* 2nd edn. (Cairo 1965), pp. 55–56.
55 From a speech quoted by Muḥammad Ḥusain Haykal in his *Tarājim Miṣriyya wa-Gharbiyya* (Cairo 1980), p. 153; first published in 1929.
56 Ibid., p. 149.
57 Lord Cromer is supposed to have supported the promotion of Qur'ānic schools as a means of diverting attention form the university project. (See Sāmiya Ḥasan Ibrāhīm, op. cit., pp. 31–32). A debate on which alternative to adopt was launched in the press at the time (see idem., op. cit., pp. 17–18 and al-Jamī'ī, op. cit., pp. 11–12). It should be noted, again, that opposition to the university project was also voiced by foreign papers including *The Times.* See Sāmiya Ḥasan Ibrāhīm, op. cit., pp. 33–34. It is not without significance that Luṭfī went out of his way to appease such hostile reactions, arguing that the university project was not a nationalist manifestation aimed at provocation, and that it had nothing to do with politics. See his article "Mā li 'l-siyāsa wa 'l-'ilm?" ("What has politics to do with knowledge?"), first published in *J,* 25 May 1907, and reprinted in idem, op. cit., pp. 170–172.
58 See the text of Tharwat's speech as reproduced in *al-Muqtaṭaf,* vol. XXXIV (1909), pp. 138–140, p. 138.
59 See the text of the speech as reproduced in ibid., pp. 141–145, p. 141.
60 Ibid., pp. 142 and 143.
61 According to the text of a call to establish the university issued by an elected preparatory committee, the university was to be "a school for the sciences and the arts admitting all students irrespective of their race or religion", and was to "have no political character and no relation to politicians". See Sāmiya Ḥasan Ibrāhīm, op. cit., p. 30.
62 The project was financed by private contributions. Response to the campaign to collect contributions came from a wide spectrum of the population, including schoolchildren. Ibid., pp. 67 ff.
63 Germain Martin, 'L'Université Egyptienne', *Revue du Monde Musulman,* XIII (1911), pp. 1–19, p. 11. This presumably eyewitness view corroborates Ṭāhā Ḥusain's report: "Life at the University when it first became available for Egyptians was like a perpetual feast … Crowds of students converged on the study rooms, rich and poor in

endless diversity, at varying stages in their education. There was every variety of garb too". *A Passage to France*, p. 31.

64 The study took initially the form of a series of lectures delivered in the late afternoon and early evening (from 4.30 to 7 p.m.) on such days and hours as were fixed and announced ad hoc. Some time later on, it was decided to provide two lectures a day. See al-Jamī'ī, op. cit., p. 25.

65 In a discussion within the University Standing Committee (presided over by the then Prince Aḥmad Fu'ād), some members were in favour of beginning with the study of literature, philosophy, history and law, while others opted for scientific and practical subjects. The issue was also debated by the press with *al-Hilāl* giving precedence to natural sciences, while *al-Jarīda* favouring history, the fine arts and literature. See al-Jamī'ī, op. cit., pp. 17.

66 This was in fact the view of Prince Aḥmad Fu'ād. See ibid.

67 According to Muḥammad 'Abduh and Luṭfī al-Sayyid, it was mainly the Arts which should be given the priority so as to counteract the predominant utilitarian character of Egyptian education. Again, Luṭfī assumed that teaching of the Arts was necessary to educate an elite of writers, philosophers and political leaders. It was mainly of the Arts that the representatives of this current of opinion thought when they spoke of the desirability of teaching theoretical disciplines. The fact that there are theoretical natural sciences seems to have received little attention.

68 For a criticism of this "literary" bias, see Shiblī Shumayyil, *Kitāb Falsafat al-nushū' wa'l-irtiqā'*, in *Majmū'at al-Ductūr Shiblī Shumayyil* (Cairo 1910), vol. I, p. 40

69 From the text of Aḥmad Zakī's speech at the inaugural ceremony, op. cit., p. 145. The italics are mine.

70 This list is to be found, with some variations, in al-Jamī'ī, op. cit., p. 26 and Sāmiya Ḥasan Ibrāhīm, op. cit., pp. 83–84.

71 Taught by Aḥmad Zakī. On this course, see Ṭāhā Ḥusain, *A Passage to France*, pp. 4 and 5.

72 Taught by Aḥmad Kamāl. See ibid., pp. 34–35.

73 Taught by the Italian orientalist Ignazio Guidi. See ibid., pp. 5–6. In a lecture on the Italian orientalists who taught in Egypt, Ṭāhā Ḥusain spoke of Guidi's course as consisting of forty lessons on the relations between Europe and the Orient in Medieval times, in which Guidi dealt with the Arab geographical and historical literature. Delivered in French (in Cairo, 19 February 1948), this lecture was published only in an Italian summarized version. See "Una conferenza". For Ṭāhā Ḥusain's remarks on Guidi's course, see ibid., p. 104. Guidi's lectures were published in book form under the title *Muḥāḍarāt fī adabiyyāt al-jughrāfiya wa'l-tārīkh wa'l-lughāt 'ind al-'Arab*, in *Majallat al-Jāmi'a al-Miṣriyya* (Cairo n.d.).

74 Taught respectively by Monsieur Pouphilet and Mr Miller. See al-Jamī'ī, op. cit., p. 26.

75 For this list, see ibid., p. 27, Sāmiya Ḥasan Ibrāhīm, op. cit., p. 98 and G. Martin, op. cit., p. 16. Apart from these main subjects, there were

two further optional courses, namely English literature and French literature.

76 Respectively taught by the Egyptian Ḥifnī Nāṣīf and the Italian Carlo Nallino, the two courses were meant to be complementary, with the former concentrating on textual analysis (more or less in the Arab classical manner) while the latter dealing with Arabic literary phenomena according to modern historical methodology. On Ḥifnī Nāṣīf, see Ṭāhā Ḥusain, *A Passage to France*, pp. 39–40. On the significance of combining the two above-mentioned subjects, see idem, *Fi'l-adab al-jāhilī*, in *MK*, vol. V, 1973, pp. 9 ff.

77 Taught by the German Enno Littmann. See Ṭāhā Ḥusain, *A Passage to France*, p. 36. See also idem "Enno Littman" (obituary of Littmann), *al-Majalla*, December 1958, pp. 11–14.

78 Taught by the Italian Gerardo Miloni. See Ṭāhā Ḥusain, op. cit., pp. 35–36.

79 Taught by Muḥammad al-Khuḍarī, an Azhari shaykh. See ibid., pp. 40–41.

80 Taught by Ṣulṭān Muḥammad.

81 Ibrahim Salama, *L'Enseignement Islamique en Egypte* (Cairo 1939) p. 265.

82 The university started from the very beginning (1908) to send students abroad, mainly to England and France, with a view to having qualified Egyptian staff. (See al-Jamī'ī, op. cit., Ch. 3 and Sāmiya Ḥasan Ibrāhīm, op. cit., Ch. 5). The decision to employ foreign teachers was not, however, a temporary measure; it was rather a matter of policy expressing Egypt's wish to maintain close cultural links with Europe. This policy had the full backing of no less a figure than Prince Aḥmad Fu'ād. See Ṭāhā Ḥusein, "Una conferenza", pp. 103 and 104. Cf. Ibrahim Salama, op. cit., p. 265, n.4.

83 He taught for one academic year (1908–1909).

84 Starting with a course on the history of Arab astronomy (1909–1910), he lectured for two more academic years (1910–1911 and 1911–1912) on the history of Arabic literature.

85 He lectured for one year (1910–1911).

86 Arriving at the same time as Santillana and Littmann, Miloni lectured throughout 1910–1911, and then having returned the following year to Cairo, he was to die there in February 1912. See Maria Nallino, "Taha Hussein e l'Italia" in *Taha Hussein, omaggio degli arabisti Italiani a Taha Hussein in occasione del settantancinquesimo compleanno*, L'Instituto Universitario Orientale (Naples 1964), pp. 53–65, p. 54.

87 According to 'Abdurrahman Badawi, *Mawsū'at al-mustashriqīn*, (Beirut 1984), p. 366, it was Goldziher and Hurgronje who, having themselves declined the invitation to lecture in Cairo, recommended the appointment of Massignon.

88 Wiet seems to have arrived in 1912, replacing Nallino in teaching the history of Arabic literature. See Ṭāhā Ḥusain, *Fi'l-adab al-jāhilī*, p. 10.

89 *The Stream of days*, pp. 33–34.

90 Ibid., p. 4.

91 See Ṭāhā Ḥusain's preface to Nallino's *Tārīkh*, p. 8.

92 Op. cit., p. 38.

93 Ibid., p. 38.
94 Ibid., p. 34.
95 Published as *'Ilm al-falak, tārīkhuh 'ind al-'Arab fi'l-qurūn al-wusṭā* (Rome 1911). On the novelty of this course as far as Ṭāhā Ḥusain was concerned, see "Una conferenza", p. 105.
96 These lectures (delivered in Arabic) were published in book form. See *Tārīkh.*
97 Ṭāhā Ḥusain's preface to Nallino's *Tārīkh,* p. 9.
98 Ibid., p. 9 ff. See also idem, "Fī dars al-adab wā tārīkhih", *al-Adab,* April, 1959, pp. 12–14, p. 13. On some of Nallino's Egyptian students, see idem, "Una conferenza", p. 106.
99 From a speech delivered by Ṭāhā Ḥusain (in French) on "What is Classical Arabic?" (Rome, 17 May 1950) and summarized under the title "Visita a Rome di Taha Husein Bey", in *Oriente Moderno,* XXX (1950), p. 100.
100 Ṭāhā Ḥusain's preface to Nallino's *Tārīkh,* pp. 8–9.
101 Ibid., p. 9.
102 Traditionally named *aghrāḍ.*
103 Ibid., pp. 9–10.
104 Nallino, op. cit., p. 18.
105 Ibid., pp. 18–19.
106 Ibid., p. 20.
107 Ibid.
108 Ibid., p. 19.
109 Ibid., p. 56.
110 Ibid., pp. 45 and 228.
111 Ibid., p. 57.
112 Ibid., p. 21.
113 Ibid., p. 61.
114 Ibid., p. 229.
115 The point is made first with reference to political poetry (see ibid., pp. 229 and 259), and then generalized so as to cover all poetry (ibid., p. 263).
116 Ibid., pp. 228–229.
117 As distinguished from traditional love poetry (*nasīb*) composed in the manner of pre-Islamic poets as a prelude to a poem on whatever subject (ibid., pp. 120 and 142 ff.), *al-ghazal,* whether libertine as was the case in Hijazi cities (ibid., p. 121 ff.) or chaste as was the case in the Arabian desert (ibid., p. 135 ff.) was treated as a subject in its own right by wholly dedicated practitioners.
118 As was explained later on by Ṭāhā Ḥusain, a ban on such an activity was imposed by Umayyad caliphs who had their seat in Damascus. See his *Ḥadīth al-Arbi'ā'* I, in *MK,* vol. II, 1974, pp. 192–193. See also Taha Hussein "La renaissance poétique de l'Iraq au IIe siècle de l'Hégire', *Bulletin de l'Institut de l'Egypte,* XXIV (1941–1942), pp. 99–106, p. 101.
119 Nallino, op. cit., p. 123.
120 See Nallino's enumeration of these factors in ibid., p. 143.
121 Nallino's relationship to Ibn Khaldūn will be discussed in the conclusion.

122 Ibid., pp. 60–61.
123 Ibid., pp. 62–63.
124 Ibid. p. 69.
125 Ibid. p. 78.
126 Ibid., p. 311. Read *mukhtalaqa* for the original's *mukhtalifa* – which is an obvious misprint.
127 Ibid., p. 313.
128 For an abridged version of these lectures, see *al-Madhāhib.*
129 Ibid., p. 24.
130 Ibid., pp. 22–23.
131 Ibid., pp. 32 and 33.
132 Ibid., p. 63.
133 It is reported by Ibn al-Nadīm and Ibn Abī Uṣaybi'a that al-Ma'mūn had a dream in which he saw Aristotle. See ibid., pp. 147–148.
134 Ibid., p. 148.
135 Ibid., pp. 149 and 157.
136 According to Santillana, (ibid., p. 67) the Ash'arites believed, like Aristotle, that the existence of a thing was the same as its essence, whereas the Mu'tazilites and Islamic philosophers were Platonists in that they drew a distinction between existence and essence, calling "existent" things that are conceived by the mind as well as possible (but strictly non-existent) beings.
137 Ṭāhā Ḥusein, "Una conferenza", op. cit., p. 105.
138 In *Tajdīd dhikrā Abi'l-'Alā'*, Ṭāhā Ḥusain points out the inferiority of Islamic philosophy as compared with Greek philosophy. He attributes this relative inferiority partly to the fact that Muslim philosophers "imitated" their Greek predecessors while not knowing their language. He hastens to add, however, that he would not deal in this connection with Renan's view that the Semitic mind is inherently incapable of philosophical investigation. See *MK*, vol. XI, p. 86, n. 1. Ṭāhā Ḥusain's final reservation, which is rather vague, may be taken to mean that he disagrees with Renan's racialist explanation of the relative inferiority of Islamic philosophy.
139 Delivered from 25 November 1912 to April 1913, these lectures, numbering forty, were published in book form. See *Muḥāḍarāt.* A fuller version of the first lecture in Massignon's course was published, with an introduction, in French. See "L'Histoire".
140 "L'Histoire", pp. 151–152.
141 Ibid., p. 152.
142 Ibid., p. 152. Cf. *Muḥāḍarāt,* p. 4, where Massignon speaks in this connection of "general categories and names of universals".
143 "L'Histoire", p. 152.
144 Massignon's immediate task as defined by himself is to establish the beginnings of an Arabic lexicon of philosophical terms. See ibid., pp. 153–154 and *Muḥāḍarāt,* p. 4.
145 "L'Histoire", p. 154; *Muḥāḍarāt,* pp. 5–6.
146 "L'Histoire", p. 155; *Muḥāḍarāt,* pp. 7–8.
147 "L'Histoire", p. 154; *Muḥāḍarāt,* pp. 5–6.

148 In his *Kitāb al-Alfāẓ al-mustakhdama fi 'l-manṭiq* ("Terms used in logic") and *Kitāb al-Ḥurūf* ("Book of letters"), both edited by Muhsin Mahdi (Beirut 1968 and 1970, respectively), al-Fārābī sets out to show that the basic concepts in Aristotle's logic and metaphysics could be derived, *mutatis mutandis*, from ordinary Arabic material and grammatical definitions.

149 "L'Histoire", p. 152; *Muḥāḍarāt*, pp. 4, 103 and 104.

150 *Muḥāḍarāt*, pp. 188 and 189.

151 This theme is, however, announced in the very first lecture (especially in the French version) where Massignon outlines his plan. See "L'Histoire", p. 155.

152 Ibid., Ch. XXXVIII.

153 See Ṭāhā Ḥusain's preface to Nallino's *Tārīkh*, p. 8, where he draws a striking contrast between Azhari shaykhs who indulged in the use of colloquial language when speaking reserving literary Arabic for reading, and the European masters who used literary Arabic for all purposes.

154 Nallino, *Tārīkh*, p. 60.

155 Ibid., p. 16.

156 Ibid.

157 Ibid., p. 63.

158 Ibid., p. 19.

159 Ibid., p. 18.

160 Cf. "L'Histoire", pp. 152–153.

161 Ibid., p. 153.

162 Ibid., see also *Muḥāḍarāt*, p. 4.

163 According to Ṭāhā Ḥusain, his Italian masters were motivated by "their love of our language and our country and their indefatigable benevolence towards [Egyptian] young men enamoured with knowledge". See his "Una conferenza", p. 107.

164 *A Passage to France*, p. 36.

165 Idem, op. cit., p. 104.

166 *A Passage to France*, p. 36.

167 To give but one example, consider Littman's paternal attitude as described by Ṭāhā Ḥusain in *A Passage to France*, p. 55 and his "Enno Littmann", p. 13.

168 See *Tajdīd dhikrā Abi'l-'Alā'*, pp. 11–12.

CHAPTER IV

The Early Writings

Having considered Ṭāhā's education in the young Egyptian university, we may now turn to his early writings which, as a matter of fact, largely coincided with and reflected that course of study. As we have seen in the preceding chapter, Ṭāhā made his debut as a writer in *al-Jarīda* of Luṭfī al-Sayyid in 1908. Soon afterwards he began to publish poems[1] and articles ranging over a wide variety of subjects: current affairs, social and educational reform, moral and religious issues, literary criticism and literary history. This varied and relatively prolific output, culminating in Ṭāhā's thesis on Abu'l-'Alā' al-Ma'arrī (1914), was no doubt prompted by Ṭāhā's accession to the world of secular knowledge, thanks to Luṭfī al-Sayyid and to the newly established university. Starting while still astride the Azhar and this latter institution, Ṭāhā's early activity as a writer was to a great extent a direct response to the intellectual effervescence and fermentation brought about by the encounter between the two cultures. By the time it reached its crowning point, precisely at Ṭāhā's post-graduation with the above-mentioned thesis, some sort of reconciliation was established between the two sides.

The young man received his main training as a writer from two men, Luṭfī al-Sayyid and 'Abd al-'Azīz Jāwīsh (1876–1929). The former, we are told, used to read and correct Ṭāhā's manuscripts before giving clearance for publication.[2] This supervisory role continued in one form or another throughout the period under consideration and was extended in a way to the above-mentioned thesis.[3] Luṭfī urged upon his trainee the need to be "temperate in words and deliberative in thought."[4] This might be taken to imply that the master pressed on his disciple the need to avoid verbosity, traditional ornamentation and Azharite pedantry, and also the necessity of resisting first impulses and avoiding half-baked ideas. Such a moderating note was of course in line with Luṭfī's temperament, legal training and philosophical inclinations, but it was also necessitated by the appearance of a fearful rival, namely, Shaykh 'Abd al-'Azīz Jāwīsh. Having given Ṭāhā his initial push, it was not long before Luṭfī had to contend with Jāwīsh's force of attraction pulling the young man in the opposite direction.

Jāwīsh was the complete opposite of Luṭfī: as an ardent follower of Muṣṭafā Kāmil, and leader in his own right of the latter's National Party,[5] he was fiercely opposed to British occupation, calling for immediate independence within the framework of pan-Islamism (under the Ottoman Caliphate). He was also a staunch apologist for Islam in the line of Muḥammad 'Abduh,[6] a militant populist committed to direct grass-roots action,[7] an agitator,[8] a brilliant polemicist and a fiery orator; a man who spoke with a gentle, persuasive voice but who could also burst into a rage, lashing out fiercely at the Azhar's leaders or his political opponents.[9]

It was also Jāwīsh who encouraged Ṭāhā to write a series of abusive articles against a well-established writer, namely al-Manfalūṭī,[10] whom Ṭāhā initially admired[11] and even imitated.[12] This piece of writing, which Ṭāhā was to regret later as being foolish and a continuous source of embarrassment,[13] was against all that Luṭfī stood for;[14] it was scurrilous, long-winded, ornate and, as criticism, of a purely verbal character.[15]

The young man's attitude towards his two irreconcilable mentors was cunningly ambivalent: he published his sober pieces in *al-Jarīda,* while reserving his excesses for the papers of the National Party.[16] In this he was undoubtedly moved by ambition and thirst for fame,[17] but there can be no doubt also that Jāwīsh's charisma corresponded to some of Ṭāhā's deeper inclinations; Ṭāhā's character was simply too complex to be satisfied with one master or to be absorbed by one all-consuming trend.

More specifically, many of his views and attitudes at the time were in line with those of Shaykh Jāwīsh, who must have represented for the young man the type of Islamic reformism initiated by Muḥammad 'Abduh.[18] At that time, we may assume, Ṭāhā's mind seems to have been still largely dominated by this current of thought; he was to be won over to Luṭfī's modernism, secularism, liberalism and political moderation only slowly and gradually. In fact, it took him three or four years to be so converted – and even then his conversion was not complete. Something of Jāwīsh's influence seems to have survived. It would seem that he, as a journalist and orator, helped Ṭāhā to discover the potentialities of literary Arabic as a direct means of communication.[19] An in-depth study of Ṭāhā Ḥusain's mature style might reveal that it owed more to Jāwīsh's diction – vigorous, fervent and flowing – than to Luṭfī's often drab and monotonous prose. It is true that Ṭāhā learnt in due course to shun vituperative criticism, but he never lost his passion for polemics, biting sarcasm or exuberance – qualities shared with Jāwīsh, and nourished in both cases by a deep-rooted Azhari tradition.[20]

For the purpose of this study, the term "early writings" may be taken to mean all of Ṭāhā's works produced prior to his departure for France, including, therefore, his doctoral thesis on Abu'l-'Alā'. With the exception of this work – the first book-length study to be produced by Ṭāhā and generally acknowledged as his first "mature" work – the writings in question have not yet received the attention they deserve. Rejected by their author[21] and still scattered in by now defunct and rare newspapers and periodicals, these works remain largely unknown or completely neglected. Writers dealing with Ṭāhā Ḥusain's early production have focused so far on writings in which he is least original, such as his poetry,[22] his views on social and political affairs,[23] or on episodes, now quaint and entertaining, relating to his feuds with his contemporaries. By contrast, little attention has been paid to another set of writings in which Ṭāhā is in his element, dealing with strictly critical and historical matters. For some scholars, such earlier writings are as good as non-existent.[24] Other scholars, who are aware of their existence and their relevance, have largely been content with quoting, reproducing or summarizing them. No serious attempt has thus far been made to analyse these texts or to situate them in the general development of their author.[25]

Thus, with the blessing of Ṭāhā Ḥusain himself, his early critical articles have been relegated to what may be described as his pre-history. To counter this tendency, a fair selection of these writings will be subjected to close examination here. They lack the polish and flowing rhythm of Ṭāhā's mature work; they are often tentative and inconclusive; sometimes fragmentary or left incomplete. It is obvious that their author is still groping for his way, at times showing signs of fatigue, of being out of his depth or ill-equipped to face the tasks he has set himself. But it is precisely on such accounts that the texts in question are of the utmost importance: they show us Ṭāhā Ḥusain's mature thinking while it is still in the making, at a most critical moment in his intellectual career, when he is still striving to assimilate modern forms of knowledge received mainly from Luṭfī al-Sayyid and his Western teachers at the Egyptian University. The writings in question show us Ṭāhā Ḥusain as he is beginning to break out of al-Marṣafī's neo-classical linguistic approach and Muḥammad 'Abduh's Islamic reformism into a new brand of modernism based mainly on the introduction of the scientific study of literary history and, more generally, the modern methodology of historical enquiry. As we cannot in the present state of knowledge undertake a thorough study of Ṭāhā's early writings, it is not possible to determine precisely when Ṭāhā launched his modernist programme. On the basis of the selection we have made, we may assume for the sake of convenience that the modernist turn took place in 1911. For some time before this development, Ṭāhā's thought tended on the whole to be conservative, notwithstanding the growing influence of Luṭfī and Ṭāhā's teachers at the University. The conservative trend is obvious in his criticism of al-Manfalūṭī, which was a degenerate form of al-Marṣafī's linguistic approach; it is also obvious in Ṭāhā's pronouncements on other matters such as mixed marriages[26] and the study of philosophy.[27]

Ṭāhā's fascination with Muḥammad 'Abduh and association with Jāwīsh would suggest that during this conservative phase Ṭāhā also sympathised with 'Abduh's Islamic reformism. Whether or not he fully adhered to 'Abduh's position is a question which we cannot answer with certainty, again for lack of sufficient knowledge of Ṭāhā's early works. What is certain, however, is that Ṭāhā's modernism can only be understood against the background of al-Marṣafī's and 'Abduh's teachings: as a break with purely linguistic criticism and fundamentalist reform.

On Criticism

Those of Ṭāhā's *early critical articles*[28] chosen for examination in what follows are four in number. With one exception, they were conceived as a series of articles. The first among them entitled, "Criticism, its nature, social impact and conditions as well as the harmful effects of its excessive practice",[29] is not first chronologically in that selected set of writings, but it may serve as a general introduction to them: it deals with theoretical matters relating to criticism in general, as distinct from more specific questions of literary history; and it clearly sets the tone for a whole new phase in Ṭāhā's critical practice, in which he turns away from abusive, purely polemical, criticism in order to reflect on the rules of method governing critical activity.

The article as it stands fulfils only a part of the programme announced in the long title.[30] In fact, it contains very little on literary criticism as such, being devoted to the generic concept of criticism, of which literary criticism is but a variety. Thus criticism is supposed to be applicable not only to all kinds of expression, statement or discourse (*anwāʿ al-qawl, funūn al-bayān, funūn al-kalām*), whether in prose or in verse, but also to all fields of knowledge, be they theoretical or practical, and to action. The concept of criticism is even extended to the natural sphere, for the kind of critical scrutiny involved in the evaluation of discourse and action is likened to, and supposed to complement, the critical work of nature, i.e. the process of natural selection at work in the biological and physical spheres. Just as the physical processes of synthesis and analysis involved in the transformation of matter conserve what is sound and useful while rejecting what is corrupt, unfit or harmful, critical thought works for the promotion of what is valuable while suppressing what is valueless.

It would appear from this that Ṭāhā's attempt to define criticism proceeds according to the logical order, originally established by Aristotle, of moving from the general to the specific. First comes criticism in general (in itself or as such) considered as a discriminatory process at work in the natural and human spheres. Secondly comes the isolation, within this latter sphere, of criticism in so far as it applies to all kinds of statement or discourse, whether scientific or literary.[31] Thirdly and finally, the scope is further narrowed down to literary criticism proper, that is to say, criticism as applicable only to literary statements, whether in prose or in verse.

We shall see in what follows that this Aristotelian manner of procedure, no doubt learnt at the Azhar and further confirmed through contact with Luṭfī al-Sayyid, is a distinctive characteristic of Ṭāhā's critical thinking. That it is now deployed is not without significance, for the whole article seems to be an exercise in appeasement aimed at winning the master over. The author goes out of his way to echo or appropriate Luṭfī's ideas, and to anticipate his objections. This is obvious where Ṭāhā considers criticism, in the human sphere, as a rational activity whose aim is "to distinguish what is good from what is bad, what is substantial from what is trivial; to disengage truth from falsity and what is right from what is wrong, liberate minds from the fetters of uncritical thought (*taqlīd*) and apathy and to assist nature in sustaining what is useful and conserving what is beneficial". Criticism, as the work of reason, is said, again, to be essential to the education of individuals and groups, and to be the surest way of achieving progress in Egypt.

Furthermore, Luṭfī's elitist views seem to be echoed when Ṭāhā sets the critic as an individual apart from the multitude. The work of reason, we are told, is bound to encounter fierce resistance from the majority of people, enslaved as they are by the power of custom and tradition. Exceptional individuals who have the audacity to question received opinions or established attitudes can do so only at the risk of being denounced as heretics and thereby endangering their own safety.

In what looks like an attempt to regain Luṭfī's favour after the Manfalūṭī affair, Ṭāhā strives to reduce the role of subjectivity in literary criticism by subjecting that activity to rules. Thus it is said to be a kind of debate (*munāẓara*) between author and critic, governed by the same rules as apply in polemics (*al-jadal*). As the aim in both cases is to establish the truth, there is no room in criticism for vituperation or rebuke. Truth can be reached only as the outcome of a moderate, calm and emotion-free enquiry based on knowledge of the subject at hand.

Having conceded that much, Ṭāhā would, however, seek an honourable compromise, insisting on the necessity of certain aspects of his own linguistic practice as a critic. It is true, so the argument goes, that a good critic ought not to be vituperative, but surely he has to avoid exaggerated praise and cheap flattery? Again, to the objection of those who claim that linguistic mistakes are not to be criticized where the subject concerned is, for instance, metaphysics (*al-falsafa al-ilāhiyya*), Ṭāhā retorts "our aim is to achieve excellence in all spheres without exception, in our words as well as our thoughts". And, in what sounds like a final plea, he says: "Should we follow the advocates of this point of view, we would be helpless, our tongues reduced to silence, our pens smashed and our hands tied, in the face of an author writing [for instance] a book on medicine or logic in the language of common people".

In the concluding section of the article, Ṭāhā enumerates a set of conditions for criticism which may be restated, with some order, as follows. Being a rational activity the aim of which is the establishment of truth, criticism should, first and foremost, be based on knowledge of the subject at hand. Apart from this basic requirement, criticism should be (a) fair-minded, moderate and calm in tone, avoiding abuse and rebuke; (b) free of passions and emotions, such as love or hate, which sway one's judgement; and (c) restrained in the proffering of praise and blame.

Against Jurjī Zaydān

Some of the ideas expressed in Ṭāhā's article on criticism, especially concerning what he calls "sound criticism" (*al-naqd al-ṣaḥīḥ*), are anticipated in another, partly earlier, work, namely the series of articles entitled "Naqd ṣāḥib *al-Hilāl*"[32] ("Criticism of *al-Hilāl*'s editor"). But these earlier statements on the subject are no more than intimations overshadowed by the highly polemical tone of their context. Also, it may be noted, the series of articles in question are not so much concerned with criticism strictly speaking as with literary history, and as such show the influence not of Luṭfī but of Ṭāhā's foreign masters at the Egyptian University, especially Carlo Alfonso Nallino.

Scholars who have dealt with this piece of writing have been misled by its overtly polemical character into thinking that it is yet another instance of Ṭāhā Ḥusain's literary feuding[33], and they have missed thereby the positive contribution it makes as it aims at setting the record straight with regard to such matters of theoretical interest as the origins, definition and explanatory character of the discipline at issue, namely the history of Arabic literature. We may therefore isolate a first objection levelled against Zaydān's claim that he was the first to have written a history of Arabic literature in Arabic and to have given the subject its Arabic name.[34] Ṭāhā agrees with Zaydān that while the ancient Arabs made pioneering efforts, compiling the major sources for that history,[35] it was European orientalists who were the first to organize the subject according to the historical method. In this respect, he argues, modern Arabs are no more than followers[36] and none of them can claim any credit for creativity or originality.[37] He rejects, however, Zaydān's claims about his own contribution, arguing that the most that he can say is that he was the first to have translated the name of the discipline – and even this is disputable.[38]

Having thus set the record straight concerning the origins of the history of Arabic literature, Ṭāhā would raise another set of theoretical objections relating to Zaydān's definition of the discipline. Zaydān's characterization of it as a history of the sciences (*'ulūm*) and letters (*ādāb*) to be found in Arabic, or, in other words, as a history of the various products emanating from the minds of Arabic speakers,[39] is regarded as defective in more than one respect. First, it disregards the history of Arabic in itself (*al-lugha fī nafsihā*), or the study of changes affecting the very essence of the language (*mā ṭara'a 'alā jawharihā min al-taghayyur*) – as distinct from the scientific and literary works vehicled by the language. Henceforth, a distinction is drawn between two major compartments within literary history: there is on the one hand the purely linguistic or philological study of the essence or matter (*mādda*) of the language concerned; on the other hand, there is the study of the sciences and literature produced in that language.[40]

Secondly, Zaydān's definition of the history of Arabic literature is said to confuse the history of science with the history of literature,[41] when in fact the two types of study ought to be set apart. While the former deals with the development of scientific thought throughout the ages and in different nations, the latter, confined as it is to the study of a given language during a given period of time or in a given nation, considers the history of science, if at all, briefly and occasionally or only with regard to certain specific questions.[42] The proper study of literary history, it is assumed, is the study of belles-lettres or, as Ṭāhā would put it, the arts of self-expression (*funūn al-qawl*) in poetry and prose.

The most fundamental objection levelled against Zaydān in the theoretical sphere, however, has to do with his conception of what would count as explanatory factors in the history of literature. Inasmuch as he divides this history into political epochs delimited by such major political events and social upheavals as the succession of sovereigns, states or dynasties, he is committed to the view that "political and social events" are the ultimate causes in literary history. This, Ṭāhā would say, is unacceptable; for him political and social events are themselves the consequences of deeper changes in the nation concerned.

What sort of changes are these? It is at this point that the argument becomes ambiguous and misleading. Ṭāhā would say that the changes in question have to do with *al-ādāb*; it is in this sphere that the ultimate explanatory factors in literary history should be sought. "There is no doubt", he writes, "that political and social events are nothing but the consequences of changes in the ideas and affairs of the nation [concerned], and that these changes are the result of changes in *al-aḥwāl al-adabiyya.* It follows therefore that literary epochs (*'uṣūr al-ādāb*) should be divided on other than political grounds, which means that *al-ādāb* should be viewed as the causes, rather than the consequences, of political events."[43] As the Arabic concept of *al-ādāb* is highly complex,[44] covering, among other things, (1) belles-lettres, or what might be described as literary phenomena (works and events) strictly speaking, and (2) social attitudes, customs and manners (morals or mores), it would seem at first sight that when Ṭāhā argues that political events are the consequences, rather than the causes, of *al-ādāb*, he has in mind the second sense of the concept, meaning thereby that the events in question, far from being the ultimate explanatory factors in literary history, are to be explained themselves with reference to the attitudes, manners and customs of the society concerned. This interpretation is borne out by the illustration that Ṭāhā proceeds to give, drawing on Ibn Khaldūn, with reference to political events in early Islamic history. The fall of the Orthodox Caliphate (*al-khilāfa al-rāshida*) and the rise of the Umayyad dynasty were not, we are told, the causes of what happened to the Islamic nation; they were rather the consequences of changes in the Arabs' purely bedouin morals (*akhlāq*) brought about by their exposure to the new civilization.[45] This happened when, after the pre-Islamic frugality and leanings towards some form of consultation (*al-shūrā*) as well as the forbearance and other-worldliness inculcated by Islam, the Arabs inherited the riches, luxuries and worldly ambitions of Persia and Byzantium. The rising craving for power and the reversion to tribal *'aṣabiyya* led to the fall of the republican regime and the rise of the monarchy – phenomena which can be discerned in their poetry, oratory and traditions.[46]

Further study of Ṭāhā's text would reveal, however, that the first sense of "*al-ādāb*" (as belles-lettres) is not entirely absent from his mind. Thus he cites, approvingly, Zaydān's assertion that Western scholars attach the utmost importance to the study of *al-ādāb* of any given language as a means of understanding the political history of the nation concerned, and that they periodize that history with reference to *al-aḥwāl al-adabiyya.*[47] They would say for instance that such and such a nation was going through the stage of heroic poetry (*al-ḥamāsa al-shi'riyya*) and that it was heading for another, literary, phase followed by yet another, philosophical one. There can be no doubt, Ṭāhā argues, that in admitting that much Zaydān recognizes that Western scholars periodize literary history according to the major changes affecting *al-aḥwāl al-adabiyya.*[48] It is obvious that the term *al-aḥwāl al-adabiyya,* so used, retains the narrow and specifically literary sense of *al-ādāb,* so much so that we may be tempted to render it as "literary conditions".

It is equally obvious, however, that this rendering, being univocal, does not do full justice to Ṭāhā's thought, for even here he still equivocates between the two senses of *al-ādāb.* He seems to assume, in other words, that *al-aḥwāl al-adabiyya* stands not only for literary occurrences or phenomena but also for "moral" conditions. For instance, a stage of "heroic poetry", where it occurs, seems to imply for Ṭāhā not only the predominance of a certain poetic genre, but also a whole range of moral sentiments and attitudes, or a whole vision of the world and a way of life. As far as he is concerned, political events, however prominent and eye-catching, definitely relate to the superstructure of society, whereas literary phenomena constitute in reality an inextricable strand in the basic social texture; they are closer to and more indicative of the "morals" of the society concerned.

To reconstruct Ṭāhā's views on the ultimate explanatory factors in literary history, bearing in mind his loaded use of the concept *al-ādāb,* does not, however, remove all the difficulties involved in his position. First, his thoughts on the matter involve a further strand relating to the "ideas" and the mental life of the nation concerned. In this vein, he says that "[literary] history . . . reveals to us the truth about the ideas and characteristics (*ṭabā'i'*) of the nation concerned as well as the psychological constitution (*al-tarkīb al-nafsī*) from which we can grasp the truth about the states and conditions affecting that nation."[49] It is in the same vein that Ṭāhā would argue that the study of literary history, being so revealing about the ultimate, psychological, causes of events, is necessary to understand the general history of any given nation.[50]

It would seem that this mental dimension of the argument might provide some sort of link between the two strands, so far distinguished, within the concept of "*al-ādāb*": both the literary and moral affairs of a given society might, in other words, be said to relate to, and be themselves interrelated through, the mental life of that society. Ṭāhā does not, however, exploit this possibility in order to introduce some sort of order into his conception of society and its structure. In fact, his position is further complicated through the addition, in what looks like an afterthought, of other social and environmental factors, also assumed to play a part in explanation. Thus poetry (in a given society), it is said, is influenced by the nature of the country or environment (*ṭabīʿat al-iqlīm*), religion, morals, customs and so forth.[51]

Like Nallino, on whom he draws heavily, his views on what counts as explanatory factors in literary history, as well as his conception of social reality in general, are eclectic and open-ended.[52] Having made the point that major political events, far from being the ultimate causes in literary history, are themselves the consequences of other deeper factors, both master and disciple fail to say exactly what sort of factors these may be and to provide, more generally, an articulated and well-structured view of society. Literary, moral, intellectual, social and material conditions are all invoked without any clear overall order.

We may now turn to the final set of objections levelled against Zaydān. They concern his actual treatment of pre-Islamic Arab history, and are aimed at forming a more critical view of the subject. As against Zaydān, who tends to glorify the ancient Arabs, magnifying their claim to civilization and assimilating to them (the accomplishments of) other races, namely the Ḥimyarites and the Babylonian house of Hammurabi, Ṭāhā strives to set the Arabs apart racially, linguistically and religiously and to portray them as being essentially a nomadic and largely primitive people with a shaky social and political organization, who made no significant contribution to science or wisdom.[53] While we need not enter into the details of Ṭāhā's arguments, mainly drawn from the lectures of Littmann (for comparative philology) and Milloni (for the ancient history of the Orient),[54] we may note how he contends that the literary achievements of pre-Islamic Arabs do not entail any significant modification of his views on the essentially primitive character of their culture. Thus, they cannot lay any claim to civilization by virtue of the excellence of their so-called "suspended" or "precious" odes (*al-muʿallaqāt*): the poets concerned either came from the upper and especially refined strata of society or were exposed to foreign influences.[55] Nor can the indisputable sublimity of Qur'ānic Arabic be placed to their credit, for its inimitability only goes to show that they were challenged and defeated on their own ground. Also, the Qur'ān itself provides clear indications of their primitive state.[56]

We may again highlight the fact that Ṭāhā takes what seems to be his first steps towards his later radical scepticism concerning the authenticity of pre-Islamic poetry. Thus he notes with amazement the discrepancies known to exist between the literary Arabic of that poetry and the recently discovered Ḥimyarite, Safaitic and Thamudic inscriptions. It is strange, he affirms, that the orientalists, who discovered these inscriptions, have noted that they contain little other than prayers to the gods, greeting messages or reports on the construction of edifices (*'amā'ir*) or the making of offerings. More strangely still, Ṭāhā continues, is the fact that none of these inscriptions is written in the Arabic language "with whose literary history we are concerned".[57] It is these observations, made with so much surprise as early as 1911, that constitute the first germs of Ṭāhā Ḥusain's theory, developed in 1926, concerning the spuriousness of the main bulk of pre-Islamic poetry. But more on that later.

Another interesting aspect of Ṭāhā's polemics against Zaydān over matters of history is that they provide a solid landmark in tracing the development of his religious beliefs. We can be sure that when he wrote the series of articles under consideration, Ṭāhā Ḥusain's views on religion conformed strictly to Islamic orthodoxy. That much is implicit in his statements concerning the miraculous character of the Qur'ān. The point becomes much more explicit as he condemns Zaydān's suggestion, derived from German biblical criticism, that the Law of Moses, as formulated in the Torah, is partly derived from those of Hammurabi.[58] Zaydān's views in this connection, said to amount to a denial of revelation or prophecy, are thought to be offensive to Muslims, Christians and Jews alike,[59] and particularly damaging to non-Muslim communities[60] as well as being logically untenable. That the Law of Moses has certain elements in common with the earlier laws of Hammurabi, it is argued, is no proof that the former is derived from the latter. It is as if Zaydān believes, which is false, that revealed laws (*al-sharī'a*) cannot be considered to have a divine source unless they are thoroughly novel, containing no vestige of previous (human) legislation. In fact, the divine origin of a holy book cannot be called into question on the grounds that it contains some human provisions for a law cannot be just unless it takes into account the way of life, customs and mores of the people concerned[61]

We may be certain, therefore, that as late as the autumn of 1911, Ṭāhā Ḥusain still believed that certain texts, namely the holy scriptures of the three monotheistic religions, were not man-made or did not stem from the human mind. We shall see below how his position on these matters evolved a little later.

The Past glories of Arabic

As the series of articles against Zaydān was drawing to an end, Ṭāhā published another article entitled "Hal tastaridd al-lugha majdahā al-qadīm?" ["Can Arabic regain its ancient glory?"][62] and constituting in a way a logical sequel to that series. It offers an extended review of the history of Arabic from pre-historical times to the contemporary period, tracing, as the title suggests, the rise and decline of the language through the ages and applying, more or less systematically, the new conception, introduced in the preceding work, of historical explanation in terms of socio-psychological factors.

Arabic, alleged to be the oldest Semitic language, is supposed to have developed at the infancy of mankind.[63] For vast stretches of time it developed in complete isolation, spoken by a nomadic people who made no significant contribution to world history.[64] The Arabic we know is therefore the language that was finally revealed to the world only a century and a half before the rise of Islam, at which stage it was already a developed, rich and highly expressive language.[65] The efflorescence of pre-Islamic poetry, with all its magnificent exuberance, was therefore the beginning of historical Arabic. Confirmed and consolidated a little later by the miraculous Qur'ān and the power of Islam, the language embarked on its irresistible advance, outliving other Semitic tongues[66] and sweeping aside in the Near East such non-Semitic languages as Greek, Latin and Persian.[67]

In spite of their magnificent poetry, pre-Islamic Arabs themselves were, we are told, an uncultivated and untutored people. It was the Qur'ān which brought to them a radical revolution in terms of language, thought, legislation, moral regeneration and political power; it was the Qur'ān which created the Arabs anew, turning them from nomadism to civilization.[68] Thus, so the argument goes, it is wrong to uphold the view, put forward by Ibn Khaldūn and accepted by some modern writers, that Arabic literature, and poetry in particular, stagnated under the Prophet and the Orthodox Caliphs, who, it is claimed, were occupied with the more urgent affairs of religion, conquest and state-building.[69]

By contrast, Ṭāhā moves closer to Ibn Khaldūn when he speaks of the transition from the "republican" regime of the Orthodox Caliphs to the "monarchical" Umayyad system,[70] or, again, when he describes the social and literary consequences of accumulated wealth and luxury under the Umayyads.[71] The new civilization, it is said, influenced the minds and tongues of Arabs, refining their ideas, vocabulary and styles. They henceforth gave expression to their passions and feelings in song. There also arose a class of poets dedicated to love poetry, as well as another class of poets specialized in the praise of wine.[72]

The flow reached its peak with the onset of the 'Abbāsid period. The Arabs, then at the zenith of their power, were tired of conquest and only too eager to settle in peace and comfort, enjoying the benefits of wealth and luxury.[73] It was also during that period that the Arab mind, by then fully mature, was ready to turn its attention to theoretical pursuits. Political schisms arising under the Umayyads now assumed a purely religious character, giving rise thereby to practitioners of dogmatic theology known as *al-mutakallimūn*;[74] oratory achieved an unprecedented degree of development and excellence,[75] while poetry became more and more varied, exquisite and inventive.[76] All in all, Arabic reached its happiest moment under the 'Abbāsids, giving expression to the widest range of human faculties.[77]

According to this scheme, the point of decline occurs at the beginning of the 4th century of the Hegira, where Arabic begins to lose its vigour and vitality and succumbs to an ever-growing obsession with stylistic mannerism and ornamentation.[78] The last great poet to appear is believed to be al-Sharīf al-Raḍī, while al-Mutanabbī and Abu'l-'Alā' are associated with the period of decline. They, it is said, were interested on the whole in ideas rather than in good style, but whenever they attended to the latter aspect, their poetry degenerated into loathsome affectation. In fact, they owe their status not so much to their poetic achievement as to their distinction in wisdom and philosophy.[79]

The period of decline, lasting well into the 19th century, is said to have witnessed the regression of Arab power as well as the shrinking influence of Arabic. History, Ṭāhā would say, had by then come full circle: foreign races (*al-'ajam*), having gained by then the upper hand, waged an all-out war on their race, religion and language; Arabic was forced to beat a retreat and to seek refuge in the mosques, where it was confined to liturgical functions, while in the outer world it was corrupted by colloquial use.[80]

In more recent times, and thanks to the pioneering and revivalist efforts of al-Ṭahṭāwī and Muḥammad 'Abduh, Arabic literature, whether in prose or in verse, has undergone some change for the better.[81] This promising revival, starting in the second half of the 19th century, seems, according to Ṭāhā, to have come to a standstill during the contemporary period. And it is at this point of the story that his judgements become particularly harsh. "Now", he writes, "the revival of Arabic in Egypt has become chaotic without a [recognized] leader [to set the pattern for others]. Hence, the rampant disorderliness in vocabulary and style: poets and writers express themselves nonchalantly, very often unconcerned with any rule or model."[82] The state of Arabic in the Azhar, traditionally the impregnable stronghold of the language, is equally unhappy and is definitely backward by comparison with its level in other modern schools.[83] But even these schools cannot be relied upon to carry out linguistic reform.[84] The only sure way to do so would be to give students a solid training in good Arabic accompanied by the study of the formal and material aspects of the language as well as the memorization of a fair amount of excellent ancient texts.[85]

As far as contemporary poetry is concerned, it is certainly more advanced as compared with poetry in the preceding century,[86] but it is still inferior when measured by the standards of ancient poetry or in the light of the present progress of humanity.[87] A stark contrast is drawn between pre-Islamic love poetry – so vigorous and virile – and modern love lyrics – said to be feeble and insipid.[88] Worse treatment still is meted out to the three major living poets, namely Aḥmad Shawqī, Ḥāfiẓ Ibrāhīm and Isma'īl Ṣabrī, who are summarily and unfairly dismissed on the grounds that their sensibility is not truly Egyptian. Some, it is claimed, are so imbued with Western ideas that they may be considered as belonging to Europe, while the others are so enslaved by ancient models that they may be considered as poets of the dead (*shu'arā' al-qubūr*, lit.: "poets of the graves").[89]

To the question, posed in the title of the article, as to whether Arabic could regain its past glories, Ṭāhā would give a positive answer – subject to certain qualifications. He seems to suggest that a true literary revival is possible provided that linguistic reform is pursued according to the essentially revivalist methods previously introduced by the early reformers such as Muḥammad 'Abduh, namely the revival of the ancient Arab heritage, the translation of Western works, the establishment of a learned body of linguistic authorities to introduce linguistic reforms and to promote literary Arabic, as well as the provision of linguistic training along the lines prescribed above.[90]

Sketchy as it is, this review of the history of Arabic literature has some importance if only because of the width of its scope, which demonstrates Ṭāhā's endeavour to apply Nallino's methodology beyond the limits of the latter's history of Arabic literature.[91] In this connection, the extension of socio-psychological explanation to the 'Abbāsid literature, foreshadowed to some extent by Nallino,[92] has a special significance for Ṭāhā's development, as it will henceforth be one of his major preoccupations as a historian of literature. There is what looks like the beginning of a new appreciation of 'Abbāsid poets for their inventiveness and innovation, but Ṭāhā is still held back by al-Marṣafī's conservative taste and, in particular, his utter hostility to al-Mutanabbī and Abu'l-'Alā' on account of their Greek, and more specifically, philosophical inclinations.[93]

Al-Marṣafī's influence can also be detected in Ṭāhā's criticisms of modern sensibility as compared with pre-Islamic vigour and vitality. A certain amount of time will have to elapse before he gains that complete mobility, offered by the new historical methodology, of ranging freely between different literary periods and schools, giving each its due fairly and open-mindedly.

The Life of literature

The last example to consider from among Ṭāhā Ḥusain's early essays is a series of articles entitled: "Ḥayāt al-ādāb" ["The Life of literature"][94] In this most important, but completely unknown piece of work, Ṭāhā takes up the theoretical task of defining the scope and nature of the discipline concerned with the history of Arabic literature. Materials from earlier works are used, but they are now reformulated, with certain refinements, in a more systematic fashion. As initially planned, the definition in question is intended to unfold in a series of five "prolegomena" (*muqaddimāt*)[95] that may be restated as follows. After a preliminary prolegomenon[96] (A) on the inadequacy of current historical knowledge, there follow four other prolegomena, three of which are said to be necessary (*lāzima*), while the fourth is described as optional (*ghayr lāzima*).[97] The three necessary ones are: (B) on the distinction between literature itself and the history of literature; (C) on the distinction between the history of literature and the history of science; and (D) criticism of traditional methods of literary criticism and literary history. The fifth, so-called "optional" prolegomenon (E), is meant to provide a study, by way of illustration, of the 'Abbāsid poet Abū Nuwās.[98]

In actual fact, however, Ṭāhā does not strictly adhere to his initial plan. The proposed study on Abū Nuwās (prolegomenon E) is never provided, although reference to the 'Abbāsid period recurs throughout the series. Again, criticism of traditional historical knowledge, proposed for separate treatment in prolegomenon (D), is largely assimilated to prolegomenon (B). Finally, the two main distinctions announced respectively in prolegomena (B) and (C) are aimed not so much at separating the terms concerned but rather at relating each pair, the one being assumed to be necessary to the other. From this it would appear that the author does not initially realize the complexity of his task; as the work progresses, he shows signs of fatigue, seems to be out of his depth and is obliged to improvise or to seek ad hoc solutions. "Ḥayāt al-ādāb" is, therefore, loose to the point of fragmentariness, and left unfinished and inconclusive. And yet, for all its shortcomings and lacunae, the work occupies a crucial and unique place in Ṭāhā Ḥusain's early writings, if not in his entire corpus, as it embodies his most determined attempt thus far to come to grips with the foundations of the new discipline while also laying the bases for his mature work, starting with his thesis on Abū'l-'Alā'. As this will become clearer below, we may now consider in some detail the proposed prolegomena – now reduced to three, namely the preliminary prolegomenon (A) followed by the two necessary ones (B) and (C).

(A) On the inadequacy of current historical knowledge of Arabic literature.

Under this heading Ṭāhā takes up the theme, already evoked in "Can Arabic regain its ancient glory?", of the relative stagnation of literary life in contemporary Egypt – as compared with what had been the case five years earlier.[99] This deplorable state of affairs, which is assumed to concern creative literature as well as literary criticism, is attributed to two factors. There is first what is described, rather darkly, as an "oppressive force" (*al-quwwa al-qāhira*) with devastating effects on the political, literary and intellectual spheres of activity.[100] Scattered hints to the effect that the force in question is primarily political,[101] having to do with constraints on the freedom of speech, would suggest that Ṭāhā may have in mind the restrictive regulations imposed at the time by the British occupation authorities. However, in a later article on Egyptian poets and elegiac poetry, Ṭāhā describes the "oppressive force" as a purely moral condition (*'illa adabiyya khāliṣa*) sapping the energy of poets and writers and weakening their talent.[102]The second factor is supposed to be the inadequacy of current knowledge of the Arab literary heritage. This monumental lore, constituted in the course of more than fifteen centuries, is hardly known to modern Arabs, barred as they are from acceding to their past by a thick barrier of accumulated historical debris. It was only recently that they had begun to discover this past, but the main blame for their ignorance should go to "our teachers of and writers on literature and literary history",[103] or, more generally, the so-called "Literary History School" (*madrasat al-ādāb*).[104]

By this label, Ṭāhā appears to designate a broad current of thought and teaching practice that includes, apart from Jurjī Zaydān, such academic historians of literature as Ḥasan Tawfīq al-'Adl and his followers.[105] Mainly influenced by German orientalism, the advocates of this trend had introduced, in both the Egyptian literary life and educational system,[106] the subject of literary history, considered as the study of poetry and prose in successive periods[107] corresponding to, and causally dependent on, the succession of dynasties or political regimes in general.[108] It is these specialists of literature and its history who are accused of being content with whatever meagre and superficial knowledge they may acquire by simply reading ancient books and memorizing samples of poetry and prose, and who are held responsible, in the main, for the general stagnation of the contemporary literary scene.[109]

Against the practice of this School, Ṭāhā would propose what he regards as a more adequate methodology for the study of Arabic literature, characterized, at this preliminary stage, as being socio-psychological and environmental. The literature of a given nation, it is said, cannot be studied without delving deep into the psychology of that nation and conducting a deep analysis of its temperament.[110] Such a study, it is again argued, requires an examination of the literature concerned insofar as it originates in a particular region (*mawṭin*) or environment (*bī'a*), undergoes its influence and is subject to its natural laws.[111] The point is further amplified by saying that such a study requires a thorough examination of environmental influences, whether they are immediate (*qarība*), i.e. emanating from the region concerned, or remote (*ba'īda*), i.e. emanating from neighbouring countries.[112] In the latter case, imitation is supposed to play an important role.[113]

The new methodology is supposed to find its best illustration in 'Abbāsid literature. Unlike its counterparts in pre-Islamic or early Islamic times, Arabic literature in Iraq under the 'Abbāsids was a highly complex mixture, the proper study of which calls for the collaboration of specialists from different disciplines, taking into account a variety of influences: Persian, Syriac, Greek and Indian.[114] It would be unfair to science, it is said, to claim that 'Abbāsid literature belongs to the Arabs alone, to the Persians alone, or to the Arabs and Persians together, as they both read and were influenced by Greek and Indian sciences.[115]

Accusing adherents of the Literary History School of having hardly any knowledge of foreign languages,[116] Ṭāhā would also say that they confined themselves to the study of Arabic in general (*min wajhin 'āmm*),[117] which is another way of saying that they examine literature in isolation from the psychology of the Arab nation, its environment and interactions with other nations.

(B) On the distinction between literature itself and the history of literature

Contrary to what may appear to be the case at first sight, the main aim of this prolegomenon is not so much to separate literature itself from history but to relate the former to the latter. Literary works and phenomena, so the argument goes, are necessarily historical; equally, the study concerned with these works or phenomena cannot be adequately carried out without taking their history into consideration. The development of any given literature, it is said, depends on the prevailing economic, political, intellectual and social conditions – all of which fall within the sphere of history.[118] The point is illustrated by examples, drawn from Nallino, with a view to showing how the effervescence of political poetry and amorous poetry (*ghazal*) under the Umayyads depended on such conditions.

Nallino is also echoed in Ṭāhā's detailed criticism of traditional Arab historiography. Thus it is pointed out that the Arab nation, which produced highly developed literature both before and after the rise of Islam, failed to make a significant contribution to the study of literary history. Traditional Arab scholarship, it is said, confined itself to the purely linguistic, grammatical and rhetorical aspects of literature.[119] This striking limitation is attributed to the Arabs' broader failure to excel in historical studies in general.[120] Like other oriental nations (ancient Egyptians, Babylonians, Phoenicians, Hebrews and the Semites in general), and unlike the Greeks and Romans, the Arabs' interest in history was restricted to relating and recording major political events (such as the deeds of kings and the deaths of great men), natural disasters, famines and pests, without seeking an explanation. Apart from this rudimentary form of historiography, the Arabs did not know history as a discipline or craft (*ṣināʿa*) through which one acquires the habit (*malaka*) of critical enquiry (*al-taḥqīq*) and the discovery of explanatory factors (*al-istinbāṭ*).[121]

Ṭāhā moves beyond Nallino, however, when he takes the further step of criticizing the performance of such great Arab historians as al-Ṭabarī, al-Masʿūdī, Ibn al-Athīr and Ibn Khaldūn even at the elementary level of recording and relating events. They, it is argued, relied almost entirely on oral traditions, neglecting the study of official papers and chancellery records.[122] Where such documents existed, the historians in question were not aware of the need to investigate their authenticity.[123] By contrast, history is said to have grown into a fully fledged science with its own rules and principles – just as logic or any other theoretical science.[124]

As he develops these criticisms of Arab historiography, Ṭāhā formulates by the same token, and also independently of Nallino, some of the methodical rules deemed necessary for truly historical research.

Suppose, he says, we want to study the history of the caliph al-Ma'mūn. It would not be enough to read the above-mentioned authorities on the subject; a critical examination of any available documentary evidence would also be necessary. Such an examination would in turn require knowledge of a number of special enquiries and disciplines.[125] Of equal importance would be the study of social life at the time of al-Ma'mūn,[126] as reflected in the then current fables, legends, poetry, speeches, proverbs, physical heritage, form of government, public opinion and economic conditions.[127]

Then follow two further rules of the highest importance, as they bear on what will become explosive issues in Ṭāhā Ḥusain's mature work. The first rule stipulates the necessity of subjecting ancient historical texts to critical examination under the authority of reason with a view to removing interpolations (*al-ziyādāt*) and exaggerations.[128] Citing examples from both Pharaonic and Islamic histories, Ṭāhā notes, in particular, that the latter history teems with exaggerations closer to fiction than to fact.[129] It is no wonder, he says, that there is so far no reliable history of Islam in Arabic.[130] The point is then made, more specifically, with reference to the history of Arabic literature, where exaggerations, interpolations and forgeries abound as a result of a variety of motives.[131] Adherents of the Literary History School are accused of meekly accepting such reports and traditions at face value.[132]

The second rule stipulates that in writing the history of a given nation, it is necessary to take into account any relevant traditions emanating from other contemporary nations, whether or not they have been in contact with the people concerned. Thus, for instance, in writing the history of Islamic conquests under the Orthodox Caliphs, it would be a grave error to rely exclusively on Arab sources.[133]

The proposed account of the necessary conditions of scientific historiography will be further amplified under the following prolegomenon. But we may note straightaway how Ṭāhā's position becomes increasingly radical and iconoclastic. As he extends his critique from the Literary History School to the whole tradition of Muslim historiography, he seems to suggest that the essential weaknesses of that contemporary current of thought are deeply rooted in Arab history and the Arab mentality.[134] Such a critique is thus doubly destructive: purporting to denounce the false modernity of that School, it also uncovers its shaky foundations in Arab traditions.

(C) On the distinction between the history of science and the history of literature.

Ṭāhā's position on this question seems to have evolved since his polemics against Zaydān. There, the overriding concern was to draw a clear demarcation line between the two disciplines, on the grounds that knowledge of the former is necessary to the latter only occasionally and incidentally. Now, by contrast, the stress is laid rather on establishing a close link between the two subjects, mainly on the grounds that there is a particular science, namely psychology, a knowledge of which is essential in all studies of literary history.

Having argued in the preceding prolegomenon (B) that it is necessary for literary study to be historical, Ṭāhā would now claim that the historical character of this type of study is primarily psychological. As this claim has already been made tentatively within the preliminary prolegomenon (A), one would expect it to be firmly established in the present prolegomenon (C), coming as it does at the end of the series. In practice, however, Ṭāhā's reasoning at this crucial stage, most opaque and inconclusive, stands in need of some analysis and reconstruction.

There is first a general observation to the effect that the diversity of forms of knowledge or disciplines show one common affinity as a result of their having one and the same source, namely the human mind.[135] This, it is implicitly assumed, is manifest in the fact that such forms of knowledge or disciplines follow the same pattern of development.[136] There follows, secondly, an attempt to show that, following the example set by philosophy as it came to explain matter with reference to atoms, literary study has developed in such a way as to realize the importance of psychological factors for the explanation of texts.

It is important to notice that it is philosophy or rational enquiry (*al-naẓar al-ʿaqlī fi'l-falsafa*) which is supposed to serve as a model. It is, in other words, philosophical disciplines (*al-ʿulūm al-falsafiyya*) which are said to have advanced in such a way as to set the pattern for literary study. The ancient Graeco-Arab philosophical account of material bodies in terms of two allegedly irreducible components, matter and form, is said to have given way to the modern chemical conception of matter, reducing material bodies to their constituent atoms. Being at first content with what is manifest, the human mind has so developed as to be no longer satisfied with less than reaching what is most basic and invisible. A similar development has taken place in the literary sphere, with the traditional account of statements (*aqwāl*), whether in prose or in verse, as compounds of matter (i.e. words insofar as they are representations of meanings) and form (syntax)[137] being replaced by a more far-reaching explanation of statements in terms of ultimate factors residing in the soul. The literary enquiry is no longer satisfied with the mere evaluation of form (style) and content (words or meanings); it would rather reach for the deeper causes of excellence in either case; that is to say, it would seek to analyse statements along the lines of the chemical analysis of matter – except that it has its own chemistry, namely psychology.[138]

One point that can be easily clarified concerns the so-called "literary" account of statements. This, it may be noted, is none other than the purely linguistic approach to literary texts, developed by ancient Arab philologists and still practised by such modern revivalists as Ṭāhā's own Azhari master al-Marṣafī, confined as it is to the (intrinsic) constituents of a literary text, i.e. its formal (phonetical, grammatical, syntactical) aspects as well as its content. The approach in question is now contrasted with, and claimed to have given way to, the modern conception of such a text as a product of psychological factors.

But the argument, so stated, is still obscure and inadequate as far as Ṭāhā's purposes are concerned, namely to establish the necessity of psychology for literary history.

Basically, the point at issue is quite simple and may be stated as follows. Modern literary study needs to invoke psychological factors in the explanation of statements because it has emulated, or ought to emulate, the natural sciences in adopting a causal approach to its object. The reason why Ṭāhā does not have much success in establishing the point in question is that he, being still under the influence of Azhari scholasticism, does not as yet draw a distinction between philosophy and (natural) science. For him, philosophy is still the monolithic subject that it used to be in classical times and the Middle Ages, covering the whole range of human knowledge. Thus he still thinks of the modern development mentioned above as if it has occurred within philosophy itself, replacing a superficial analysis in terms of manifest constituents by a more refined and deeper analysis in terms of remote, hidden constituents. In other words, Ṭāhā is trying to establish a point for which he does not as yet possess the necessary conceptual tools. The development he is trying to describe is in fact that which took place in modern times, when the natural sciences replaced the philosophical, purely conceptual, explication of what it is to be a material object by an empirical explanation accounting for how such an object comes into being as a result of causal factors. It is this type of development which led to the invocation of atoms in the explanation of matter; and it is through a similar kind of development in the literary field that recourse to psychological factors can be explained and justified.

Sometimes the point is made by saying that a line of verse, for instance, is the product of material as well as mental factors (*'awāmil māddiyya wa-ma'nawiyya*).[139] The introduction of the former kind of factor does not, however, compromise the predominance of psychology. A literary work is supposed to be a direct result and mirror of the mind of its author, or a direct outcome of a combined effort involving all the psychological powers and mental faculties of the latter.[140] But these very powers and forces are ultimately reducible or traceable to subjective as well as objective influences. Such a line of verse, Ṭāhā would again say, is a direct reflection of a certain character or temperament (*mizāj*) of the poet's mind, but this character or temperament is itself the outcome of mental as well as material factors.[141] Underlying a literary work, there is an effort directly traceable to the artist's mind, but which in the final analysis is the fruit of collaboration between the artist and his environment or, as Ṭāhā would put it, his "time" (*zamān*).[142] Literature mirrors not only the mind but also life.[143]

A further complexity emerges when the necessity of psychology, so far affirmed with regard to literary history, is extended to history as such. Historiography, it is claimed, can no longer be confined to the mere relation and recording of events; it needs to adopt an analytical approach whereby such events are traced back to their obscure origins in the human psyche; history, it is now asserted, is but a manifestation of the social self or collective mind (*al-nafs al-ijtimā'iyya*).[144] Already foreshadowed in Ṭāhā's polemics against Zaydān,[145] this apparently innocent generalization now reveals a new critical edge in line with Ṭāhā's growing radicalism. Adding a further item to what he sees as necessary conditions for historical enquiry, he argues that it would not be enough to relate the episodes and traditions of Islamic history, to draw lessons from them (*al-'ibar wa'l-'iẓāt*) or even to subject them to critical examination with the aim of removing accretions (*fuḍūl*) in the manner of the critically-minded (*al-muḥaqqiqūn*) among ancient historians; for when all these conditions have been satisfied, there would still be a further necessary condition, namely to clarify the otherwise obscure link between those episodes and traditions and the Islamic mind. Satisfying this condition, says Ṭāhā without mincing his words, is the only means of "removing the miraculous character of many an episode in Islamic history"[146]; it is only then that these events could be said to be understood or known. The point is driven home again when he affirms that there is no place in logic or history for miracles, and that these may be relegated to religious disciplines.[147] He himself, Ṭāhā says, would have undertaken a study of the noble Qur'ān to show how it affected the minds of men throughout the ages, had it not been for the clamour and controversy that would arise as a result.[148]

Thus far the necessity of the history of science for literary study has been explained with reference to psychology. In the ninth and final article in "Ḥayāt al-ādāb", which ends the series rather abruptly,[149] the point is again made with reference to several other disciplines,[150] among which philosophy attracts special attention. The need for some knowledge of this subject is supposed to arise on two accounts, first, that philosophy (strictly speaking) is related to psychology,[151] and, secondly, that literature is known sometimes to be subject to the influence of philosophical disciplines. Here again, the 'Abbāsid period in the history of Arabic literature is taken to be a case in point. As opposed to pre-Islamic literature, which drew on indigenous experience and customs[152] as well as early Islamic literature, which was influenced by newly developed or introduced knowledge and traditions,[153] 'Abbāsid literature, standing at the zenith of Islamic contact with other civilizations, felt the full impact of philosophical disciplines, mainly in translation. The whole intellectual climate of the period was so impregnated with philosophical ideas that no man of culture could have remained indifferent to them or escaped their impact. In fact, many poets of the period made a point of cultivating the subject, giving expression to such ideas in a philosophically loaded form. No serious student of the period in question can ever hope to come to grips with such a complex and sophisticated literature without some knowledge of philosophy.

Given this, adherents of the Literary History School come in for a final jab, as they are castigated for their indifference and outright hostility to philosophy. Even if for the sake of argument they were allowed to pretend to ignore the atheism of Muṭī' [Ibn Iyās], Ḥammād ['Ajrad] and Ibn al-Muqaffa', the Mu'tazilism of al-Jāḥiẓ and the reactionary tendencies of al-Sayyid al-Ḥimyarī, they could not avoid the study of philosophy. It is after all an Arab subject, written in Arabic, traditionally taught on a wide scale in Islamic schools and mosques and still receiving some (scanty) attention in the Azhar. One can perhaps understand the hostility of theologians to philosophy, but there can be no excuse for those scholars who present themselves as students of the history of literature and the history of science to ignore philosophy, take pride in so doing and denounce it for corrupting minds and tongues.

This apology for philosophy, so divergent from Ṭāhā's views on the subject in 1909, heralds the final work of Ṭāhā Ḥusain's early period, namely his doctoral thesis on Abu'l-'Alā' al-Ma'arrī – a most representative figure of 'Abbāsid literature and poet-philosopher par excellence.

The Encounter with the Sage of Ma'arra

On 5 May 1914, Ṭāhā Ḥusain was awarded a doctorate for his thesis on Abu'l-'Alā' al-Ma'arrī. This work, published a year later under the title *Dhikrā Abi'l-'Alā*[154] ["In Memory of Abu'l-'Alā'"], has a claim to be regarded as a first in many senses. Being the first thesis ever submitted to, and passed by, the nascent Egyptian University, it was also the first work of Ṭāhā Ḥusain to be recognized by him as worthy of publication in book form. In his preface to the first edition,[155] he leaves the reader in no doubt as to the importance he attaches to his study on Abu'l-'Alā'. His decision to have it published, he affirms, was motivated by an "altruistic" concern that both contemporary and posterior generations be well-informed about his intellectual development, for the work in question represented his life at the age of twenty-five.[156]

In a much wider perspective, albeit with the same tone of pride, we are informed that the work, being the first in Arabic literature to adopt a modern historical methodology, constitutes a major landmark in Egyptian literary life. So strict and rigorous is the book's adherence to a well-defined plan that it may, so it is claimed, be considered as a kind of logic if not actually a logic [an organon?] of literary history.[157]

To all this we may add that the publication of *Dhikrā Abi'l-'Alā'* marked the beginning of Ṭāhā Ḥusain's international fame.[158]

There is no doubt, therefore, that this study on Abu'l-'Alā' constitutes a breakthrough in Ṭāhā Ḥusain's intellectual production. It does not, however, involve a complete break with the earlier, less polished and less fortunate articles. It is no more than the culmination of the theoretical and methodological effort carried out starting with the polemics against Zaydān in 1911. While in his earlier works he set out the principles and rules of the new historical methodology, his thesis on Abu'l-'Alā' provides a first, admittedly major, illustration. It is true that the detailed study on the Sage of al-Ma'arrā is preceded by a "Preface" (*muqaddima*) and a "Prologue" (*tamhīd*) expounding the theoretical and methodological premises for the whole work. But Ṭāhā's statements to this effect are a final reformulation of conclusions more or less reached in the earlier articles. The polish and self-assurance of the first mature work are simply signs of a certain measure of stability attained through the gropings, rehearsals and improvisations of the articles. It is thanks to the toil contained in these minor writings that the author could finally reap the fruits of his labours.

In the "Preface", Ṭāhā reviews and pronounces a final judgement on the different schools of literary thought thus far known to him, giving each its due and retaining from each such ingredients as deemed valuable or useful. Thus the merits and shortcomings of the linguistic approach, as represented by its modern advocate, al-Marṣafī, are weighed against those of the modern historical methodology taught by European masters at the Egyptian University. Previously made to look outmoded in the light of modern scientific development, the linguistic approach is now given a limited but necessary role in literary study. It is found wanting on two accounts: first its strict attachment to the classical model of excellence as exemplified by the pre-Islamic desert-dwelling poets and to a lesser extent by their emulators in later ages, and secondly its exclusive concern with linguistic, and mainly rhetorical, aspects.[159] By contrast, the historical methodology is commended for its open-mindedness and wider scope: it treats all forms of literary expression from whatever age and of whatever quality on an equal footing. It also covers many aspects of the subject and hence requires some knowledge of several disciplines: the philosophical and religious sciences, history and geography, comparative philology, individual and collective psychology, modern European languages and literature as well as Western methodologies and orientalist writings.[160]

The contrast, so far drawn in favour of the historical methodology, is however counteracted by a further move towards a more balanced view. Thus the linguistic approach is thought to be indispensable for training students in literary composition and cultivating their taste for the Arabic literary heritage.[161] By the same token, the historical form of procedure is found insufficient: it is in this vein that European sources on Abu'l-'Alā', thought to satisfy the requirements of history and the spirit of criticism, are said to be an unreliable guide to Abu'l-'Alā''s biography or to his literary and philosophical doctrines. Orientalist students of the ancient Arab poet, it is claimed, could not unravel the intricacies of his obscure language or fathom the depths of his thought, as they suffer from the major handicap of not mastering his language, or even classical Arabic for that matter.[162]

The final conclusion to this even-handed apportioning of praise and blame is that an adequate study of Arabic literature should combine the two approaches, with the linguistic one constituting an essential moment of textual comprehension and appreciation. In other words, the ideal literary study should be based on a two-pronged strategy, where a historical explanation in terms of psychological and environmental factors is accompanied by textual analysis (in the manner of al-Marṣafī).[163]

Having reached this conclusion, Ṭāhā, we may notice, is in a position to dismiss the Literary History School – now designated as "the doctrine advocated by the majority of teachers of literature in Egyptian schools" – summarily and decisively. It is, says Ṭāhā, a "distorted and confused" (*mushawwah* and *mukhtaliṭ*) doctrine: neither ancient nor modern and neither useful in cultivating literary faculties nor helpful in inculcating modern methodologies.[164]

In the "Prologue" to the work under consideration, Ṭāhā does no more than generalize the causal logic shown in "Ḥayāt al-ādāb" to underlie the historical point of view. Thus the thesis that literary works are products and reflections of the minds and environments of their authors is turned into a well-rounded view of the world as a deterministic system in which individual authors lose their autonomy, being assimilated to a mere product of the whole. "The purpose of this work", writes Ṭāhā, "is not to depict Abu'l-'Alā''s life apart, but to study the life of the Islamic mind (*nafs*; lit.: soul) at that time, for the man with all his states (*aṭwār*) was but the necessary product and ripe fruit of a combination of causes which constituted his temperament and on which he had no control or rule."[165] Some of these causes, we are told, are material (*māddiyya*), while others are immaterial (*ma'nawiyya*); some are [directly] related to man, whereas others are not so related.[166] It would be a grave error to imagine that a man is independent of his surroundings, and immune to the influence of past and present conditions. Such an independent being can have nothing to do with this world, composed as it is of interrelated and interacting entities and having no place for accident – everything being the consequence of a preceding cause and the cause of some subsequent event.[167]

Calling this doctrine "determinism in history" (*al-jabr fi'l-tārīkh*), Ṭāhā sees it as implying that the movement of history is ineluctable (*jabriyya*), leaving no room for free choice or will; that events of whatever magnitude or kind cannot be exclusively attributed to individual agents however high-ranking they may be; that they should be equally, or even primarily, attributed or referred to the whole of which the individual concerned is a part. Any historical event, be it a poem, a speech or an epistle, is a tissue (*nasīj*) of social as well as natural (*kawniyya*; lit.: cosmic) causes amenable to investigation and analysis – just as matter is subject to chemical action.[168]

A literary work cannot be ascribed solely to its author, for this latter individual is himself the product of his epoch.[169] More elaborately, the ultimate factors accounting for such an individual like Abu'l-'Alā' and his works are said to be the Islamic nation's, soul or mind,[170] a particular space (or physical environment) and a particular time (epoch or period). Again, Abu'l-'Alā' is said to have been the product of a certain period of time, a certain space (region) as well as certain political, social, economic and religious conditions.[171]

This form of determinism goes hand in hand with what might be described as a positivist or scientistic view of knowledge, according to which history is considered as a purely descriptive science (*waṣfī lā waḍ'ī*) just like any other theoretical or experimental discipline. The role of a historian, it is claimed, consists in describing what there is rather than creating something new,[172] proffering no praise or blame;[173] it is no different from that of a philosopher, mathematician or a natural scientist. In such forms of knowledge the facts concerned are eternal, constant and necessary (*qadīma, thābita, wājiba*); what is contingent (*'āriḍ*) is only human knowledge.[174]

The style in which these ideas are expressed has about it an air of finality, being laconic, magisterial and almost epigrammatic. It is a symptom of the stability achieved through the simple refinement and generalization of earlier positions: Ṭāhā now feels that he has at last mastered the principles of historical methodology, that having established those principles in their final form there is for him no more to do but to try and apply them to the particular case of Abu'l-'Alā'.

As for the choice of subject, it can be fully understood only in the light of earlier development. In "Can Arabic regain its ancient glory?", Ṭāhā still thinks that the fourth century of the Hegira marks the beginning of Islamic decline; that later poets, such as al-Mutanabbī and Abu'l-'Alā', are lesser poets on account of their Greek and philosophical leanings. These positions are, however, eroded gradually as Ṭāhā comes to realize the full implications of his newly adopted historical methodology. He now sees that the exclusion of a literary period or school is incompatible with the historical spirit. There is, moreover, an increasing emphasis on the importance of the 'Abbāsid period for its linguistic and intellectual achievements, its interaction with other civilizations, its concern with theoretical and specifically philosophical matters and, above all, its poetic inventiveness. The complete dependence of literary phenomena on political factors is denied: the progress or decadence of any given period is no longer to be measured by political criteria alone. The fourth and fifth centuries come to be considered as the zenith of 'Abbāsid culture, notwithstanding the rampant political disintegration. Philosophy comes to be seen as something like the highest form of 'Abbāsid intellectual effervescence and as an integral part of Arab culture. More specifically, al-Mutanabbī is partially rehabilitated as his brand of philosophical poetry is seen as a sign of intellectual refinement and sophistication (if compared with the traditional nomadic wisdom of the pre-Islamic poet Zuhayr Ibn Abī Sulmā)[175].

Ṭāhā's own account of the reasons leading to his choice of subject is misleading inasmuch as it is silent on the determining role of factors relating to his earlier development. He, we are told, had originally found Abu'l-'Alā' repugnant and would have chosen another subject,[176] but he was finally drawn to him mainly for two reasons. The first is that he thought that he could make a significant contribution to the study of a subject arousing such wide interest among scholars both in the East and the West. While the former debated whether the author of *al-Luzūmiyyāt* was a true Muslim or an unbeliever, the latter translated his works into several European languages and paid a great deal of attention to his philosophy and originality. Secondly, both the author and his subject had been afflicted early in life with, and considerably influenced by, the handicap of blindness.[177] These two reasons, whether considered individually or together, do not tell us the whole story. On the purely academic level, Ṭāhā's interest in Abu'l-'Alā' could not have been determined by his sole concern for originality; his choice must have been, partly, determined by an awareness, however dim at the beginning, that the subject offered an ideal opportunity to break with the narrow confines of al-Marṣafī's classicism and to illustrate the historical methodology with its characteristic wider range, even-handedness and concern for interaction and acculturation. From the personal point of view, Ṭāhā's identification with his subject could not have been completely based on that common affliction. Ṭāhā must have been aware well before embarking on his study of Abu'l-'Alā'[178] that the ancient poet-philosopher, who fearlessly faced the full consequences of his doubts with regard to received traditions[179] and orthodox faith, could offer him some guidance on the thorny theological and philosophical problems that were beginning to trouble him. In other words, by choosing to partake in the then raging debate on Abu'l-'Alā''s controversial religious and philosophical doctrines, Ṭāhā sought to face the loss of the innocence of his own orthodox faith. Abu'l-'Alā' was not only a blind man of letters like himself, he was also a kindred spirit in many respects: he had a great deal to say on the human condition and on the kind of conduct to adopt (given that condition).

Among the factors leading to Ṭāhā's choice of subject we must also count the influence of Luṭfī al-Sayyid. It was he who aroused the young man's interest in the subject;[180] and although he read Ṭāhā's thesis on Abu'l-'Alā''s only after its completion,[181] it would seem that the work was not written without some guidance from him. In fact, the work carries in more than one way an indirect tribute to the "teacher of the generation". Hence, for instance, the emphasis laid on Abu'l-'Alā''s knowledge of, and debt to, Greek philosophy. Again, he is thought to be primarily a philosopher[182] and a founder of philosophical poetry;[183] his teachings are expounded in a systematic fashion like those of a philosopher in the Peripatetic tradition.[184] More specifically, he is thought to be a rationalist,[185] an Aristotelian advocating the eternity of space, time and matter,[186] an Epicurean in his ethics[187] and a critic of the monarchical system.[188] That Ṭāhā's work also embodies other influences, mainly that of his foreign masters at the Egyptian University, does not diminish the importance of Luṭfī's contribution to this stage of the young man's development, as the adoption of the new historical methodology, with all its critical, positivist and scientistic ramifications, was in line with Luṭfī's modernist orientations and explicit teaching. To study Abu'l-'Alā' at all, so methodically and so systematically, not shunning the thorny issues of religious doctrine,[189] or going out of his way to appease orthodox sensibilities,[190] may be considered as yet another battle cry in the war for modernism. All in all, the thesis on Abu'l-'Alā' constitutes Luṭfī's final victory over Jāwīsh and reformism in general.

Concerning Ṭāhā's actual treatment of Abu'l-'Alā', we may note first the long – excessively long – journey he makes before dealing with the subject proper. After the "Prologue", in which he sets out his conception of the world as a deterministic system, there follow five main chapters (described as *maqālāt*; "essays"): the first, "Zamān Abu'l-'Alā' wa-makānuh" (Abu'l-'Alā''s epoch and country) on the poet's environment as defined by his nation, people or race,[191] its history and its natural environment; the second, "Ḥayāt Abu'l-'Alā'" (Abu'l-'Alā''s biography) dealing in ample detail with his tribe, family, upbringing and further development; while the third, fourth and fifth chapters cover his literary, scientific and philosophical works, respectively. This manner of procedure is obviously in line with the author's scientific concerns. Starting with environmental factors, followed by psychological ones (the poet's experience of life and psychology), and proceeding thence to Abu'l-'Alā''s works, the author hopes to show that both the man and his works are the necessary outcome and true reflection of his surroundings as well as psychological make-up. Taking into account the life of Islamic society or mind in the designated space and time, as well as Abu'l-'Alā''s own life, we are supposed to have all the factors inevitably leading to that outcome.

The book, so designed, is disproportionate. As one critic has complained, too much space is given to historical and biographical matters at the expense of Abu'l-'Alā''s works.[192] Also, having waded through so much detail before coming to this final and most relevant part of the study, we may feel disappointed. For one thing, there is no reason to believe that the author's determinism has been firmly established; the most that he can claim is to have situated Abu'l-'Alā''s works in their historical context.[193] Secondly, Ṭāhā's discussion of these works is rather old-fashioned, both in its traditional classification of Abu'l-'Alā''s poetry according to "themes" such as panygeric, elegy, love poetry, etc., and its mainly rhetorical orientation.[194]

Another critic objects to the work's predominantly philosophical character, presenting Abu'l-'Alā' as a systematic philosopher with definite and final views, rather than as a poet with a specific experience.[195]

These cogent criticisms do not, however, take into account that underlying the uneven distribution of attention there is some sort of structural unity. Strangely enough, the book reproduces, in reverse, the ever-widening view of the world we have already encountered in Ṭāhā Ḥusain's autobiography as related in *al-Ayyam.*[196] Instead of Ṭāhā's own progression into the wider world, we now find Abu'l-'Alā''s movement in the opposite direction, whereby the universal circle gradually narrows down to its centre as the protagonist retreats to his final self-imposed seclusion. Though in line with the adopted logic of explanation as well as Abu'l-'Alā''s life journey, this latent structure seems to reflect concerns other than strictly logical or scientific ones. For instance, the figure of Abu'l-'Alā' standing at the centre of such a circle seems to embody certain aspects of Ṭāhā Ḥusain's humanism. This implication becomes clearer as we move from the cosmic dimension to the historical or cultural framework, where the author attempts to define the main co-ordinates for his subject, namely Abu'l-'Alā''s people or nation, in that particular space and at that particular time. Thus, in a series of ever-widening definitions, Abu'l-'Alā' is related to humanity at large. First, the "Arab race" is found to be too narrow a term to characterize Abu'l-'Alā''s people.[197] Secondly, the "Islamic nation", initially deemed preferable,[198] is also found to be too narrow, and is replaced by the Islamic nations.[199] But even this loose designation is in turn rejected unless it is so redefined as to include all those who came under the Muslims' rule, inhabited their land or were closely linked with them.[200] This must be so, we are told, as Abu'l-'Alā' extended his interest to adherents of non-Muslim sects and creeds and even studied the Greeks, who were so remote in space and time. The scope of the study, it is again said, must in fact be extended from the Far East to the Far West and from several centuries before Christ to modern times.[201] By virtue of his extensive knowledge, all-englobing preoccupations and continued relevance, Abu'l-'Alā' is therefore entitled to be considered in the widest possible frame of reference. He, it is assumed, is a universal figure standing at the crossroads of the most diverse cultures and traditions. And we are required to see this as the circle shrinks down to its narrowest, where we find Abu'l-'Alā' confined in his house in Ma'arrat al-Nu'mān.[202] Having renounced the world, after a disastrous foray into Baghdad, he spends the last fifty years of his life as a semi-recluse,[203] a twice-bound captive[204] composing, among other things, his major masterpiece, namely "*al-Luzūmiyyāt*"[205] on all matters relating to the human condition.

It is also at that same point that Ṭāhā's work on Abu'l-'Alā', purporting to be rigorously scientific, fully reveals its deeply personal character. Suggested by the structural affinity with *al-Ayyam*, this character becomes manifest, as the scholarly and historical manner of procedure comes to an end, rather abruptly, giving way to a lyrical and subjective mode of writing.[206] The author is now at the doorstep of Abu'l-'Alā''s abode in Ma'arrat al-Nu'mān: "Let us now stop at a particular house in Ma'rrat al-Nu'mān of which history has left no description."[207] Having gained access to the inner recesses of the house, the author finds himself face to face with his subject musing at length on life and human destiny.[208] Ṭāhā's call for his reader to stop at the history-forsaken dwelling evokes that long poetic tradition, going so far back as pre-Islamic times, of weeping over deserted encampments (*al-bukā' 'alā al-aṭlāl*) in an elegaic prelude, where the bard bids his companion(s) to stand by and give support at the unbearable scene of desolation.

This dramatic turn, obviously standing for the author's identification with his subject, is not accidental to Ṭāhā Ḥusain's thought: being somehow built into the very design of the present work,[209] it will also be a characteristic of the author's second major work on Abu'l-'Alā', entitled *Ma' Abi'l-'Alā' fī sijnih*" (1939). In this book, written a quarter of a century after the early thesis, Ṭāhā expressly turns his back on historical erudition, adopting instead another approach based on sympathy and compassion.[210] Almost halfway through the book, and again abruptly, he pays Abu'l-'Alā' another visit. "And", relates the author, "I was admitted into the Shaykh's [i.e. Abu'l-'Alā''s] audience as he sat, presiding over a large and spacious room, on a well-worn mat, dictating to a group of people, while many others simply listened in amazement . . .".[211]

Understandable in the later, overtly impressionistic work, the above-mentioned turn must appear paradoxical in the earlier thesis, committed as it is to so-called objective or scientific criticism.[212] But this paradox, as many others, must be accepted as an integral part of Ṭāhā's thought: the earlier work, purporting to be historical and scientific, already contains the seeds of his later impressionism. In fact, it may be argued that such a shift towards a more subjective stance was inevitable for someone who embraced al-Marṣafī's critical approach.[213]

It should be clear at the end of this review of Ṭāhā's early works that *Tajdīd dhikrā Abi'l-'Alā'* was not, as is generally assumed, the beginning of his career as a critic and literary historian. Considered rightly as the first fruit of Ṭāhā's maturity, the work was, and can only be understood as, the crowning of the exploratory and foundational enquiry into matters of method, which was carried out in the earlier essays.

Though relegated by their author to limbo, these essays were to serve ever after as a (hidden) reservoir of seminal ideas and intuitions. Thus the emphasis laid on the 'Abbāsid period was reflected later in a variety of ways. Abu'l-'Alā', who was a late 'Abbāsid poet, was chosen as the subject for Ṭāhā's first book. In the early twenties, Ṭāhā was to inaugurate his major studies in the history of Arabic literature with a work wholly devoted to the period and having as its hero Abū Nuwās, who is supposed to be the representative of the age.[214] Equally, Ṭāhā's sceptical views on pre-Islamic poetry and his historical approach to miracles and the Qur'ān were to have far-reaching repercussions in his subsequent works. And more generally, Ṭāhā's positivism as developed for the first time in the early essays was to preoccupy him ever after.

Notes

1 It would seem that Ṭāhā's first work to be published was a poem which appeared in *J*, 1 January 1908. See Muḥammad Sayyid Kilānī, *Ṭāhā Ḥusain al-shā'ir al-kātib* (Cairo 1963), p. 17.

2 Ṭāhā Ḥusain, "al-Marḥūm al-Ustādh Aḥmad Luṭfī al-Sayyid", *Majallat Majma' al-Lugha al-'Arabiyya*, XVIII (1965), pp. 113–116, p. 114.

3 Ṭāhā Ḥusain, *A Passage to France* (Leiden 1976),p. 28.

4 That is how I render Ṭāhā Ḥusain's "*al-qaṣd fi'l-alfāẓ wa'l-anāta fi'l-tafkīr*" as compared with Kenneth Cragg's translation as "effective style and sustained thinking". See ibid., p. 19.

5 P.J. Vatikiotis, *The History of modern Egypt from Muhammad Ali to Mubarak* (London 1991), pp. 205, 229.

6 See his *al-Islām dīn al-fiṭra wa'l-ḥurriyya* (Cairo 1983).

7 Anwar al-Jundī, *'Abd al-'Azīz Jāwīsh, min ruwwād al-tarbiya wa'l-ṣiḥāfa wa'l-ijtimā'* (Cairo 1965), p. 64.

8 See Vatikiotis, op. cit., pp. 208– 209.

9 Ṭāhā Ḥusain, *A Passage to France*, p. 20.

10 Ibid., pp. 20–21. Entitled "*Naẓarāt fi'l-naẓarāt*", and devoted to al-Manfalūṭī's collection of essays, "*al-Naẓarāt*", the series was started in *Miṣr al-Fatāt*, 3 August 1909 and resumed in *al-Sha'b*, 20 April 1910.

11 Ṭāhā Ḥusain, op. cit., p. 21.

12 See Kilānī, op. cit., p. 82 ff. for examples illustrating Ṭāhā's imitation of al-Manfalūṭī.

13 Ṭāhā Ḥusain, op. cit., p. 21.

14 Luṭfī showed his disapproval by remaining completely silent over the whole affair. See ibid., p. 22.

15 Ibid., p. 21.

16 Ibid., pp. 8, 25. Some of these papers, namely *al-'Alam* and *al-Hidāya*, had Jāwīsh as their editor-in-chief.

17 In his *Ma' Ṭāhā Ḥusain*, vol. II, (Cairo 1968), p. 57, Sāmī al-Kayyālī reports that some forty years after his campaign against al- Manfalūṭī, Ṭāhā Ḥusain confessed that his criticism of the former had been motivated by his desire as a "hot-headed" young man to achieve notoriety at the expense of a prominent writer. Notice also that the young man made a habit of criticizing his prominent contemporaries. Thus he took to task Ḥāfiẓ Ibrāhīm, 'Abd al-Raḥmān Shukrī, Muṣṭafā Ṣādiq al-Rāfi'ī, Rashīd Riḍā, 'Uthmān Mahdī and, as we shall see in the sequel, Jurjī Zaydān. On these feuds, see Kilānī, op. cit., pp. 99 ff.; 'Abd al-Ḥayy Diyāb, *al-Turāth al-naqdī qabl madrasat al-jīl al-jadīd* (Cairo 1968), pp. 78 ff.; Muḥammad Abu'l-Anwār, *al-Ḥiwār al-adabī ḥawl al-shi'r*, 2nd edn. (Cairo 1987), pp. 100 ff.; Anwar al- Jūndī, "Ṣafaḥāt majhūla min ḥayāt Ṭāhā Ḥusain, 1908–1916", in *Ṭāhā Ḥusain kamā ya'rifuh kuttāb 'aṣrih* (Cairo n.d.), pp. 43–62, pp. 50 ff.; 'Abd al-'Alīm al-Qabbānī, *Ṭāhā Ḥusain fī al-ḍuḥā min shabābih, 1908–1913* (Cairo 1976), pp. 126 ff.; Aḥmad 'Ulbī, *Ṭāhā Ḥusain, rajul wa-fikr wa-'aṣr* (Beirut 1985), pp. 258 ff.

18 It is against this background that we should perhaps understand Jāwīsh's vehemence against the conservatism of the Azhar's autho-

rities. For Jāwīsh's contacts with Muḥammad 'Abduh, see Anwar al-Jūndī, op. cit., pp. 42–43.

19 It was Jāwīsh who initiated Ṭāhā into journalistic work proper, public speech and teaching (literature). See Ṭāhā Ḥusain, op. cit., pp. 24, 25, 26.

20 After a short spell of study at the Azhar, Jāwīsh went to Dār al-'Ulūm from which he graduated in 1897. See Anwar al-Jūndī, op. cit., pp. 41–42.

21 Ṭāhā Ḥusain never cared to collect any of his works prior to his book on Abu'l-'Alā'.

22 On Ṭāhā's poetic activity which came to an end in 1913, see Kilānī, op. cit., 'Abd al-'Alīm al-Qabbāni, op. cit., al-Kayyālī, op. cit., pp. 43 ff; and Aḥmad 'Ulbī, op. cit., pp. 273 ff.

23 On these views in which Ṭāhā was no more than a follower of Qāsim Amīn and Aḥmad Luṭfī al-Sayyid, see Kilānī, op. cit. pp. 134 ff. and pp. 156–157. Ṭāhā's early writings on social and political matters should, however, be of some historical interest in a full study of his evolution from a traditional or conservative standpoint to a modernist outlook.

24 This is the case of Cachia (*Taha Husayn: his place in the Egyptian renaissance* (London 1956)) and Jābir 'Uṣfūr (*al-Marāyā al mutajāwira. Dirāsa fī naqd Ṭāhā Ḥusain* (Cairo 1983)), who assume that Ṭāhā Ḥusain's career as a critic and literary historian begins with his doctoral study on Abu'l-'Alā'. This assumption is made explicit by Miftah Tahar who, having assimilated the whole of Ṭāhā Ḥusain's critical writings prior to the study in question to the famous abusive polemics mentioned above, argues that these writings are devoid of any literary value. See his *Ṭāhā Ḥusayn, sa critique littéraire et ses sources françaises* (Tunis 1976), p. 45 and ibid., n. 1.

25 For rudimentary moves in this direction, see Abu'l-Anwār, op. cit., pp. 105 ff.; 'Abd al-'Azīz al-Dusūqī, *Taṭawwur al-naqd al-'Arabī al-ḥadīth fī Miṣr* (Cairo 1977), pp. 252 ff. and Ahmad Buhasan, *al-Khiṭāb al-naqdī 'ind Ṭāhā Ḥusain* (Beirut 1985), pp. 32 ff.

26 In 1911, Ṭāhā Ḥusain published a series of articles in *H,* 1 January and 1 March 1911, in which he proscribed the marriage of Muslim men with Christian and Jewish women for the harmful effects it could have on the children. See Kilānī, op. cit. p. 153 and Cachia's preface to Ṭāhā Ḥussein's *An Egyptian childhood* (London 1981).

27 In 1909, Ṭāhā castigated students of philosophy as arrogant people who would not heed the orders of God, giving their obedience to "human demons". These people, he argued, "have delved deep in philosophy only to come out empty-handed and impoverished". See Ṭāhā Ḥusain, "Waylī min ghadī", *Miṣr al-Fatāt,* 15 September 1909. As cited by Kilānī, op. cit. p. 31.

28 This term will be henceforth used as a convenient way of designating the articles in question.

29 "Al-naqd ḥaqīqatuh atharuh fi'l-umam shurūṭuh wa-maḍārr al-ghuluww fīh", *al-Bayān,* 1911, pp. 377–383. The exact date of publication within this year is somewhat uncertain: it is given as 24 August by Abu'l-Anwār, op. cit., p. 105 and ibid., n. 3 and as 1

September by Ḥamdī al-Sakkūt and Marsden Jones, *A'lām al-adb al-mu'āṣir fī Miṣr*, I, *Ṭāhā Ḥusain*, 2nd edn. (Cairo-Beirut 1982), p. 134. Having examined the 1911 volume of *al-Bayān* in the Egyptian National Library, I could not establish a more accurate dating.

30 At the very end of the text, said to have been no more than a summary discourse on "criticism in itself" (*al-naqd fī nafsih*), further instalments are promised on literary and scientific criticism (*al-naqd al-'ilmī wa 'l-adabī*) relating to all kinds of statement (*funūn al-kalām*), the first of which should deal with the criticism of poetry. According to al-Sakkūt and Jones (op. cit., p.134), a second article in the series was published in *al-Bayān*, 1 October 1911; but neither Abu 'l-Anwār (op. cit., p. 105, n. 3) nor myself could find such a sequel.

31 A third class of statement, namely philosophical, is also recognized, but this addition does not introduce any drastic change into Ṭāhā's classification, for at this stage he does not draw a clear distinction between philosophy and science.

32 The series consists of three main articles, published in *H*, respectively in June-July, August-September and October-November 1911 and all devoted to a detailed review and refutation of Jurjī Zaydān's *Tārīkh adāb al-lugha al-'Arabiyya* ("History of Arabic Literature"), vol. I. A reply from Zaydān, then owner and editor of the monthly *al-Hilāl*, published in the August-September issue of *H* ("Radd 'alā intiqād", pp. 624–631), drew from Ṭāhā Ḥusain a "reply to the reply" ("Radd 'alā radd"), also published in the same issue.

33 See, for instance, Anwar al-Jūndī, op. cit., pp. 50, 51 and 52.

34 For this claim, see Zaydān, op. cit., ed. Shawqī Ḍayf, (Cairo n.d.), p.8.

35 Ṭāhā's agreement with Zaydān over this point is, however, partial, as he would question the latter's views on what would count as such major sources. See "Naqd ṣāḥib *al-Hilāl*" I, *H*, June-July 1911, pp. 450 ff.

36 Ibid., p. 453.

37 See Ṭāhā Ḥusain, "Radd 'alā radd", *H*, August-September 1911, p. 637.

38 Ibid. Ṭāhā's questioning of Zaydān's claims is no doubt based on his awareness that the latter had a forerunner, namely Ḥasan Tawfīq al-'Adl who, having studied the subject in Germany, taught it at Dar al-'Ulūm. See below, p. 89.

39 Jurjī Zaydān, op. cit., p. 8.

40 The distinction, implicitly drawn in "Naqd ṣāḥib *al-Hilāl*" I, *H*, June-July 1911, pp. 454 ff., is clearly established in "Naqd ṣāḥib *al-Hilāl*" II, *H*, August-September 1911, pp. 603–604.

41 Ibid.

42 One such question would be to study the introduction into Arabic of new terms and concepts as a result of translating Greek and Indian astronomical works. See ibid., p. 604.

43 "Naqd ṣāḥib *al-Hilāl*" I, *H*, June-July 1911, p. 458.

44 See Nallino, *Tārīkh*, pp. 21 ff. Cf. F. Gabrieli, *EI*[2] art. "Adab".

45 Ṭāhā Ḥusain, op. cit., pp. 458–459.

46 Ibid., p. 459.

47 "Naqd ṣāḥib *al-Hilāl*" II, *H,* August-September 1911, p. 606.
48 Ibid.
49 "Naqd ṣāḥib *al-Hilāl*" II, *H,* August-September 1911, p. 605.
50 Ibid.
51 "Naqd ṣāḥib *al-Hilāl*" I, *H,* June-July, 1911, pp. 460–461.
52 For an assessment of Nallino's position, see above ch. III, pp. 55 and 56.
53 "Naqd ṣāḥib *al-Hilāl*" II, *H,* August-September 1911, pp. 621 ff.
54 See ibid., p. 612, where these two foreign masters are explicitly cited.
55 Ibid.
56 Ibid., p. 622.
57 Ibid., p. 609. Information on the then newly-discovered Semitic inscriptions and the discrepancies observed to exist between their language and Arabic was transmitted to Ṭāhā by Nallino (see above, ch. III, p. 57) and, most probably, by Littmann.
58 "Naqd ṣāḥib *al-Hilāl*" III, *H,* October-November 1911, p. 826.
59 Ibid.
60 Muslims' faith in their religion is supposed to be unshakable, whereas non-Muslim young people are said to be more inclined to emulate westerners in everything, including atheism. See ibid., pp. 826–827.
61 Ibid., p. 828.
62 Originally delivered as a lecture on 19 October 1911, the article was published in *H,* October-November 1911, pp. 761–803.
63 Ibid., p. 763. The oldest known Semitic language is of course Akkadian and not Arabic.
64 Ibid., pp. 767–768.
65 Ibid., p. 768.
66 Ibid., p. 764.
67 Ibid., p. 784.
68 Ibid., pp. 777–778.
69 Ibid., p. 778.
70 Ibid., pp. 781–782.
71 Ibid., p. 783.
72 Ibid., pp. 783–784.
73 Ibid., p. 786.
74 Ibid., pp. 786 and 787.
75 Ibid., p. 787.
76 Ibid., pp. 788–789.
77 Ibid., p. 791.
78 Ibid., pp. 791–792.
79 Ibid., p. 792.
80 Ibid., pp. 794–795.
81 Ibid., pp. 796–797.
82 Ibid., p. 797.
83 Ibid., pp. 797–798.
84 Ibid., pp. 798–790.
85 Ibid.
86 Ibid., p. 800.
87 Ibid.

88 Ibid., pp. 786 ff.
89 Ibid., p. 771.
90 Ibid., pp. 801–802.
91 Nallino's *Tārīkh* stops at the end of the Umayyad period.
92 Relying mainly on Ibn Khaldūn, Nallino introduces the theme of accumulated wealth and increased luxury and refinement under the Abbasids. See ibid., pp. 36–37
93 According to al-Marṣafī, as expounded by Ṭāhā Ḥusain, al-Mutanabbī and Abu'l-'Alā' "went deep into the study of philosophical doctrines and their style had about it a Greek note setting them apart from the conventions of desert-dwelling Arabs". See Ṭāhā Ḥusain, *Tajdīd dhikrā Abi'l-'Alā',* in *MK,* vol. X, 1974, p. 10.
94 Published in *J* between 15 January and 8 March 1914, the work was meant to contain nine instalments. Strangely enough, article VI in the series is missing and it looks as if it was never published, although al-Sakkūt and Jones, op. cit., p. 137, give its date as 5 February 1914.
95 See the last few paragraphs of "Ḥayāt al-ādāb" I, *J,* 15 January 1914.
96 Described as "necessary" (*lāzima*), this first prolegomenon is also said to be insufficient (*lā takfī*), and may, for the sake of clarity, be characterized as "preliminary" – to distinguish it from other subsequent prolegomena also said to be necessary.
97 Ibid.
98 Ibid.
99 "Ḥayāt al-ādāb" I, *J,* 15 January 1914.
100 Ibid.
101 See for instance the complaint that "politics has extinguished the energy (*jidhwa,* lit: "firebrand" or "flame") of literature".
102 "Shu'arā'unā wa 'l-rithā'", *J,* 10 February 1914.
103 Op. cit.
104 Although the scholars and writers concerned are supposed to study literature as well as literary history, the term actually used to designate them is rather restrictive, meaning literally "the literary study school" – which is probably a way of suggesting, as Ṭāhā would in fact argue, that they are no more than students of literature or that they are not truly historians of literature, as their conception of history is superficial.
105 On al-'Adl, see Aḥmad al-Shāyib, *Adab al-lugha al-'Arabiyya bi-Miṣr fī al-nisf al-awwal min al-qarn al-'ishrīn,* 2nd edn. (Cairo 1966), pp. 6, 7, 8. See also Kāmil Sa'fān, *Amīn al-Khūlī fī manāhij tajdīdih* (Cairo 1982), pp. 68–69 and 188–189, as well as al-Sakkūt and Jones, op. cit., pp. 27–28. In an article entitled "Fī dars al-adab wa tārīkhih", *al-Adab,* April 1959, pp. 12–14, p. 12, Ṭāhā Ḥusain designates al-'Adl (without naming him) and Jurjī ṣaydān as the main representatives of the movement in question.
106 Cf. Nallino, op. cit., pp. 103–104, where he refers to works recently published in Egypt on the history of literature, pointing out their educational character as textbooks "currently used in Egyptian schools". Ṭāhā Ḥusain was, however, the first to set such a current

of thought and teaching practice as a target for criticism in the name of (what he took to be) truly historical and scientific methodology.

107 On the purely chronological character of the School's conception of historiography, see the opening lines of "Ḥayāt al-ādāb" IX, *J*, 8 March 1914.

108 See "Ḥayāt al-ādāb" I, *J*, 15 January 1914, where Ṭāhā Ḥusain points out that the scholars he has in mind confined themselves to observing the political condition of the Islamic caliphate. See also "Ḥayāt al-ādāb" VII, *J*, 7 February 1914, where it is suggested that adherents of the School take into account only political factors.

109 See ibid., where Ṭāhā Ḥusain suggests that superficial knowledge of ancient literature necessarily leads to ignorance with regard to modern literature – the two bodies of literature being connected.

110 Ibid.

111 Ibid.

112 "Ḥayāt al-ādāb" II, *J*, 19 January 1914.

113 Ibid.

114 Ibid.

115 Ibid.

116 An obviously unfair accusation insofar as al-'Adl and Zaydān are concerned.

117 "Ḥayāt al-ādāb" I, *J*, 15 January 1914.

118 "Ḥayāt al-ādāb" III, *J*, 21 January 1914.

119 Ibid.

120 For Nallino's criticisms of traditional Arab historiography, see his op. cit., pp. 56–57 and 228–229. See also above, ch. III, p. 54.

121 "Ḥayāt al-ādāb" III, *J*, 21 January 1914.

122 Ibid.

123 Ibid.

124 Ibid.

125 Apart from the investigation of authenticity, historical criticism is supposed to require a knowledge of ink, paper and script. See ibid.

126 Ibid.

127 Ibid.

128 "Ḥayāt al-ādāb" V, *J*, 29 January 1914.

129 Ibid.

130 Ibid.

131 This point which will be a major theme in Ṭāhā Ḥusain's later criticism of the authenticity of pre-Islamic poetry is also made by Nallino, op. cit., pp. 69, 78 and 313. See also above, p. 57.

132 "Ḥayāt al-ādāb" V, *J*, 29 January 1914.

133 Ibid.

134 "The School concerned with our ancient literature is based on a set of illusions as old as this literature, which it is high time to dispel." Ibid.

135 See the opening lines of "Ḥayāt al-ādāb" VII, *J*, 7 February 1914.

136 This implicit assumption is made explicit in "Ḥayāt al-ādāb", IX, *J*, 8 March 1914.

137 This is how I render Ṭāhā Ḥusain's "*al-niẓām al-jāmi' li'l-alfāẓ*" – an expression reminiscent of 'Abd al-Qāhir al-Jurjānī.
138 Ibid.
139 "Ḥayāt al-ādāb" VII, *J*, 7 February 1914.
140 Ibid.
141 Ibid.
142 Ibid.
143 Ibid.
144 "Ḥayāt al-ādāb" VIII, *J*, 28 February 1914.
145 See above p. 81, where Ṭāhā speaks of a psychological constitution proper to a nation.
146 Op. cit.
147 Ibid.
148 Ibid.
149 In the final paragraph of the article, the reader is promised further instalments of the series, but these were never published.
150 Knowledge of Semitic languages, modern European languages and literature, as well as philosophical disciplines, is said to be necessary to literary study.
151 Ṭāhā Ḥusain, ibid., assumes that psychology is one of many disciplines falling under the title "philosophical sciences" (*al-'ulūm al-falsafiyya*).
152 See the contrast drawn in this connection between Zuhayr Ibn Abī Sulmā's poetry of wisdom – Bedouin, unaffected and unsophisticated – and that of al-Mutanabbī, said to draw on written philosophical knowledge as translated in Arabic and to involve fine logical operations and forms of expression.
153 Apart from inherited traditions, early Islamic literature is believed to have undergone the influence of newly developed religious disciplines and political doctrines, as well as a variety of mythological, astronomical and medical lore acquired through contact with other nations. Ibid.
154 Subsequently (i.e. starting from 1930) modified into *Tajdīd dhikrā Abi'l-'Alā'* ["Abu'l-'Alā': remembrance renewed"].
155 Dated 14 December 1915, this preface was added to the original text as part of getting it ready for publication.
156 *Tajdīd dhikrā Abi'l-'Alā'*, in *MK*, vol. X, 1974, p. 16.
157 Ibid.
158 See R.A. Nicholson's praise for the work in his *Studies in Islamic poetry*, reprint (Cambridge 1969), p. 51. See also his reference to Ṭāhā Ḥusain, ibid., p. 142.
159 Ṭāhā Ḥusain, op. cit., p. 10.
160 Ibid., p. 11.
161 Ibid., p. 12.
162 Ibid., pp. 33 and 253.
163 Ibid., p. 15.
164 Ibid., p. 12.
165 Ibid., p. 20.
166 Ibid.

167 Ibid., pp. 20–21.
168 Ibid., p. 24.
169 Ibid., p. 21.
170 Ibid., p. 23.
171 Ibid., p. 36 ff.
172 Ibid., p. 21.
173 Ibid., pp. 225 and 230.
174 Ibid., p. 21.
175 "Ḥayāt al-ādāb" VIII, *J*, 8 March 1914.
176 Ṭāhā Ḥusain, op. cit., p. 15.
177 Ibid., p. 15.
178 Ṭāhā Ḥusain's knowledge of Abu'l-'Alā' goes as far back in time as his study under al-Marṣafī in the Azhar. See ibid., p. 10.
179 For a statement of Abu'l-'Alā''s critical attitude towards received traditions, see ibid., pp. 263–264.
180 See Ṭāhā Ḥusain, "al-Marḥūm al-Ustādh Aḥmad Luṭfī al-Sayyid", p. 115.
181 Ibid. See also idem, *A Passage to France*, p. 28.
182 Idem, *Tajdīd dhikrā Abi'l-'Alā'*, pp. 219–220.
183 Ibid., pp. 228–229.
184 Ibid., p. 267 ff.
185 Ibid., p. 262 ff.
186 Ibid., pp. 268 ff and 277.
187 Ibid., pp. 309–310. It was Luṭfī who first informed Ṭāhā that Abu'l-'Alā' borrowed his theoretical and practical philosophies from Epicurus. See Ṭāhā Ḥusain, "al-Marḥūm al-Ustādh Aḥmad Luṭfī al-Sayyid", p. 115.
188 *Tajdīd dhikrā Abi'l-'Alā'*, pp. 310–311. It was also Luṭfī who first drew Ṭāhā's attention to Abu'l-'Alā''s critical view of monarchs. See Ṭāhā Ḥusain, op. cit., p. 115.
189 Abu'l-'Alā' is represented as a theist who firmly believes in the existence of God (ibid, pp. 279–280) as an immobile mover (ibid., p. 280) in (eternal) space and time (ibid., pp. 283 ff.), but denies prophecy. (ibid., pp. 295 ff).
190 See ibid., pp. 31–32, where Muḥammad Ḥilmī Ṭammāra is criticized for the attempt he makes in his *Tārikh Abu'l-'Alā'* to please the religious and Azhari authorities by forcing Abu'l-'Alā' into the circle of believers.
191 Ṭāhā Ḥusain, ibid., pp. 38–39, speaks of the Islamic nation (*al-umma al-Islāmiyya*), Abu'l-'Alā''s "people" (*sha'b*). He also refers to the Arab race (*al-jins al-'Arabī*), but argues that the Arabs in the Syria of the fourth century had lost their racial purity. He equally speaks of Abu'l-'Alā''s "generation" (*al-jīl*), a term he obviously borrows from Ibn Khaldūn.
192 Miftah Tahar, op. cit., p. 54.
193 Ibid., p. 53.
194 Ibid. Cf. Muḥammad Mandūr, *Fī'l-mīzān al-jadīd* (Cairo 1977), p. 130.
195 See Mandūr, ibid., pp. 103–131.
196 See above chapter I.

197 Ṭāhā Ḥusain, op. cit., pp. 22 and 38–39.
198 Ibid., p. 22.
199 Ibid., pp. 23 and 40–41.
200 Ibid., p. 41. A similar process of continually redefining the term "Arab" until it covers all nations and peoples inhabiting Islamic lands (provided that Arabic is their main language for writing on scientific matters) is to be found in Nallino, *'Ilm al-falak, tārīkhuh 'ind al-'Arab fī 'l-qurūn al-wusṭā* (Rome 1911), pp. 16–17.
201 Ṭāhā Ḥusain, op. cit., p. 23.
202 Abu'l-'Alā''s birthplace – a country town to the south of Aleppo.
203 Though hardly ever venturing beyond the bounds of his house, Abu'l-'Alā' received visitors and students.
204 Referring to himself as "the twice-bound captive" (*rahīnu'l-maḥbasayn*) of seclusion and blindness, Abu'l-'Alā' also describes himself (in *al-Luzūmiyyāt*) as a captive of three prisons, the third being the forced abode of his soul in the "evil" body.
205 A series of poems of varying length in which the poet imposes on himself unnecessary constraints (*luzūm mā lā yalzam*) with regard to rhyme.
206 On this point, I am indebted to Jābir 'Uṣfūr, op. cit., pp. 335 ff.
207 Ṭāhā Ḥusain, op. cit., p. 170.
208 Ibid., pp. 170–171.
209 Notice how the turn, involving as it does a return and a visit to Abu'l-'Alā', is anticipated right at the beginning of the first chapter, where Ṭāhā affirms, in a lyrical vein, the need to review Abu'l-'Alā''s epoch out of fidelity and loyalty, just as the old ruins need to be revisited by their former inhabitants.
210 Ṭāhā Ḥusain, *Ma' Abi'l-'Alā' fī sijnih*, in *MK*, vol. X, 1974, pp. 331 ff.
211 Ibid., p. 379.
212 Cachia, op. cit., pp. 143 and 144.
213 As has already been pointed out in Chapter II, al-Marṣafī's critical approach contains, besides textual analysis, another component, namely that of appreciating or "savouring" (*tadhawwuq*) the literary qualities of a text.
214 See "al-Qudamā' wa'l-muḥdathūn: Abū Nuwās", in *Ḥadīth al-Arbi'ā'* II, in *MK*, vol. II, 1974. Article first published in *al-Siyāsa*, 23 January 1923.

CHAPTER V

Back to the French Sources

As a reward for his success in obtaining a doctorate degree for his thesis on Abu'l-'Alā', Ṭāhā Ḥusain won a scholarship to study in France, where he was to spend about five years, from November 1914 to October 1919. Before moving on to consider this final stage in Ṭāhā's formal education, it would be appropriate to look more closely at the earlier period of his education at the Egyptian University (1908–1914), with a view to ascertaining to what extent he was then already familiar with, and committed to, French modes of thought.

This question has never been properly investigated even by scholars who have dealt specifically with the influence of French thought on Ṭāhā,[1] or those who have detected the influence of Hippolyte Taine on the above-mentioned thesis.

Some scholars write carelessly, as if such an influence was never exerted at all or in any significant way before Ṭāhā's departure for France. Thus one scholar depicts Ṭāhā's development in terms of two symmetric compartments, namely his traditional education at the Azhar on the one hand and his discovery *in Paris* of Western science, rationality and humanism on the other hand.[2] In more emphatic terms, another scholar affirms that Ṭāhā's European outlook (*'aql*; lit.: mind) and his option for French culture were formed during his study years in Paris.[3]

Both the failure to examine this question in depth and the tendency to assume that Ṭāhā's European orientations were formed only in France have one common source, namely the relative neglect of Ṭāhā's education at the Egyptian University and of his early critical writings during the intermediate period between Ṭāhā's schooling at the Azhar and his study years in Paris.[4]

In fact, Ṭāhā's encounter with Western culture and his attraction to France in particular must have started in 1907 when, while still a student at the Azhar, he began to frequent Luṭfī al-

Sayyid's circle. The latter, a francophone by education, was also a francophile. The same could perhaps be said of the senior members of his circle who were, like Luṭfī, graduates of the French School of Law in Cairo and who were invited to lecture at *al-Jarīda*'s "school".[5] Outside this circle, there was Jāwīsh of course, who was also a francophile, although an anglophone by education. It was he who put into the young man's head the idea of studying in France.[6]

Ṭāhā Ḥusain recalls how the idea took hold of him so strongly that he began to look upon it not as a mere dream but as a reality that had to come about.[7] This need not be surprising in view of so many signs and indications pointing in that direction. The cultural prestige of France had been enormous in Egypt since the nineteenth century. As a student at the Egyptian University, Ṭāhā was given the choice to study either French or English; he opted for the former. When the going proved to be rough, he took private tuition in the language[8]; and the moment he felt that he had achieved some proficiency he applied for a scholarship to study in France.[9]

As we have seen in the preceding chapter, the encounter, clash and interaction between Ṭāhā's traditional schooling at the Azhar and modern Western culture were at their strongest when he was admitted to the Egyptian University in 1908. It was during the following two years that, while continuing to study at the Azhar, he also attended the courses given by both Egyptian scholars and orientalists in modern areas of knowledge according to modern teaching methods; and it was then that he became intoxicated, as never before or ever after, by the ensuing intellectual fermentation.

Three years after that date, the Western turn became clearly defined; the early critical writings began to appear, and were concerned with indicating what was required for the study of Arabic literature to be truly scientific, historical or modern. In what follows, we shall first recapitulate our review of these writings in order to show that the turn was specifically towards France.

We are therefore concerned with Ṭāhā's development during the period extending from 1907/8, time of his first encounter with Luṭfī al-Sayyid and his subsequent enrolment at the Egyptian University, to 1914, when Ṭāhā completed the drafting of his thesis on Abu'l-'Alā'. It was during this period that Ṭāhā Ḥusain came to be exposed for the first time, and in an intensive way, to modern forms of knowledge and modes of thought; it was also then that he produced his early writings, including those critical essays in which he began his lifelong endeavour to introduce the scientific or historical study of Arabic literature.

As far as we know, this initiative seems to have taken place sometime in the middle of the period under consideration, namely in 1911, with the publication of the series of articles on Zaydān. At this stage Ṭāhā was dissatisfied with his own practice of verbal criticism, a degenerate form of al-Marṣafī's neo-classical linguistic approach to literary texts; and he began to search for a more principled critical practice. This first enquiry into the rules of "sound criticism" was soon overtaken by a growing concern with literary history; it was in this sphere that Ṭāhā henceforth sought the right rules of method. His refutation of Zaydān's views on the history of Arabic literature thus constituted the beginning of a sustained attempt to introduce a more modern or a genuinely historical version of the subject.

Hence, the period under consideration divides naturally into two major phases. There was first a preliminary period extending from 1907/8 to that point in time in 1911 at which the critical essays began to appear. This, we may say, was a period of relatively passive receptivity, during which Ṭāhā digested the new secular and modern ideas of Luṭfī al-Sayyid and his teachers at the Egyptian University, including a number of prominent orientalists. In the meantime, he maintained a neo-classical and generally reformist stance under the direct influence of al-Marṣafī and Jāwīsh.

The 1911 critical essays which brought to a close this phase of receptive learning and conservative convictions appeared within a short space of time, suggesting an outburst of creative energy and signalling a major turning point in Ṭāhā's career. It was then that he inaugurated his lifelong modernist course, gradually beginning to reject all ahistorical conceptions of the Arab cultural heritage. If Zaydān's position appeared to be naively or half-heartedly historical, the traditional Arab approach to literary texts, being purely linguistic, lacked the historical dimension altogether. By extension, Muḥammad 'Abduh's reformism was also objectionable, as it was essentially a revivalist doctrine bent on demonstrating the autonomy and eternal relevance of Islamic canonic texts. In opposition to all these positions, Ṭāhā saw the history of Arabic literature as a discipline *sui generis*, with a logic of its own, unknown to the Arabs, irreducible to their ways of thinking and entailing a historical criticism of their cultural heritage.

The second major phase, which covered the years 1911–1914 and saw the publication of his early critical essays, was therefore modernist and critical in character. But Ṭāhā's development during this period did not run smoothly; in 1914 his thought underwent a remarkable shift towards a more stringent conception of literary history as well as a more radical critique of the Arab cultural heritage. Early in that year he published the series of articles entitled "Ḥayāt al-ādāb"; at the same time, we may assume, the drafting of the thesis on Abu'l-'Alā' must have been well under way. There was, therefore, a second set of writings marking a second major transition in Ṭāhā's early thought.

There were, we may say, two sub-phases within this critical period, represented by two series of publications, the first appearing in 1911, while the second in 1914. In the first stage Ṭāhā moved from an attitude of relatively passive receptivity to one of active assimilation, a process in which he sought to account for the scientific study of Arabic literature through the analysis, reconstruction and adaptation of his teachers' views, especially those of C.A. Nallino. His originality in this phase consisted in dwelling on the fundamental question of method, otherwise implicit or fragmentarily treated, in those views, and in seeking new applications for the new methodology. However, the answer he provided remained within the conceptual limits established by Nallino.

In 1911, Ṭāhā wrote as a follower of the Italian master; like the latter, he accounted for what it was to study Arabic literature scientifically in loose and open-ended terms. Having rejected Zaydān's view that literary phenomena were to be explained with reference to the political order of things, and having suggested that such an explanation must be sought at a deeper level of fact, Ṭāhā did not know in hard and fast terms the nature of this alternative basis of explanation. His use in this context of the Arabic concept *al-ādāb* constituted a clear indication that he did not have any fixed views on the subject. Being highly ambiguous, the concept in question covered various types of potential explanatory factors (apart from literature, the prevailing manners, morals, customs and ideas); besides, it left the door open for the additional influence of the physical environment. As long as

Ṭāhā was committed to such a diversity of factors, which were not fitted into any definite order or structure, he adhered to what might be called Nallino's open-ended objectivism.

Something similar could be said of Ṭāhā's critical comments at this stage on the Arab literary heritage, which, like those of Nallino, were muted and mild.

As early as the first article on Zaydān, Ṭāhā noted that ancient Arab scholars had compiled the necessary source materials for the scientific study of Arabic literature, whereas the credit for organizing the subject according to historical principles should go to orientalists. But this observation, indicating the absence of historical methodology from the Arab cultural heritage, did not give rise to any harsh criticism; on the contrary, it apparently implied an acknowledgement of the Arab contribution as being after all a pioneering effort in what was assumed to be a common pursuit or collaborative enterprise. In fact, Ṭāhā was hardly aware at this stage that the Arab contribution was qualitatively different from, or inferior to, the Western one .Thus the Arabs were said to have been the first to write on the history of literature;[10] and *Kitāb al-Aghānī* in particular was praised for being "the real source and true reference for the history of Arabic letters strictly speaking" (*al-ādāb al-'Arabiyya al-khāliṣa*)[11]

In "Hal tastaridd al-lugha majdahā al-qadīm?", Ṭāhā regretted that ancient Arab scholars, though well-placed in time to enquire into the Semitic origins of Arabic, had devoted their energies to the compilation of linguistic materials, leaving to orientalists, or to the comparative philologists amongst them, the task of investigating the linguistic side of the history of Arabic literature.[12] The tone became slightly more heated as Ṭāhā sarcastically rebuked (presumably) later scholars who had wasted so much effort on futile enquiries about the use of Syriac in the afterlife.[13] But despite the touch of regret or irony, Ṭāhā's criticisms of traditional Arab scholars remained restrained.

More serious criticisms arose as a result of actually applying the historical methodology to Arabic literature, but these were limited to the pre-Islamic Arabs on account of their primitive culture, and were counterbalanced by a highly favourable appraisal of the achievements of the Islamic era, including the civilizing role of the Qur'ān and the splendours of the Abbāsid period.

The same criticisms were also counterbalanced by high praise for pre-Islamic poetry. The authenticity of this lore was never questioned at this stage. It is true that Ṭāhā was already aware that there were discrepancies in terms of language and religious content between pre-Islamic poetry and the mainly Ḥimyarite inscriptions found in different parts of Arabia, above all in the Yemen and Ḥaḍramawt. But from these discrepancies, simply noted with a sense of wonder, Ṭāhā merely concluded that the known pre-Islamic poets could not have been (Yemenite) Qaḥṭānis and must have been (Northern) ʻAdnānis.[14] While his attention was drawn to those discrepancies, partly by Nallino, Ṭāhā did not even share the latter's limited scepticism concerning the authenticity of poetry attributed to the Tabābiʻa.

Such was Ṭāhā's position until the appearance in 1914 of the second set of early writings, signalling the occurrence of a remarkable shift beyond Nallino to a more stringent account of the scientific study of Arabic literature and a radical critique of Arab culture.

Ṭāhā's views on the nature of historical methodology now became much more articulate and stringent. He was, more than ever, aware that the new discipline had a logic of its own which he strove to expound in a series of prolegomena and critical procedures. No longer content with simply enumerating the various types of explanatory factors at work in literary history, he sought to give an answer to the more fundamental question about the *nature of explanation* involved. Thus literary history was supposed to explain the why of literary utterances in terms of their efficient causes – as opposed to the classical, Greek and Arab, analysis in terms of intrinsic, material and formal, constituents.

In drawing this contrast, Ṭāhā made it clear that literary history was a science in the manner of natural sciences, with chemistry as the paradigm case. Psychology also had a central role to play, but this was conceived of according to the chemical model: psychology, wrote Ṭāhā, was the chemistry of the soul. Like chemical analysis, psychological investigation sought the deeper, hidden causes of its own objects. Reaching beyond any given literary work for its invisible causes within the writer's soul, i.e. the many faculties and powers involved in the act of creation, the process of explanation moved deeper still, seeking, beyond the individual subject, the ultimate external causes which determined these faculties and powers and hence determined and explained the literary work itself.

It is important to stress the novelty of the psychological dimension so introduced. In 1911, Ṭāhā showed some interest in psychological matters, for he spoke of ideas, feelings and passions proper to nations as being among the explanatory factors involved in literary history. But psychological factors were simply enumerated among other types of factor, without being distinguished as a specific class, let alone a privileged one. He also spoke of a "psychological constitution" proper to a nation; but he made no attempt to use this idea as an organizing principle. In the 1914 writings on the other hand, the psychological dimension was assumed to constitute the core or focal point within the system of double causation described above; for the whole system was now organized around the concept of a collective mind proper to the nation concerned. In other words, the above-mentioned ultimate factors in literary history, now neatly divided into those which were material or physical (*māddiyya*) and those which were moral (*ma'nawiyya*), were all supposed to revolve around a nation's soul or mind – this being the true subject of history. It was in this sense that Ṭāhā maintained that none of Abu'l-'Alā' al-Ma'rri's works could be attributed to the poet-philosopher alone, as both he and all his actions were a product of the Islamic nation. He affirmed that all events in Islamic history were manifestations of the Islamic mind.

In this fashion, Ṭāhā moved beyond Nallino's *open-ended objectivism* to what might be called *systemic objectivism*, an overtly scientistic conception of the history of Arabic literature as a deterministic system revolving around a collective mind proper to the Islamic nation.

The transition went hand in hand with wide-ranging and radical criticisms of Arab culture. No longer confined to Zaydān, Ṭāhā's strictures regarding a lack of historical spirit were directed at the Literary History School, ancient Arab philologists and historians and also at the Arabs at large as Orientals and Semites. Ṭāhā now suggested that the true historical spirit was a more or less Western monopoly; that by comparison the Arab contribution to the study of literary history and history proper was poor. Arab historians at their best or most critically-minded, so the argument went, confined themselves to oral traditions and were not aware of the value of written documents for the scientific study of history.

This last point deserves special attention, as it implies that Ṭāhā was already aware that modern historical investigation, as distinct from traditional Arab historiography, was based on the study of written documents. He was also aware, be that in a rudimentary fashion, that modern historical investigation applied to documents a series of technical or critical procedures furnished by "special" (or auxiliary) disciplines.

Other criticisms were addressed to the Arab cultural heritage as it came under scrutiny in the light of historical methodology, thus stringently defined. As such an object of study, this heritage was no longer treated as an autonomous and self-validating body of texts, but was reduced to, and judged as, a product of historical conditions governed by iron-clad necessity. In this way, serious doubts began to arise concerning the authenticity of pre-Islamic poetry. Ṭāhā now developed Nallino's views concerning the various motives behind poetic forgery and multiplied the examples illustrating the point. Cases of fabricated poetry, he maintained, were common and numerous in the Arab literary sources.[15]

It is obvious that Ṭāhā's position on the subject evolved beyond Nallino's limited doubts. The trend was all the more remarkable when we also note that the newly expressed scepticism ranged more widely: it did not spare traditional Arab sources on Islamic poetry or on Islamic history, teeming with all sorts of exaggerations and fantasies, as Ṭāhā maintained. Nor did this scepticism spare received reports on miracles, including the ones attributed to the Prophet.[16]

This brings us to the most radical feature of Ṭāhā's early thought as it was expressed in 1914, namely his position on supernatural phenomena. In 1911 he dealt with the subject in perfect conformity with Islamic orthodoxy, rejecting Zaydān's suggestion that the Mosaic Law was derived from the Babylonian laws of Hammurabi and affirming the divine origin of religious legislation and revealed scriptures. But in 1914 Ṭāhā could no longer maintain this straightforward position, given that he now assumed that history was but a manifestation of the social self. He therefore insisted on the need to clarify the relatioship between wonders reported in Islamic history and the minds of Muslims. And although he was not forthcoming as to the nature of this clarification, there can be no doubt that the process culminated in two unorthodox conclusions concerning miracles and the Qur'ān, respectively.

With regard to miracles, the process led to dispelling their wondrous character.[17] Ṭāhā cited in this connection the example of the astounding victories won by early Muslims over much stronger forces, namely the Meccan polytheists as well as the Persians and Byzantines. As against Ibn Khaldūn, whom he must have had in mind,[18] he did not think it enough to invoke the Muslims' strength of faith or the political decline in the two ancient empires. The process of clarification must, according to Ṭāhā, proceed further. What he had in mind was far from clear, but it is obvious at any rate that he rejected what Ibn Khaldūn would have put forward as a further argument, namely that the early Muslims had divine support.

"(At that time)," writes Ibn Khaldūn, "Islam was winning the hearts of the people and causing them to be willing to die for it in a way that disrupted the customary course of affairs. That happened because people observed with their own eyes the presence of angels to help them, the repeated appearance of heavenly messages among them They were thoroughly frightened and perturbed by a sequence of extraordinary miracles and other divine happenings, and by frequent visitations of angels."[19] Ṭāhā would have none of this; without revealing the identity of his interlocutor, he retorts rather impatiently: "Don't talk to me about miracles and events which violate the customary course of things (*khawāriq al-'ādāt*). These matters have nothing to do with history or logic and are better relegated to religious disciplines".[20]

To clarify the link between miracles and group psychology thus amounted to the exclusion of such happenings from the realm of history. Concerning the Qur'ān on the other hand, Ṭāhā drew a different conclusion, equally unorthodox, but moving in the opposite direction. To clarify the link between the Book and the minds of Muslims was to make a point of studying its verses insofar as they bore on their minds throughout history. This is not very informative; and Ṭāhā was not to be drawn any further, for the question, as he went on to explain, was thorny and potentially explosive. But what he was driving at seems to be clear; namely that the Qur'ān must always be studied *in history* or in its social environment or context. This conclusion, together with the observation concerning the discrepancies between pre-Islamic poetry and ancient Arabian inscriptions, already contained the germ of Ṭāhā's generalized scepticism of the late 1920s concerning the authenticity of pre-Islamic poetry.[21]

With this recapitulation of Ṭāhā's development during the years 1907/8–1914, we are in a better position to ascertain the general orientations and sources of his critical thought. When he began in 1911 to introduce the historical study of Arabic literature, he assumed that the principles according to which the subject was historically organized had been laid down by orientalists, and he accordingly sought these principles in the teachings of his foreign teachers, mainly Nallino. At this stage, he accounted for the history of Arabic literature in terms of Nallino's open-ended objectivism, namely the view that events and phenomena within that history must be explained not with reference to the political order of things (the succession of reigns) but with reference to a deeper level of reality involving, in a loose and unstructured way, the prevailing social mores (manners, morals, customs and ideas) as well as environmental conditions. And as long as Ṭāhā's ideas on the subject were couched in these general terms, his criticisms of the Arab cultural heritage either with regard to the absence of the above-mentioned historical principles from it or as a result of applying them to its study, remained limited and mild.

While it is not our intention to study the origins of Nallino's open-ended objectivism, we may point out tentatively and provisionally[22] that the doctrine in question seems to draw on a variety of sources, some of which are certainly French. For by siding with the history of customs, manners and ideas as distinct from political history, Nallino was in fact party to a debate which broke out in the last decades of the nineteenth century, dividing German and French historians into two camps: the advocates of political history and the advocates of a general history of civilization.[23] As far as France is concerned, the debate may be traced back to Voltaire. He was probably the first to denounce political history, *l'histoire des batailles* as he would sarcastically say, in favour of a broader and fuller kind of history in terms of the whole moral life of any given period, or, in other words, a history of civilization.[24] A more recent pioneer of this kind of history would be Saint-Simon.[25]But we might narrow the scope further, and relate Nallino's doctrine to historians of civilization who did not simply consider political factors within a broader perspective, but sought to explain them causally with reference to deeper types of social factors. If this is so, then the most likely prototype for Nallino's programme would be perhaps Fustel de Coulanges (1830–1889), who, while assuming that political phenomena could be so explained,[26] would not commit himself to any system or synthesis into which all types of explanatory factor may be fitted neatly. As pointed out by Cassirer, Fustel insisted that for the historian there must be only facts, nothing but facts and warned against "vague generalities" and premature syntheses. For him, history is indeed a science, but it is a science of facts or a science of observation.[27] In a nutshell, Nallino's open-ended objectivism may be classified as a mild form of positivism.

If this is so, it follows that, in adopting this position in 1911, Ṭāhā came under the influence of French thought as early as this date, except that he did so through Nallino, and within the conceptual limits of his doctrine.

In 1914, however, Ṭāhā went beyond these limits. His conception of the history of Arabic literature underwent a significant shift towards systemic objectivism, i.e. the view that literary history constituted a deterministic system based on collective psychology; and a radical critique of Arab literary history, which was a correlate of that stringent form of objectivism. In doing so, we may say, Ṭāhā was committed to a tough-minded or full-blooded version of positivism, which has rightly been traced back to Hippolyte Taine (1828–1893). Nallino, who never mentioned Taine in his lectures on the history of Arabic literature, must be held to be indebted *up to a point* to Taine. Like the latter who was the first to put forward the idea of (literary) history as a science,[28] Nallino assumed that the discipline must be based on causal explanation, but he would not press the point so as to commit himself to Taine's scientism (the idea that the subject in question must be a science in the manner of natural sciences). Nor would Nallino commit himself to Taine's determinism or collective psychology. Thus if we are to assume, as perhaps we should, that Nallino actually took Taine into account in developing his own open-ended objectivism, then we must bear in mind that in doing so Nallino also sought to avoid Taine's excesses.

But it is precisely these excesses which Ṭāhā came to embrace wholeheartedly in 1914. No longer content with Nallino's mild positivism, the author of "Ḥayāt al-ādāb" and *Tajdīd dhikrā Abi'l-'Alā'* reached beyond the Italian orientalist for the full-blooded doctrine in its French version.

Something similar could be said of Ṭāhā's rudimentary knowledge at this same stage of the codified methodology of modern historical enquiry and criticism, which in turn exceeded the limits of Nallino's teaching and seems to have had its roots mainly in French positivist sources.

We may now proceed to investigate in some detail how it was possible for Ṭāhā to establish direct links with France. This enquiry which we propose to carry out for the first time comprises two main tasks. First, to show more clearly the positivist ingredients that went into the making of Ṭāhā's systemic objectivism and to identify as much as possible the channel(s) through which these ingredients were transmitted to him. Secondly, to examine in some detail the French sources of Ṭāhā's early knowledge of positivist historical methodology and criticism and again to identify the channel(s) through which this knowledge was passed on to him.

The question concerning these channels arises in both cases, once it is admitted that the information concerned was not obtained through Nallino. Ṭāhā's knowledge of French was not sufficient to enable him to tackle the French sources in the original; nor does he seem to have had at his disposal Arabic translations or adequate accounts of the doctrines involved in either case.

Both tasks are bound to encounter serious difficulties. For apart from the numerous gaps in our knowledge of the period under consideration, Ṭāhā does not offer his reader much help concerning his sources. His acknowledgements, where they occur, are made in very general and misleading terms. An example of this is Ṭāhā's unqualified homage to Nallino, which has hitherto led scholars to assume that Ṭāhā's early views on literary history were largely if not entirely learnt from Nallino and that they coincided more or less with those of the Italian orientalist. On the other hand, Ṭāhā's implicit references are either so fleeting and elusive as to pass unnoticed or else so disproportionately pronounced as to magnify the importance of the debt. For these reasons we need to read Ṭāhā's texts with the utmost care. The effort required is worth the trouble, as it reveals a new chapter not only in Ṭāhā's development but also in the history of modern Arab thought.

The first positivist influence to be detected in Ṭāhā's systemic objectivism relates to the scientistic dimension of this doctrine and may be traced, at least in part, to Auguste Comte's (1798–

1857) famous law of the three states. This is the kind of influence that can easily pass unnoticed in view of the fact that Ṭāhā simplifies and adapts the law in question in "Ḥayāt al-ādāb".

Comte's law, meant to depict the development of the human mind in the first place, stipulates that all forms of knowledge must pass through three stages in order to achieve full maturity: (1) a *theological stage,* in which the human mind, aspiring to reach the inner nature of beings as well as their first and final causes, presents them as the outcome of supernatural agents; (2) a *metaphysical stage,* in which these agents are replaced by "abstract forces, real entities or personified abstractions inherent in the different beings of the world"; and (3) a *positive stage,* in which "the human mind, recognizing the impossibility of obtaining absolute truth, gives up the search after the origin and hidden causes of the universe and a knowledge of the final causes of phenomena. It endeavours now only to discover . . . the actual laws of phenomena that is to say their invariable relations of succession and likeness".[29]

In what is assumed to be an indispensable complement to the fundamental law, Comte argues that sciences do not reach the positive stage all at once; they only do so in conformity with the diverse nature of their subject matter, or according to an order determined by the degree of generality, of simplicity and of reciprocal independence of phenomena. Thus astronomy, having as its subject matter the most general, the simplest and most independent phenomena, was the first science to reach positive maturity. Then followed in succession and for similar reasons physics, chemistry and physiology.[30] Finally, at the end of the series, Comte delimits a further space to be filled by a new science, namely "social physics" or sociology. Being concerned with the most special, most complex and most dependent of all phenomena, sociology is the last to achieve positivity.[31]

Comte's law, together with its complement, are rewritten by the author of "Ḥayāt al-ādāb". Like Comte, he prescribes for all forms of knowledge one single course of development, since they all spring from the human mind. Literary study, he thus argues, has evolved along the same lines as the "philosophical study of matter". While in classical times, material objects were accounted for in terms of their intrinsic, material and formal, components, in modern times the human mind would be content with nothing less than an explanation of these same objects with reference to their deeper causes. Similarly, the literary study of statements, whether in verse or in prose, has evolved from the classical mode of explication, in terms of material and formal components, to the modern mode of explanation seeking to discover the causes of these statements in the minds and surroundings of writers.

Ṭāhā's argument reflects Comte's law, albeit in a simplified, modified and somewhat garbled form. While doing away with the theological state altogether, and replacing sociology by literary study as the youngest discipline to achieve full maturity, Ṭāhā, as we have already seen, misdescribes the transition from the metaphysical (read philosophical) form of explanation in terms of abstractions to the scientific (read positive) form of explanation in terms of causal factors and laws. That the transition is so misdescribed is due to the fact that the author of "Ḥayāt al-ādāb" has not grasped the qualitative difference between traditional philosophy and modern natural science. Comte conceives of the march towards positivity as a process in which the mind renounces its theological and metaphysical ambitions and confines itself to the more modest, but more fruitful, study of causal laws governing observable phenomena. Ṭāhā, by contrast, has in mind an advance from a philosophical form of analysis confined to the constituents at hand to yet another form of philosophical analysis reaching for what is remote or ultimate. But there can be no doubt that Ṭāhā uses Comte's law as a model in order to drive home the point that literary study is the last branch to join the modern family of sciences, especially chemistry.

Fortunately, the question of how it was possible for Ṭāhā to obtain knowledge of Comte can easily be answered. Apart from the fact that positivist ideas in general were in the air in Egypt at the time,[32] Comte's law in particular was known to Luṭfī al-Sayyid.[33] To this we may add that Massignon dealt with Comte's law in his lectures delivered at the Egyptian University in 1912–1913 (i.e. well before the publication of "Ḥayāt al-ādāb").[34]

By contrast, Taine's influence on Ṭāhā constitutes a daunting challenge to any investigator who wishes to ascertain its true extent and identify its channels of transmission. Although Taine is never mentioned by name in any of Ṭāhā's early writings known to us, the author of "Ḥayāt al-ādāb" and *Tajdīd dhikrā Abi'l-'Alā'* makes a point of echoing Taine's introduction to his *History of English literature* and the first chapter of his *Philosophie de l'art* in such a pronounced way that it verges at times on paraphrase or semi-quotation.

Like Taine, Ṭāhā assumes that history is a science of observation and explanation: to the former's assertion that "science neither pardons nor proscribes: it verifies and explains",[35] corresponds the latter's statement that "The work of a historian consists in the search for causes: it is descriptive (*waṣfī*) rather than creative (*waḍʿī*) indicating what is the case without inventing anything ... Thus we do not allow ourselves to praise or blame people ... for to proffer praise or blame is not part of the historian's work".[36] To Taine's definition of the historical spirit as "sympathy for all forms of art and all schools",[37] corresponds Ṭāhā's postulate that "that who studies literature for its own sake must study both what is good and what is bad and must master both what is meagre and what is substantial on an equal footing and without discrimination".[38]

There is some divergence between the two on the question of which natural science should serve as the primary model for literary history. Taine, who was well aware of the progress made by the biological sciences of his time and probably bore in mind that physiology was the last science to reach positive maturity according to Comte, thought that (literary) history should emulate zoology and botany in the first place.[39] Ṭāhā, on the other hand, favoured chemistry. But this divergence leaves room for some agreement, as Taine avails himself sometimes of chemical analogies. Thus his view that moral qualities such as "vice and virtue are products, like vitriol and sugar; and [that] every complex phenomenon has its springs from other more simple phenomena on which it hangs."[40] is echoed by Ṭāhā's statement that "a historical event ..., a poem ..., a speech ... or an epistle ... are all but a tissue of social and natural causes, just as amenable to investigation and analysis as matter is to the work of chemistry".[41] Again Taine's statement that "no matter if the facts be physical or moral, they all have their causes"[42] is reflected by Ṭāhā's contention that "every effect, be it physical or moral, every phenomenon, whether social or natural (*kawniyya*; lit.: cosmological), ought to be reduced to its origins and traced back to its primary sources ... that is to say, the assembly of causes [which brought it about]".[43]

Both authors are opposed to the exclusive ascription of events to individuals, for they both assume that all events are ultimately caused by extra-subjective forces. "A work of art", Taine writes, "is not a mere play of imagination, a solitary caprice of a heated brain, but a transcript of contemporary manners, a type of a certain kind of mind".[44] Rewritten by Ṭāhā, the dictum reads: "We do not believe that individuals are the sole agents behind events; we believe rather that events are the outcome of an assembly of factors [beyond individuals]".[45]

The divergence between Taine and Ṭāhā on the nature of the ultimate causes of events (Taine's "contemporary manners, etc." as opposed to Ṭāhā's "assembly of factors") is of little or no importance, being simply a matter of wording: both assume that the ultimate causes in question are integral parts of one deterministic system revolving around a collective mind.

This brings us to the most striking correspondence between Taine and Ṭāhā. To the former's conception of history as a system determined by the famous triad, *race, milieu* and *moment,* there corresponds Ṭāhā's own conception of Islamic history as being a system revolving around the Islamic nation or people (*umma, sha'b*) in regions of space (*makān, iqlīm*) and at different epochs (*zamān*). But it is precisely at this point that problems begin to arise regarding the exact role played by Taine in shaping Ṭāhā's thought. It is here, where the correspondence between the two authors seems to be complete, that other influences and forces can be seen to have come into play, rendering the situation much more intricate. Ṭāhā himself warns us that his determinism in history (*al-jabr fi'l-tārikh*) is a complex hybrid involving various strands. In introducing this doctrine, he says, he is simply following many philosophers, both European and Muslim.[46] The doctrine, we are told again, draws on two main sources, the one is philosophical (or to be more accurate scientific – philosophical),[47] while the other is religious (or better still theological). According to the former source, free will is incompatible with a conception of the world as a system governed by thoroughgoing causality, while according to the latter source, free will is incompatible with God's omnipotence and omniscience.[48]

Each one of these two "sources" constitutes a broad current with several tributaries. On the theological side, which is purely Islamic, we may surely count Abu'l-'Alā's own contribution,[49] which in turn presupposes a whole tradition of debate on free choice and predestination going back to the *Mutakallimūn.*[50] Needless to say, the subject was familiar to Ṭāhā Ḥusain, if only because of his training in *tawḥīd* at the Azhar. When he writes that man cannot "appropriate" (*yamtalik*) the causes [influencing social life], nor can he "repel" or "acquire" them (*la yastaṭī'u lahā daf'an wa-lā iktisāban*), he thinks as an uncompromising *jabrī* (adherent of predestination) who rejects even the Ash'ari doctrine of *kasb* (acquisition or appropriation), a compromise solution the purpose of which is to retain for human beings a semblance of efficacy and moral responsibility by contending that their actions, though created by God, can nevertheless be acquired or appropriated by them.[51]

As for the scientific-philosophical source, it is a mixture of Islamic and Western influences, involving, besides Taine's contribution, a possible Stoic component transmitted by Santillana,[52] and an Islamic component which may be traced back to Ibn Khaldūn,[53] and also to what he describes as the "philosophers'" [i.e. Muslim Peripatetics'] doctrine that there exists an essential and necessary causality.[54]

In view of this complexity, the question necessarily arises as to the specific role of Taine's influence. Falling within the scientific-philosophical current of deterministic thought, this role consists apparently in introducing the historical, or to be more precise, the literary historical dimension;[55] for of all the determinists so far cited, it was Taine who first applied determinism to the explanation of literary phenomena in particular. The said role, it may further be added, consists also in basing determinism, thus restricted, on the assumption of a collective mind. In other words, Ṭāhā's determinism in history owes to Taine, as distinct from any other Islamic or Western source, its literary historical character as well as its collective psychologism.

But having thus pinpointed what is distinctively Tainean in Ṭāhā's determinism, we need to note further that Taine's influence, diffuse and pronounced as it may be, does not run very deep. Miftah Tahar was the first to point out that one should not exaggerate the identity of views between Taine and Ṭāhā Ḥusain.[56] We may now show how the two positions diverge on the most fundamental level. At first sight, the two appear to be in perfect agreement inasmuch as Ṭāhā's three basic concepts, "nation", "region" and "epoch", correspond to Taine's triad, *race, milieu* and *moment.* On closer examination, however, the correspondence turns out to be purely verbal.

Each term in Taine's triad is heavily loaded, and the whole set is so carefully designed as to give substance to his claim that there is for each people a collective soul with a specific constitution, a so-called elementary moral condition[57] involving three major faculties. Thus *race* stands for inner, native or hereditary dispositions, i.e. primitive or primordial spiritual forms implanted in the nature of a people by millennia of evolution;[58] *milieu* on the other hand stands for acquired dispositions, well-established habits of mind, so to speak, imposed on a people under the prolonged pressure of external surroundings or circumstances;[59] while *moment* stands for the long predominance of a master idea, a pattern of thought or an ideal of man in the cultural climate of a people.[60]

Taken together, the three faculties making up the mental structure of a people are supposed to derive from, or to be developed through, a people's experience in histor; but once developed, whether as innate dispositions, acquired habits of thought or "momentarily" dominant ideas, they become, so the argument goes, autonomous forces acting independently of their external origins; it is they rather than these latter conditions which, according to Taine, jointly determine and explain all works of art and indeed all events in the history of any given people or culture. It is in this sense that history for Taine is a psychological problem, just as astronomy, in its elements, is a mechanical and physiology a chemical problem.[61] In fact, there is, according to him, a form of psychological mechanics involving the three factors, the "internal mainsprings", the "external pressure" and the "acquired momentum", which determine all motion in history and which, had they been measurable, would have made it possible to deduce as from a formula the specific character of future civilization.[62]

By contrast, none of Ṭāhā's basic concepts have any psychological implications; and taken together, the three concepts do not give substance to his claim that there is a mind or soul appropriate to the Islamic nation. The claim in question remains verbal inasmuch as Ṭāhā makes no attempt to show that the Islamic mind has a specific constitution. For him, as we have seen in the preceding chapter, the Islamic nation does not constitute a distinctive racial group; it is rather a multitude of ethnic, religious and cultural groups held together by loose ties. Their unity is ensured by no mental structure of well-defined and fixed dispositions and master ideas. Thus the psychological dimension, built into Taine's system, is practically absent in Ṭāhā's system. In the latter case, to study the Islamic nation in different regions and epochs amounts in fact to the study of the above-mentioned groups in their natural and social surroundings. And that is what Ṭāhā actually does in his study on Abu'l-'Alā'.

In other words, Ṭāhā adopts no more than the outer shell of Taine's system. Having reached this conclusion, we may now proceed to consider the other part of the puzzle, namely the question of how it was possible for Ṭāhā to obtain his knowledge of Taine. His French was inadequate; it is highly improbable that this knowledge was gained from an Arabic source, whether a translation[63] or an account of some sort or another.[64]

To solve the problem, some scholars have suggested that Ṭāhā became aware of Taine through informal discussions with Nallino.[65] In practice, this could have taken place only in 1910–1912, the period the Italian orientalist spent in Cairo lecturing on the history of Arabic literature. While this hypothesis cannot be entirely ruled out, it does not have any solid backing either. The only piece of evidence in support of it is Ṭāhā's reference, in 1911, to the idea of a "psychological constitution" proper to a nation,[66] which is highly reminiscent of Taine's "moral constitution". However, there are two reasons why this evidence is not conclusive. First, the idea in question, occurring only once, is not developed sufficiently to prove the presence of a Tainean influence. Secondly, even if such an influence were to be established, that fact would not of itself be proof that Nallino was the transmitter. Given that Nallino never mentions Taine and that we have no sufficient knowledge of Ṭāhā's early period in Cairo, the field is open for other hypotheses. Luṭfī al-Sayyid, who was familiar with positivism and who in a sense supervised Ṭāhā's thesis on Abu'l-'Alā',[67] could have passed to Ṭāhā the necessary information on Taine. Also, as I shall presently show, Massignon was well placed to serve as a channel for this information. To be on the safe side, I am inclined to think that Ṭāhā's knowledge of Taine and of positivism in general was obtained piecemeal through a protracted process of research and a number of different channels, including probably Luṭfī al-Sayyid, Nallino in a minor role, if at all, and with Massignon as the principal contributor.

Massignon was ideally suited to play a crucial role in initiating Ṭāhā into Taine's doctrine. Apart from the fact that he was French, his course of lectures, delivered in 1912–1913, was close in time to the second set of Ṭāhā's early writings (1914); and, as we have already seen, he was instrumental in the provision of information on Comte's law of the three states. As far as Taine is concerned, Massignon does not have much to say; the French critic is mentioned only once as being one among many Western advocates of materialist determinism.[68] But Massignon's discussion of determinism as such and of its various ramifications both in the West and in Islam appears to have had a decisive influence on Ṭāhā's systemic objectivism and to have offered an ideal context for the provision of specific information on Taine.

Massignon must have had a part to play in suggesting to Ṭāhā his hybrid conception of determinism in history (*al-jabr fi'l-tārīkh*). It is important to note in this connection how the Arabic term used by Massignon to designate materialist determinism, *al-ijbār al-māddī* (materialist compulsion) conflates the Islamic theological idea of *jabr* (predestination) and the (partly) Western scientific-philosophical idea of natural necessity. In another passage devoted to the different meanings of *al-irāda* (will), Massignon applies his customary procedure of drawing parallels and affinities between Western and Islamic traditions, citing on the same footing the Mu'tazilites' and Māturidītes' *ikhtiyār* (*liberté* or free will) and, significantly, the Ash'arites' *kasb ma' istiṭā'a* (acquisition accompanied with the ability to act), along with *jabr* and *ḍarūra* (necessity).[69]

It goes without saying that Massignon did not initiate Ṭāhā into such Islamic doctrines; what he must have done, through the above-mentioned procedure, was rather to alert Ṭāhā to the continued relevance of these doctrines in the modern context, especially where the conception of history as a deterministic system is concerned. Thus, in a remarkable statement on the world as viewed by reason, Massignon says laconically in a manner so reminiscent of the author of *Tajdīd dhikrā Abi'l-'Alā'*: "According to the judgement of reason ... the chain of causes is continuous; the world is a closed domain (*dār mughlaqa*) and the realm of determinism is governed by the principle of the conservation of energy".[70] This point of view, Massignon implies, has certain affinities with the Islamic doctrine of *jabr*; and he opposes to it Ibn 'Arabī's dictum that "God never ceases to create" as well as Bergson's idea of creative duration; for, Massignon argues, the totality of the universe hitherto is still incomplete and is poised (*māthila*) for the future.[71]

Again, Massignon makes it clear that Western determinism is incompatible with accidents and miracles. Thus, in a discussion of the different meanings of "nature" in Western thought, he refers to the Aristotelian distinction between *physis,* which stands for the totality of things governed by law, and *tyché* (*al-fa'l* or *al-ṣudfa*) which stands for that which is subject to no law.[72] In the same context, Massignon points out that determinists maintain that being natural is incompatible with being "supernatural", when this term is taken to mean that which violates the customary course of things, such as miracles.[73]

These ideas, which were reflected in Ṭāhā's systemic objectivism, might have offered Massignon an ideal opportunity for introducing specific information on Taine, except that this information went unrecorded for one reason or another. There are here two possibilities. First, that the information was given within the lecture room, but was not written down. Massignon the lecturer, we may note, did not read from a script, preferring instead to improvise in the light of the needs and responses of his students. According to Ṭāhā Ḥusain, the French orientalist found it difficult to render the technical terms of modern philosophy into Arabic, and he used to interrupt his delivery every few minutes in order to question the students and to make sure that they had understood.[74]

In a report, so far unpublished, on his mission in Cairo, Massignon gives more details on his teaching method. His duty, as he put it, was to get to know his audience and to communicate with them in Arabic. For this purpose, he thought, he had better abandon the idea of teaching through [formal] lessons carefully written and carefully delivered, and give instead spoken lectures, showing no fear of addressing a sudden apostrophe to the best among them in order to stimulate general attention. He took it upon himself, again he writes, to learn with his students how to think together, allowing them to perceive both the ideas pursued and the verbal expression while still in the making, with all the inevitable hesitations and false steps.[75]

Given this manner of proceeding, together with the fact that the published text of Massignon's lectures is based on the notes taken by one student,[76] it was perhaps inevitable that some of Massignon's pronouncements went unrecorded or were drastically abbreviated.

Secondly and alternatively, the information on Taine could have been provided in a purely informal manner. We know for a fact that informal discussions took place between Massignon and

Ṭāhā. The latter, who befriended almost all his foreign teachers, seems to have had still closer contacts with Massignon. A special relation seems to have developed between master and student. According to Ṭāhā Ḥusain, Massignon for some mysterious reason used to single him out for questioning before anybody else. A few days after the beginning of the course, a strange kind of friendliness (*ulfa*) grew up between the two. Massignon wanted to know everything about Ṭāhā and started inviting him to his lodgings, where they met frequently and had ample discussions.[77]

Thanks to Massignon's report mentioned above, we know now the mystery behind that friendliness. Generally speaking, Massignon felt a special affinity with Azharites, having been himself a former Azharite of sorts,[78] and, what is more important, being convinced that the Azharites among his students were more promising than their fellow students, who were graduates of government schools: it is they, more than the latter category, who had learnt to reason in their mother tongue; it is from their ranks that future writers and philosophers were likely to emerge. More specifically, Massignon, with his keen perception, could not fail to spot Shaykh Ṭāhā, that "aveugle clairvoyant", as an exceptional student with a mind of the highest calibre. Massignon was specially impressed by Ṭāhā's articles in *al-Jarīda,* and his remarkable performance in the oral examination at the end of the course; for unlike all his fellow students, who had learnt their lecture notes word by word with the admirable ease of Orientals, Ṭāhā expounded the Kantian antinomies of pure reason[79] with such a perfect choice of expression.

In the informal discussions that took place between the French orientalist and his Egyptian student, they could not have failed to take up some of the subjects dealt with in the lectures, especially the ones of common interest, such as determinism and its different facets in the two cultures. Ṭāhā, we may also assume, must have played an active part, given his Azhari background and dialectical skills; and it is highly probable that in the ensuing exchange, Massignon provided, *in Arabic,* the required information on Taine, together with supporting textual references.

Thus far the evidence adduced in favour of the hypothesis that it was Massignon who initiated Ṭāhā into Taine's doctrine is based on the proven fact that the former played an essential part in giving substance to and shaping Ṭāhā's systemic objectivism. The hypothesis can now receive further confirmation from the fact, equally important and also demonstrable, that Massignon appears to have served as a channel for Ṭāhā's early knowledge of yet another aspect of the positivist tradition, namely codified positivist historical methodology and criticism. Against those who believe that this aspect had been unknown to Ṭāhā until he went to the Sorbonne[80], we can show beyond the shadow of a doubt that he became acquainted with the field in question while still in Egypt, mainly through Massignon.[81]

For this purpose we need to turn to Massignon's treatment of *uṣūl al-tārīkh* (the principles of history) or the *méthode historique* in lecture XXVI and also in a section of the concluding lecture XL. The subject covers both questions of method strictly speaking and philosophical speculations on the course and ends of historical events.[82] When Massignon inaugurates the discussion with the statement that history, previously a branch of literature, has come to be a science *sui generis* with a philosophy of its own, the term "philosophy of history", just like *uṣūl al-tārīkh*, is meant to have the same wide extension.

The first thing to note here is the importance attached to the philosophy of history through the sheer amount of space allocated to it, the use of the Arabic term *uṣūl al-tārīkh*[83] as a designation, and the stress laid on the subject as a necessary correlate of the emergence of history as a science. This very prominence seems to have had a powerful impact on Ṭāhā, contributing to his sharpened awareness of the importance of the subject. Thus he seems to echo Massignon when he claims for his work on Abu'l-'Alā' the status of a logic of literary historical enquiry.[84]

It was also from Massignon that Ṭāhā derived the idea that modern historical enquiry is essentially a critical investigation of written documents, and that it developed for this purpose a set of "special" sciences. Massignon classifies these sciences as follows: (a) archaeology; (b) the study of [ancient] writings, comprising epigraphy and palaeography; (c) diplomatics and the authentication of sources (*critique des sources*; *taṣḥīḥ al-isnād*); (d) computation of calendar (*comput*; *'ilm al-ṭuqūs*)[85] and genealogy; and (e) historical geography and comparative mythology.[86]

From this classification of auxiliary sciences, as they are commonly called, Ṭāhā retained the idea that they include a science (obviously palaeography) "which teaches you about the different kinds of ink used in different ages, the different kinds of paper (*qirṭās*) as well as the different kinds of script (*aqlām*), and, no less importantly, teaches you the rules of calligraphy (*al-khaṭṭ*) as it changed through the ages".[87]

Massignon's reference, within the same classification, to diplomatics (*'ilm al-farāmīn*) may also have been Ṭāhā's source for the point he makes concerning the necessity of studying archives and chancellery records in an adequate historical enquiry.[88]

Further information on modern historical methodology seems to have been derived from section 2 of Massignon's concluding lecture (XL) which is devoted to a discussion of the problem of history and witnesses (*al-tārīkh wa'l-shuhūd*), said to cover three methodological questions (*masā'il uṣūliyya*). The interesting thing about this discussion is that it appears to take issue with a certain tradition of historiographical thought, which came to be represented at the turn of the century by Langlois and Seignobos, especially in their famous manual on positivist historical methodology, *Introduction aux études historiques* (1898). To bring out more clearly the relevance of this discussion to Ṭāhā, we may consider the three questions, arranged here according to a different order of priority:

(1) Which are more reliable, oral testimonies or written ones?

Under this heading, Massignon criticizes the modern European practice, going back three hundred years, of showing, he says, too much respect for written documents (*al-mutūn al-maktūba*); and he commends the Islamic preference for the spoken word (*al-ḥadīth*) or oral reports in collecting the Prophet's traditions. For Massignon, reliance on this latter type of report, when accompanied by criticism of the transmitter's character, is sounder than reliance on written documents, even when supported by [palaeographic] criticism of the characteristics of paper, writing and seal. In other words, as against the Western bias for the critical investigation of written testimonies by means of auxiliary sciences, Massignon shows preference for the typically Islamic criticism of oral testimonies known as *al-jarḥ wa'l-ta'dīl* (disparaging and declaring trustworthy).[89]

(2) Which testimonies are more credible, those given by ordinary uneducated people or rather those given by the literate elite?

Massignon's preference goes to the former class of testimony; for while ordinary people are apt to speak their mind openly and with no ulterior motive, educated people are easily swayed by their own ideas, giving to theories the priority over the facts.[90]

The point is then illustrated with reference to the question of miracles, on which, says Massignon, historians are divided: while there is a first group of historians who admit the occurrence of historical events described as miracles in numerous reports backed by diverse chains of transmission (*musnada*) in all nations and ages, there is a second group who would deny the very possibility of such events, cast doubt on all reported miracles and would simply rule them out[91] without giving, according to their own theory, a scientific reason based for instance on the criticism of document, writing or witnesses. This, contends Massignon, is a [methodological] drawback (*nuqṣān*); a good historian should be ready to admit any report concerning a historical event as long as it is supported by an authentic chain of transmission, and even if it clashs with his own personal point of view.[92]

(3) Who is more trustworthy, a witness giving testimony in secret or a witness giving testimony in public?

Most scholars, Massignon points out, believe that historical accounts often contain what is called official lies (*mensonge officiel, al-kadhib al-rasmī*). Among the examples given are "the inscriptions made by Assyrian kings, which contain numerous lies" and "Napoleon's proclamations to his soldiers".[93] In view of this, comments Massignon, it would be better for the historian to take into account public as well as secret testimonies, collating the ones against the others.

To illustrate the point, Massignon advises his listeners not to accept the Ash'arites' denunciations of their Mu'tazilite adversaries without checking them against the latters' writings found in the Yemen.[94] His Arabic at this point is both clumsy and cryptic, but the essential point may be restated as follows: Never trust the Ash'arites' official depiction of their Mu'tazilite enemies without taking into account the proscribed and virtually clandestine writings of this latter vanquished party.

For this discussion of the three methodological questions to be fully appreciated, it is necessary to note how it reflected Massignon's preoccupations at the time. He was then fully engaged in what was to become his lifetime commitment to the cause of al-Ḥallāj, and he must have had taken the decision to apply in his thesis on al-Ḥallāj's passion[95] the Islamic criticism of oral traditions as transmitted through the non-official testimonies of the mystic's persecuted followers and through popular legend. It is in this context that we should read Massignon's objections to what he regarded as a characteristically Western bias for written, preferably official, sources and for scientific opinion.

The fact that he discusses these issues in terms of concepts such as "witness" and "testimony" shows that his criticisms were particularly aimed at a group of methodological theorists who had recently given historical criticism a juridical turn, treating documents as testimonies and the authors of these as witnesses. Initiated by Père de Smedt in his *Principes de la critique historique* (1883), the move was taken up by other scholars, especially Charles Seignobos who, while accepting the juridical point of view, subjected it to a set of "scientific" reservations and criteria.[96] Viewed from this angle, Massignon's otherwise terse and cryptic comments begin to reveal their secrets.

With regard to question (1), the main, if not the only, target for criticism seems to be Langlois and Seignobos, who are known to have consecrated the Western historical practice of only trusting the written word. For them, the historian works necessarily with documents; where there are no documents, there is no history.[97] They would not qualify this judgement even when they take into account "the ancient collections of Arab tradition [which] give lists of their successive guarantors".[98] This is undoubtedly because Langlois and Seignobos believe that whereas writing fixes a statement and ensures its being transmitted faithfully,[99] oral tradition is by its nature a process of continual alteration, which degenerates inevitably into legend[100] and from which it is impossible to extract any trustworthy information by any procedure.[101]

Concerning question (2), Massignon's criticisms do not seem to be addressed to Langlois and Seignobos alone. They would certainly come under attack inasmuch as they advocate the point of view of the educated elite, in this case the scientists, as against the uncultured multitude. For both authors, legend, as we have just seen, is inextricably bound up with oral tradition; "it arises", they write, "among groups of men with whom the spoken word is the only means of transmission, at least in barbarous societies, or in classes of little culture, such as peasants and soldiers".[102]

Concerning miracles, both authors would again come within the range of Massignon's criticisms, for although aware that testimonies about miracles "have filled the documents of every people",[103] and that such facts could be established through historical examination, Langlois and Seignobos would still reject them or hold them to be improbable as long as they contradict the findings of science.[104] However, the two authors would not claim that miracles are impossible (or that they are possible for that matter),[105] nor would they say that miracles should be rejected prior to critical examination; and to this extent they do not seem to qualify as the primary target of Massignon's criticisms. So he probably had in mind some other writer(s) with a more extreme position on the subject.

Finally and as far as question (3) is concerned, Massignon's criticisms, if any, could have only been aimed at someone who advocated reliance on public testimonies exclusively or mainly. It is only in this case that Massignon's rejoinder concerning the need to collate such testimonies against secret ones would naturally follow. If this is so, then the most likely target of this criticism would be Père de Smedt (rather than Langlois and Seignobos), who advises the critical historian to show prudence in using (private) memoirs and secret reports.[106]

Be that as it may, there can be no doubt that Massignon's discussion of these methodological questions had an influence on Ṭāhā, except that this influence did not always work according to Massignon's intentions. For on the first two of the three issues discussed by Massignon, Ṭāhā can be shown to have adopted the very "positivist" position that the former combated. On question (1), we have already seen how Ṭāhā took to task critically-minded Arab historians, including Ibn Khaldūn, for their exclusive reliance on oral traditions and their failure to realize the scientific importance of documents. On question (2), Ṭāhā's contention that miracles have no place in history or logic comes so close to the extreme position that Massignon criticized, namely that reports about miracles should be excluded without examination.

As far as question (3) is concerned, Ṭāhā tends on the whole to agree with Massignon. Thus the latter's remarks about the official lies propagated by Assyrian kings is developed and amplified by Ṭāhā when he denounces the fantastic exaggerations and unfounded claims inscribed by the Pharaohs of Egypt and the Assyrians on their respective monuments, with the sole purpose of glorifying and even deifying the sovereign.[107] Again, Massignon's warning against exclusive reliance on the official point of view may have had an influence on Ṭāhā Ḥusain when he argues that in writing on Islamic conquests under the Orthodox Caliphs, it would not be sufficient to take into account the relevant Arab sources only, and that it would also be necessary to consider other versions given by conquered nations.[108]

It would seem therefore that Massignon's influence was crucial on Ṭāhā's writings of 1914. While it cannot be conclusively proved that he supplied Ṭāhā with the required information on Taine, the likelihood of this hypothesis is considerably enhanced by the fact that the French orientalist supplied so many of the ingredients of Ṭāhā's systematic objectivism and his knowledge of positivist historiography.

The fact that Massignon's influence did not always work according to his intentions, that his own combat against positivism made it possible for Ṭāhā to discover and side with the opposite camp, brings us to a final point about the timeliness and appropriateness of Massignon's teachings. He was unique among Ṭāhā's foreign teachers in that he knew better than any of them how to bring into sharp focus the relations, whether harmonious or antagonistic, between modern European culture and Islamic traditions. Massignon did not do so out of mere erudition or a neutral interest in comparative study: he was in fact practising what he was to call the "science of compassion", which, whatever its limits,[109] sought to do full justice to the traditions in question, highlighting their continued relevance or their relative merits by comparison with European culture. It is in this spirit that Massignon was able to see that Islamic theological and mystical doctrines were relevant in a discussion of Western materialist determinism, and to set the Islamic criticism of transmitters (*al-jarḥ wa 'l-ta'dīl*) against the Western critique of written sources, giving his preference to the Islamic side. This manner of presentation was most timely and most appropriate in Ṭāhā's case; it was in a sense all that he needed in order to reach his final positivist position. For Ṭāhā, as a former Azhari in search of modernism, nothing could have been more stimulating or enlightening than that debate as conducted by Massignon. All that Ṭāhā had to do was to turn the latter's argument the other way round, resetting it in favour of the modern positivist camp. Massignon's science of compassion was counteracted by Ṭāhā's search for modernism.

We should, however, resist the temptation of giving all the credit to Massignon. Since Ṭāhā's views are never a mere reflection of those of Massignon, we can never rule out the possibility that other influences were involved. This caution is all the more necessary in view of the many gaps in our knowledge: we have no complete collection of Ṭāhā's early writings, no complete record of the lectures he attended at the Egyptian University, no exhaustive survey of contemporary periodical literature, no account whatsoever of Ṭāhā's informal discussions with his foreign teachers, and no detailed information on what went on within Luṭfī al-Sayyid's circle. These numerous gaps should impose an element of caution.

To sum up: by the time Ṭāhā was ready to leave for France in November 1914, he had already established his own brand of modernism on stringent positivist bases. The first step along this path had been taken in the 1911 articles, written mainly under the influence of Nallino and more or less within the limits of his mild and open-ended objectivism. A second and final step had been taken in the 1914 writings, in which Ṭāhā adopted systemic objectivism, a position about which he had probably learnt from Massignon, but which did not coincide with the standpoint of either orientalist. In so doing, Ṭāhā had managed to establish direct links with France.

Later, when he went to the Sorbonne, which was then dominated by positivism, he was to study under Seignobos as well as other prominent positivists such as Durkheim and Lévi-Bruhl. What he was to learn there was new in many respects, but it was also familiar and relevant, as he was already a convinced positivist who had made up his mind about some of the issues occupying his masters. By the same token, he was to discover that he was deeply involved in the then rampant debates within the positivist camp. More specifically, the existence of different, sometimes antagonistic, factions of positivists was to shake his belief in his own systemic objectivism. From that point onward, he was to embark on an endless process of readjustment and revision. But try as he might, some of the positions he had reached in his early writings were to die hard, if at all.

Notes

1 For instance, Kamāl Qulta, *Ṭāhā Ḥusain wa-athar al-thaqāfa al-Faransiyya fī adabih* (Cairo 1973), p. 94 ff.; Miftah Tahar, *Ṭāhā Ḥusayn, sa critique littéraire et ses sources françaises* (Tunis 1976), p. 45 ff.; and Anouar Louca, "Taha Hussein et l'Occident", *Cultures,* II (1975), pp. 118–142.
2 Anouar Louca, "Taha Hussein ou la continuité de deux rives", *Qantara,* July-August 1992, dossier spécial, pp. vii-viii.
3 Aḥmad 'Ulbī, *Ṭāhā Ḥusain, qiṣṣat mukāfiḥ 'anīd* (Beirut 1990), p. 107.
4 A most striking example is that of Aḥmad 'Ulbī who offers in his *Ṭāhā Ḥusain, rajul wa-fikr wa-'aṣr* (Beirut 1985) what must count as the most detailed study so far of the period in question, but relies exclusively on secondary materials.
5 For a list of their names, see Muḥammad Ḥusain Haykal, *Mudhakkirāt fī al-siyāsa al-Miṣriyya* (Cairo 1990), vol. I, p. 32.
6 Ṭāhā Ḥusain, *A Passage to France* (Leiden 1976), p. 49.
7 Ibid., pp. 44 and 49.
8 Ibid., pp. 46 ff.
9 Ibid., pp. 50 ff.
10 "Naqd ṣāḥib *al-Hilāl*" I, *H,* June-July 1911, p. 453.
11 Ibid. By this Ṭāhā means Arabic *belles-lettres* as distinct from Arabic science.
12 "Naqd ṣāḥib *al-Hilāl*" III, *H,* October-November 1911, pp. 766–767
13 Ibid., p. 767
14 "Naqd ṣāḥib *al-Hilāl*" II, *H,* August-September 1911, pp. 608 and 623.
15 "Ḥayāt al-ādāb" V, *J,* 29 January 1914.
16 Ibid.
17 "Ḥayāt al-ādāb" VIII, *J,* 28 February 1914.
18 For Ibn Khaldūn's pronouncements on the subject, see *The Muqaddima. An Introduction to history,* tr. Franz Rosenthal (London 1986), vol. I, pp. 320–321 and 330.
19 Ibid., p. 437.
20 Ṭāhā Ḥusain, op. cit.
21 It was partly as a development of these early reflections that Ṭāhā Ḥusain contended in *Fi'l-shi'r al-jāhilī* ("On pre-Islamic poetry") (1926) that the Qur'ān was the first authentic document in Arab history, which provided a true picture of the linguistic and religious conditions prevailing in Arabia before Islam. Later, in 1928, he argued that the Qur'ān was the only authentic text of Arabic prose of the early history of Islam. See Taha Hussein, "De l'emploi dans le Coran du pronom personnel de la troisième personne comme démonstratif. Mémoire présenté au XVII Congrès d'Orientalistes" (Paris 1928), p. 4.
22 We shall have more to say on the subject in the conclusion.
23 See Ch.-V. Langlois and Ch. Seignobos, *Introduction to the study of history,* tr. G.G. Berry (London 1912), p. 237. See also Ernst Cassirer, *The Problem of knowledge. Philosophy, science and history since Hegel* (New Haven-London 1969), pp. 265 ff.

24 On Voltaire's pioneering contribution to the debate on political history versus history of civilization, see Ernst Cassirer, op. cit., pp. 265–266. In his *Essai sur les mœurs,* Chap. LXXXIV, Voltaire writes: "je considère ... le sort des hommes plutôt que les revolutions du trône. C'est au genre humain qu'il eût fallu faire attention dans l'histoire : c'est là que chaque écrivain eût dû dire: *Homo sum*; mais la plupart des historiens ont écrit des batailles". As quoted by J. Ehrard et G. Palmade, *L'Histoire* (Paris 1964), p. 44.

25 "Hitherto", writes Saint-Simon, "*history* has been badly divided. The different successive periods recognized by the School are very unequal in length, and the epochs to which these divisions correspond are not based on the general series of the development of the human intelligence, but are always determined according to secondary or local events. Historians have fixed their attention on political, religious or military facts; they have not adopted a sufficiently elevated point of view". Italics in the original. The quotation is part of an extract from *Introduction aux travaux scientifiques du XIX siècle,* 2 vols., 1807–8, as selected by Keith Taylor, in *Henri Saint-Simon (1760–1825) Selected writings on science, industry and social organization* (London 1975), p. 94. See also the pertinent remarks made by Durkheim on Saint-Simon's conception of history in *Socialism and Saint-Simon,* tr. Charlotte Sattler, ed. Alvin Goulder (London 1959), pp. 102 and 103.

26 In his *Cité antique,* Fustel tries to show that religious faith was the determining factor behind the whole social and political constitution of society in ancient Greece and Rome, but he would not generalize this model to all societies at all times. For him, the basic social stratum throughout history is not religion, but the inner being of man. "If", he writes, "the laws of human association are no longer the same as in antiquity, it is because there has been a change in man. There is, in fact, a part of our being which is modified from age to age; this is our intelligence. It is always in movement, almost always progressing, and on this account, our institutions and our laws are subject to change." See Numa Denis Fustel de Coulanges, *The Ancient city,* with a forward by Arnaldo Momigliano and S.C. Humphreys (Baltimore-London 1991), p. 4.

27 Cassirer, op. cit., pp. 320–321. See also ibid., p. 318.

28 Gerard Delfau and Anne Roche, *Histoire/Littérature; Histoire et interprétation du fait littéraire* (Paris 1977), p. 51 ff.

29 Auguste Comte, *Introduction to positive philosophy,* ed. Frederick Ferré (Indianapolis 1988), p 2.

30 Ibid., p. 10.

31 Ibid., p. 12.

32 Albert Hourani, *Arabic thought in the liberal age 1898–1939* (Cambridge 1984), p. 138 ff.

33 See Jamal Mohammed Ahmad, *The Intellectual origins of Egyptian nationalism* (Oxford 1968), p. 102.

34 *Muḥāḍarāt,* p. 135. It may be noted also that Massignon (ibid., p. 167) deals with Comte's classification of the sciences.

35 Hippolyte Taine, *Philosophie de l'art* (Paris 1985), p. 19. As quoted by René Wellek, *A History of modern criticism 1750–1950* (Cambridge 1983), p. 39.
36 Ṭāhā Ḥusain, *Tajdīd dhikrā Abi'l-'Alā',* in *MK*, vol. XI, 1974, p. 24.
37 Taine, op. cit., p. 39, as quoted by Welleck, op. cit., p. 39.
38 Ṭāhā Ḥusain, op. cit., p. 11.
39 H.A. Taine, *History of English literature,* tr. H. Van Laun (Edinburgh 1871), vol. I, p. 6. See also idem., *Philosophie de l'art* (Paris 1985), pp. 16–17.
40 Taine, op. cit., p. 5.
41 Ṭāhā Ḥusain, op. cit., p. 24. See also idem, "Ḥayāt al-ādāb" VII, *J*, 7 February 1914.
42 Taine, *History of English literature,* vol. I, p. 6.
43 Ṭāhā Ḥusain, *Tajdīd dhikrā Abi'l-'Alā',* p. 24.
44 Taine, op. cit., p. 1.
45 Ṭāhā Ḥusain, op. cit., p. 24.
46 Ibid., p. 24, n. 1.
47 I owe this qualification to Miftah Tahar, op. cit., p. 50.
48 Ṭāhā Ḥusain, op. cit., p. 288.
49 Ibid pp. 286 ff.
50 Cf. Miftah Tahar, op. cit., p. 51.
51 See L. Gardet, *EI*[2] art. "Kasb". See also W.M. Watt, *Islamic philosophy and theology* (Edinburgh 1979), p. 86.
52 Expounding the Stoics' monism, Santillana writes "... The whole [system] depends on the cause of all causes ... The world as a whole is a cause and is caused and there is no place in it for accident or coincidence ... Fate is nothing but the succession and connection of causes. Nothing happens unless it is predetermined in the past, and nothing will happen in the future unless it has its reason in the present". Santillana, *al-Madhāhib,* p. 83.
53 "This world, with all the created things in it," writes Ibn Khaldūn, "has a certain order and solid construction. It shows nexuses between causes and things caused, combinations of some parts of creation with others ..." *The Muqaddima,* vol. I, p. 194. See also ibid., vol. III, p. 34 for Ibn Khaldūn's belief in thoroughgoing causality, i.e. the thesis that "causes continue to follow upon causes in an ascending order, until they reach the causer of causes".
54 Ibid., vol. I, p. 188.
55 Ibn Khaldūn, as we have just seen, advocated determinism in history. This fact was expressly recognized by Ṭāhā in his dissertation on the Arab historian. See T. Hussein, *Etude analytique et critique de la philosophie sociale d'Ibn-Khaldoun* (Paris 1917), p. 45, where Ibn Khaldūn is said to have anticipated Montesquieu on the idea of determinism in history.
56 Miftah Tahar, op. cit., p. 49.
57 Taine, *History of English literature,* vol. I, pp. 5, 10 and 19.
58 Ibid., pp. 10–11. There are, according Taine, three main races or groups of races: the Aryans, the Chinese and the Semites. See ibid., pp. 8–9.

59 Ibid., p. 9 and pp. 11–12.
60 Ibid., pp. 12–13.
61 Ibid., p. 19.
62 Ibid., p. 14.
63 See Miftah Tahar (op. cit., p. 50 and ibid., n. 23) who points out that no translation of Taine's works is mentioned by J. Tajir in his *Ḥarakat al-tarjama bi-Miṣr khilāl al-qarn al-tāsi' 'ashar* (Cairo n.d.) or by J.E. Sarkis in his *Dictionnaire encyclopédique de bibliographie arabe* (Cairo 1930).
64 The main, if not the only, such account to have been revealed so far is the one to be found in Quṣṭākī al-Ḥimṣī's *Manhal al-wurrād fī 'ilm al-intiqād* (Cairo 1907) vol. I, p. 89 and p. 151. On this point, see Jābir 'Uṣfūr, *al-Marāya al-mutajāwira. Dirāsa fī naqd Ṭāhā Ḥusain* (Cairo 1983), pp. 62–63, n. 72. But the information provided by al-Ḥimṣī on Taine is too rudimentary to account for Ṭāhā's more specific knowledge of the subject. Notice also that Rouchdi Fakkar in his *Aux origines des relations culturelles contemporaines entre la France et le monde arabe* (Paris 1973), has surveyed the Arabic periodical literature in the nineteenth century and has found no contributions on Taine.
65 The suggestion, made by Miftah Tahar (op. cit., p. 50), is taken up as a foregone conclusion by Aḥmad Būḥasan in his *al-Khiṭāb al-naqdī 'ind Ṭāhā Ḥusain* (Beirut 1985), p. 61.
66 See above, ch. IV, p. 81.
67 See above, p. 102.
68 Massignon, op. cit., p. 134.
69 Ibid., op. cit., p. 95. For Ṭāhā's rejection of the Ash'arites' views on *kasb*, see above, pp. 131–132.
70 Ibid., op. cit., p. 140.
71 Ibid.
72 Ibid., pp. 51–52.
73 Ibid., p. 52.
74 Ṭāhā Ḥusain, "Ustādhī wa-ṣadīqī Louis Massignon", in *Dhikrā: Louis Massignon* (Cairo 1963), pp. 27–30, p. 27.
75 L. Massignon, "Rapport : Mission d'études sur le mouvement des idées philosophiques dans le pays de langue arabe". A photocopy of this report, typewritten in Paris in July 1913, has been made available to me by courtesy of Daniel Massignon and Christian Destrenau. The latter has produced, in collaboration with Jean Moncelon, the latest biography of Massignon. It was they (see C. Destrenau and J. Moncelon, *Massignon*, Paris, 1994, p. 104) who drew my attention to the existence of this report. To be henceforth referred to as "Rapport".
76 Namely Tawfīq Mar'ashlī. See the opening paragraph in the editor's preface to Massignon's *Muḥāḍarāt.*
77 Ṭāhā Ḥusain, op. cit., p. 27.
78 Massignon attended a course in logic at the Azhar in 1910. See Destrenau and Moncelon, op. cit., pp. 86–87. Given by Shaykh Dusūqī, the course is dealt with by Massignon in his "Rapport".
79 For Massignon's treatment of this subject, see his *Muḥāḍarāt*, p. 39.

80 In an article entitled, "Malāmiḥ min al-ru'ya al-tārīkhiyya 'ind Ṭāhā Ḥusain", *al-Ḥayāt al-Thaqāfiyya* (Tunis), No. 55, 1990, pp. 25–32, 'Umar Miqdād al-Jumaynī holds the view (see pp. 25–26) that Ṭāhā's positivist conception of history as a science could not have been derived from his teachers, whether Egyptian or foreign, at the Egyptian University, and that the conception in question was acquired only later at the Sorbonne thanks to Charles Seignobos and others.

81 Nallino's role in this respect was of less importance, in view of the fact that, unlike Massignon, he did not address the subject explicitely.

82 *Muḥāḍarāt*, pp. 133, 134, 135.

83 A highly suggestive term as it must have reminded Ṭāhā of the Islamic discipline, *uṣūl al-fiqh* (principles of jurisprudence) for its fundamental importance as a kind of logic for jurisprudence. In his *Etude analytique et critique de la philosophie sociale d'Ibn-Khaldoun* (Paris 1917), pp. 34–35, Ṭāhā argues that the idea of establishing a new science of sociology (as an auxiliary discipline for history) might have been suggested to Ibn Khaldūn by *uṣūl al-fiqh*. It may be noted again that in *Tajdīd dhikrā Abi'l-'Alā'* p. 32, Ṭāhā speaks of *al-fiqh al-tārīkhī* to mean roughly the true historical spirit or historical criticism.

84 Ibid., p. 16.

85 Massignon's use of *'ilm al-ṭuqūs* (lit.: the study of rites) as a name for the discipline concerned is odd and hard to explain.

86 Massignon, op. cit., p. 132.

87 Ṭāhā Ḥusain, "Ḥayāt al-ādāb" IV, *J*, 26 January 1914. Cf. Massignon's characterization of palaeography (op. cit., p. 132) as the study of [ancient] writings on paper (*qirṭās*). See also his reference (ibid., p. 208) to "the investigation of the characteristics of paper (*qirṭās*), script (*khaṭṭ*) and seal".

88 Ṭāhā Ḥusain, op. cit.

89 See J. Robson, *EI*^{2} art. "al-Djarḥ wa'l-Ta'dīl".

90 Massignon, op. cit., p. 208.

91 Ibid., p. 208. This is how I read roughly Massignon's obscure "*wa-yaqṭa' dhikrahā 'anhā*".

92 Ibid.

93 Ibid., p. 207.

94 Ibid.

95 The work was begun in Cairo in 1907. See Louis Massignon, *La Passion de Ḥallāj, martyr mystique de l'Islam* (Paris 1975), vol. I, p. 17, n. 2. On the same page Massignon points out that the course of lectures he delivered in Cairo in 1912–1913 allowed him to press on with his study on the origins of al-Ḥallāj's technical lexicon.

96 See Ch. Seignobos, *La méthode historique appliquée aux sciences sociales* (Paris 1901), p. 30 ff. See also Langlois and Seignobos, op. cit., p. 156 ff.

97 Ibid., p. 17.

98 Ibid., p. 178.

99 Ibid., p. 180.

100 Ibid., p. 180–181. Cf. Seignobos, op. cit., p. 76.
101 Langlois and Seignobos, op. cit, p. 183.
102 Ibid., p. 181.
103 Ibid., p. 207.
104 Ibid., p. 206 ff.
105 "Science knows nothing of the possible or the impossible . . .", ibid., p. 206, n. 2.
106 P. Ch. de Smedt, S.J., *Principes de la critique historique* (Liège-Paris 1883), p. 120.
107 Ṭāhā Ḥusain, "Ḥayāt al-ādāb" V and VII, *J*, 7 February 1914 and 28 February 1914, respectively. It should be noted, however, that in making this point, Ṭāhā was also influenced by Nallino, who, in his *Tārīkh* (pp. 228–229) criticized Arab historical works for relying mainly on official sources or the testimony of the victorious side.
108 "Ḥayāt al-ādāb" V, *J*, 7 February 1914.
109 See Edward W. Said, "Islam, the philological vocation, and French culture: Renan and Massignon" in Malcolm H. Kerr (ed.), *Islamic studies: A tradition and its problems* (California 1980), pp. 53–72.

CHAPTER VI

The Twilight of Positivism

The Sweet voice

On 14th November 1914 Ṭāhā Ḥusain's long-cherished dream of being able to study in France came true, as he left Alexandria by ship on his first journey ever out of Egypt. He, together with a number of fellow students, were sent to Montpellier rather than to Paris, where they could study safely away from the dangers of war. For Ṭāhā, the journey meant the beginning of a completely new life. As soon as he was on board, he took off his Azhari garments in order to sport a Western suit.[1]

As the purpose of his mission was to obtain a *licence* in the Arts – in history in particular – he needed to be proficient in French and Latin. His studies in Montpellier were therefore preparatory, covering French, French literature and history,[2] apart from private tuition in Latin.

However, Ṭāhā's stay in Montpellier did not last long, for he, together with his companions, were abruptly called back to Cairo as a result of a severe financial crisis affecting the Egyptian University. Less than a year after his departure for France,[3] Ṭāhā was back in Cairo, with his dreams shattered and also with a broken heart. For it was in Montpellier that Ṭāhā met Suzanne Bresseau, the girl from Burgundy who was to be his reader before becoming his fiancée and then his wife.[4]

On their first encounter, one memorable day in May 1915, she was intimidated by his blindness,[5] while he was enchanted by her voice as he listened to her recite some verses by Racine.[6] It was then that he felt the doors of a new kind of happiness were opening for him. It was she, the "sweet voice" as she came to be called, who held the key.

Although his stay in Cairo was not idle,[7] the lovesick Ṭāhā was in utter despair, pouring his heart out in prose and verse.[8] Luckily for him, the Egyptian University soon made financial recovery and sent him back to France towards the end of 1915. This time, however, he was to go to Paris to study at the Sorbonne. It was possible for him there to be with his sweetheart again. But before going any further in relating Ṭāhā's love story, we need to pause momentarily in order to consider certain developments relating to the Montpellier period.

Reflections on al-Khansā'

Little is known about Ṭāhā's life in Montpellier. The period tends to be glossed over by Ṭāhā Ḥusain as well as by his biographers. His first encounter with Suzanne (vaguely described), the list of courses he attended at the University, his achievement of proficiency in French and his first steps in the study of Latin – these are more or less the bare facts relating to the period. The rest is obscure; so far we know almost nothing about the intellectual climate prevailing at the university and hardly anything about his teachers there.

This obscurity can be partly dispelled, however, if we take into account a series of two articles on the life of the pre-Islamic poetess al-Khansā', which Ṭāhā wrote during his brief return to Cairo, but which carry clear marks of the Montpellier period.

Published under the title "Ḥayāt al-Khansā'" (the life of al-Khansā')[9] and dedicated to al-Ānisa Ṣubḥ (Miss Ṣubḥ),[10] the two articles, neglected until fairly recently,[11] shed new light on the evolution of Ṭāhā's thought in Montpellier and even herald subsequent developments in Paris and thereafter.

The main thesis put forward in "Ḥayāt al-Khansā'" is that the poetess, and indeed all pre-Islamic poets, have no historical character or are not historical figures. As the author makes it clear, if he chooses to limit his discourse to the poetess, it is only because the subject is of special interest to Miss Ṣubḥ, who would dispute his claim as regards al-Khansā'[12] and who played a role herself as a female talent in the intellectual and emotional life of the nation.

We may recall that earlier on in 1914 Ṭāhā had already expressed doubts concerning the authenticity of some of the lore described as pre-Islamic poetry. His scepticism is now extended to the historical status of <u>all</u> pre-Islamic poets. As far as he is concerned, they are the subject of prehistory, or what in his view comes to the same thing, legendary figures (des *personnes légendaires*).[13] This thesis is reached as a conclusion to two premises, the first of which concerns the absolute necessity of written documents to history. In Ṭāhā's view, history according to its "modern practitioners and methodological theorists" (*aṣḥābuh wa-wāḍi'ū manāhijih min al-muḥdathīn*) is only what can be critically derived from a written source; where there is no such a source, there is no history either.[14] The thesis, so attributed, can be legitimately traced to Langlois and Seignobos.[15]

The second premise is an observation to the effect that al-Khansā', and other pre-Islamic poets for that matter, lived before the advent of history, at a time when writing was not common among the Arabs.[16]

This is certainly a radically new development. Notice how Ṭāhā's position has evolved over the years. In 1911 he assumed that the efflorescence of pre-Islamic poetry marked the beginning of historical Arabic.[17] Later, in 1914, he associated prehistory with the absence of writing,[18] a thesis which implies that pre-Islamic poetry pertains to the prehistory of Arabic. But that conclusion was not drawn. Nor did Ṭāhā think at the time that prehistorical figures were necessarily legendary. His new conclusion, now explicitly drawn and applied to pre-Islamic poetry, seems to be the fruit of new information obtained in Montpellier, either through access to Langlois and Seignobos' work or from secondary sources, such as lectures or reading materials intended for students.

To describe a poet as a prehistorical figure does not imply, however, that the study of his work cannot be profitable for literature and history. Thus, according to the author of "Ḥayāt al-Khansā'", there is much to be learnt from the study of Homer's two great epic poems on the social and civic life of the Greeks during their archaic age (*jāhiliyya*). In fact, what can be learnt from Homer concerning that period is much more than whatever could be learnt from Pindar about his own age. As a poet who lived in a period when writing was common, Pindar is not the only or the most reliable source available to historians.[19]

Ṭāhā has only two reservations to make concerning knowledge obtained through the study of prehistorical poets. First, the texts concerned must be subjected to a "special" [critical] treatment; secondly, it must be borne in mind that the conclusions reached are only probable, as historical investigation can yield "indubitable truth" only when it is applied to written sources.[20]

With regard to al-Khansā' in particular, reports about her were only written down more than a century after her death. Ṭāhā therefore argues that it is possible, if not absolutely certain, that the traditions relating to her life and work were tampered with through forgetfulness[21] and/or carelessness of copyists and revisers.[22] What is even worse is that, according to Ṭāhā, the trustworthiness of the two major written sources on the poetess, namely Ibn Qutayba's *al-Shi'r wa'l-shu'arā'* and Abu'l-Faraj al-Iṣfahānī's *al-Aghānī*, need not be taken for granted. Apart from the need to investigate the attribution of these documents, the conditions of their reproduction and the possible mistakes of their copyists[23], the partiality and integrity of the two authors are not above doubt: the former is known through his work on *al-imāma wa'l-siyāsa*[24] for his Shī'ite bias,[25] while the latter is known for his loose morals.[26] On this latter point, Ṭāhā applies, as he himself acknowledges, the Islamic critical method of *al-jarḥ wa'l-ta'dīl* – adapted to literary purposes.[27] But it should be obvious by now that Ṭāhā's criticism of the two Arab sources on al-Khansā' bears the imprint of Langlois and Seignobos, as it follows some of their rules for the textual criticism of documents.[28]

Other influences are also detectable in Ṭāhā's remarks concerning Homer and Pindar, which demonstrate some awareness of the Homeric question. This awareness, it should be noted, was not first acquired in Montpellier and may be explained with reference to the influence of Arab sources, especially Sulaymān al-Bustānī's introduction to his translation of the *Iliad*, first published in 1904. That the author of "Ḥayāt al-Khansā'" was already familiar with the work in question is shown by the fact that, like al-Bustānī, he draws a parallel between the Greek archaic age and the Arab *jāhiliyya*, between Greek pre-classical poetry on the one hand and pre-Islamic poetry on the other.[29]

But al-Bustānī makes no significant references to Pindar and, unlike Ṭāhā, shows no reservations concerning the historical value of the *Iliad*[30]. Further knowledge on the Homeric question seems to have been acquired in Montpellier. But in what source(s) could have Ṭāhā found this additional knowledge? The question is intriguing and difficult to answer. The view that the Homeric poems, as well as legends in general, could, and should, be critically studied with a view to uncovering the kernel of truth hidden in them can be traced back to Alfred and Maurice Croiset's *Introduction à la littérature grecque* (1887). But apart from the fact that this view was not at the time the exclusive property of the Croisets (it had been put forward previously by several French and German classical scholars)[31], it is highly unlikely that Ṭāhā, as a mere beginner in Montpellier, could have tackled their monumental work (5 volumes). The most that could be said is that Ṭāhā obtained the knowledge in question from some secondary source deriving from the Croisets and/or other primary sources.

Thus far we have been concerned with the negative aspect of "Ḥayāt al-Khansā'". Now we may consider the positive side, which is no less intriguing. Taine, whose systemic objectivism was silently adopted in *Tajdīd dhikrā Abi'l-'Alā'*, is now mentioned by name and criticized for the first time. Ṭāhā proposes to study al-Khansā' according to an entirely new method. He would not, he says, conduct the enquiry in the traditional, and still prevailing, manner of narrating and collecting received reports; nor would he adopt the methodology of the philosophy of history which is not based on sound principles.[32] There is presumably a third way, which is that of Taine (in a revised version). "I subscribe", Ṭāhā writes, "to Taine's view, according to which al-Khansā' would be nothing but the fruit of her age and the result of her milieu ... But I would not give the whole credit to the age and the milieu, embracing thereby the extreme position of this critic-philosopher (*al-nāqid al-ḥakīm*); for besides these two factors, I take into account the psychological condition of the individual and the group."[33]

Before leaving for France, we may recall, Ṭāhā acknowledged the role of individual psychological factors in the process of literary creation. At the time, the admission of these factors was not incompatible with his Taineian objectivism, as he maintained that they were ultimately the outcome or extension of extra-subjective ones, whether physical or moral (i.e. relating to collective psychology)[34]. The situation is completely different now, as Ṭāhā assumes that the introduction of psychological factors, especially individual ones, constitutes a revision of Taine's position, now judged to be extreme. In making this assumption he is right, since the factors in question are no longer thought to be reducible to extra-subjective ones. "By the psychological condition," he writes, "I mean what the poet may possess as a characteristic issuing from his soul, and whose relation to the environment cannot be established by any historical or scientific means. We may be certain that the good poet or the talented writer has a [distinctive] character setting him apart from his contemporaries; it is also certain that the work of the poet or the writer is a manifestation of this character".[35] But this revision of Taine's system cannot be a mere coincidence, for it faithfully echoes Gustav Lanson's views on the necessity and irreducibility of the role played by subjective factors in the creative process.

It would seem, therefore, that "Ḥayāt al-Khansā'", written under the impact of Ṭāhā's experience in Montpellier, is a highly significant piece of work in more than one way. First, it reflects new influences which, with varying degrees of certainty, could be traced back to scholars (Seignobos, Alfred Croiset and Lanson) who were to teach Ṭāhā at the Sorbonne. Given that all these scholars belong in one way or another to the positivist tradition of thought, the text in question, like the earlier, "Ḥayāt al-ādāb", constitutes yet another example of Ṭāhā' endeavour to gain access to the original and most up-to-date sources of positivist thought.

Secondly, "Ḥayāt al-Khansā'" adds further weapons to Ṭāhā's sceptical arsenal relating to pre-Islamic poetry. Having equated what is not written with what is prehistorical and legendary, and having applied this dictum to pre-Islamic poets, Ṭāhā is only one step short of his 1926 scepticism concerning the authenticity of the bulk of pre-Islamic poetry. Furthermore, in his work on al-Khansā' he deploys the critical procedures of positivist historiography and adapts the traditional doubts concerning the unity and authorship of Homer's works to pre-Islamic poetry. Thirdly, and finally, the work in question heralds Ṭāhā's later adherence to Lanson's synthetic view of the types of factors involved in the creation of literary works.

A Love story

Arriving in Paris on 1st January 1916, Ṭāhā re-established contact with Suzanne almost immediately. After a few nights in a hotel, he went to live in a spare room at the family flat, in Avenue Denfert Rochereau,[36] within walking distance from the Latin Quarter. From then onward, his life was to take an entirely new turn, both emotionally and intellectually.

In the third volume of *al-Ayyām*, largely devoted to the Paris period, Ṭāhā Ḥusain gives a great deal of information on his studies at the Sorbonne, but very little is said, in concrete terms, about the French capital as he experienced it for the first time. It is rather strange for him to be almost completely silent on the environment, the space, that witnessed his great love story, and which he was to sing ever after. The same vagueness is again noticeable in *Adīb*, a novel also concerned with the same period, except Ṭāhā's role there is that of witness and narrator. Instead, we find in *Adīb* beautifully drawn and highly evocative scenes of Ṭāhā's native land in Upper Egypt.

The third volume of *al-Ayyām* contains none of the graphic descriptions of the physical world and none of the lively portraits of human beings which give the first two volumes their novel-like character and their beauty. Published in the form of memoirs,[37] the final part of Ṭāhā's autobiography proceeds as a series of reminiscences or anecdotes intermingled with occasional lyrical effusions concerning the love affair and its associations. Consequently, the basic structure underlying the first two volumes and which reflects the hero's attempt to break out of his confinement into the wider world, is no longer maintained. And yet, strangely enough, the third part of the story contains all the ingredients which, had they been fully exploited, could have made a masterpiece along the lines of the original design. Of Ṭāhā's confinement in Paris there can be no doubt. He himself relates how sometimes he used to spend the whole day in his room, lonely and helpless unless Suzanne came to see him;[38] and how, having confessed his love to her, he had to spend a whole month in Paris while she was away making up her mind.[39] During those long hours or days of waiting, he had to struggle with his old "companion" Abu'l-'Alā' who warned him of dependence on others,[40] painting for him a picture of the world as a place ruled by divine order, but untouched by God's grace. There is a passage in the work under discussion, where the author describes how he sometimes felt so alone that he doubted not only the existence of external nature but also his own existence. It was only through his beloved, he writes, that he regained his confidence in his identity and access to the world.[41]

So how are we to explain his failure to develop the narrative according to its original design? Why was it that by the time that he came to write the third instalment in his autobiography he had lost his verve or "virulence" as Jacques Berque put it?[42] It is probable that Ṭāhā Ḥusain was then hard pressed and distracted by other projects and preoccupations. It is also possible that he chose not to reveal in detail his life in Paris, including the part relating to his love story;[43] maybe he did not want other people to retain of his beloved woman anything but an abstract notion[44] as a sign of divine grace, a source of light and a "sweet voice".

Be that as it may, we know that after a month of waiting Ṭāhā received a positive signal from the south of France, informing him that he might join Suzanne and the family there. On his arrival, however, he discovered that the family still had certain fears and reservations: he was a foreigner, a blind man and, to make matters worse, a Muslim.[45] But thanks to the intervention of a maternal uncle who was a priest, the remaining obstacles were removed. After a stroll in the fields with the suitor, the clergyman had this to say to his niece: "You may go ahead with what you intend to do. Have no fear. In this man's company, no matter how high you raise the level of conversation, he will always surpass you".[46]

The picture is somewhat clearer with respect to the intellectual side of the story. Living with Suzanne's family constituted for Ṭāhā one of the four "schools" he attended in Paris, the three others being the Sorbonne, the Collège de France and the Sainte-Geneviève Library. Every evening after dinner the family (in this case Suzanne, her mother and sister as well as Ṭāhā) would have a reading session, with one of the ladies reading aloud from a novel, a play or a short story. In this way, Ṭāhā was introduced to the nineteenth-century French drama, as well as to works by Anatole France, Paul Bourget and [Marcel?] Prévost.[47]

Being herself a student at l'Ecole Normale de Sèvres, Suzanne was of great help to Ṭāhā in his studies. Apart from being part-time reader, she helped Ṭāhā improve his French, study Latin and, most important of all, draft his dissertation for the Doctorate. Without her moral and intellectual support, Ṭāhā's achievements, which were remarkable as we shall see immediately, would not have been possible.

He was sent to France in order to obtain a *licence* in history. This he did in July 1917, or less than three years after his arrival in Montpellier. His success was all the more remarkable in view of the fact that he was the first Egyptian ever to obtain that degree. During the same month of that year he was given permission to publish his thesis on Ibn Khaldūn,[48] which was submitted for the University Doctorate.[49] A year after his success in the oral examination which he had to pass (in 1918) in order to obtain this degree,[50] Ṭāhā was granted a higher diploma for which he had to write, under the supervision of Gustave Bloch, a dissertation on lawsuits brought against provincial governors for crimes of *lèse-majesté* in the Roman Empire, according to Tacitus.[51] The list is impressive. If we count the time spent in Montpellier as no more than a preparatory period, then we may say that Ṭāhā made all these achievements in the record time of four years.

The New Sorbonne

The subject of Ṭāhā Ḥusain's education and intellectual development in Paris constitutes a potentially vast area of enquiry to which we cannot do full justice here. We shall have to be selective and hope that the choices made will be justifiable. For this purpose we have two important criteria to guide our investigation, firstly, the findings already reached in relation to Ṭāhā's university education and early writings in Egypt. At the time of his arrival in France, he was not a neutral observer or a mere achiever avid for further knowledge and academic distinction. Rather, he was a convinced positivist who, moreover, put his ideas into print. Secondly, as we shall shortly show, positivism was then the major intellectual force in French academic life and at the Sorbonne in particular. Thus, instead of following the current practice of studying the subject piecemeal and according to the influence exerted by each thinker or teacher whom Ṭāhā came to know in Paris, we shall investigate such influences under a set of themes or issues which, while not claiming to exhaust the whole field of research, appear to be of the highest relevance, given the above-mentioned criteria.

In what follows, the reader will find almost an exhaustive list of the courses Ṭāhā attended and the masters who taught them, at the Sorbonne:[52]

Greek history	Gustave Glotz
History of Greek literature	Alfred Croiset[53]
Roman History	Gustave Bloch
Medieval and Byzantine history	Charles Diehl
Modern history	Charles Seignobos
The French Revolution	Alphonse Aulard
Sociology	Emile Durkheim & Celestin Bouglé (after Durkheim's death in 1917)

French literature	Gustave Lanson
Geography	M. Albert Demangeon
Cartesian philosophy	Lévi-Bruhl

Apart from these courses, Ṭāhā studied psychology under Pierre Janet and Qur'ānic exegesis under Paul Casanova at the Collège de France. Casanova and Durkheim together supervised Ṭāhā's thesis on Ibn Khaldūn.

Many of these subjects were completely new to Ṭāhā, and he had to make a special effort in order to catch up with his French fellow students. Also, given his earlier education at the Azhar and the Egyptian University, he was particularly ill-prepared for the study of Greek and Roman history. As for physical geography, it obviously posed special problems in view of his condition. These difficulties required a great deal of hard work and adaptation. And yet many things about the Nouvelle Sorbonne, as the University of Paris came to be called around 1902, must have appealed to him. Through a series of reforms introduced under the Third Republic, university education in France was freed from subservience to the needs of general education and utilitarian professional training, in order to be reoriented, according to the German model, to disinterested research. The new system was underpinned by a republican and laic ideology which was anti-clerical, anti-aristocratic and favourable to the production of a meritorious elite.[54] Though arriving several years after the introduction of these reforms, Ṭāhā could not have been unaware of their effect, as some of his teachers had been instrumental in putting these reforms into effect and/or providing their ideological rationale. Leaving republicanism apart, these reforms and ideological orientations could not have failed to recall for him the intellectual and sociological aspirations surrounding the establishment of the Egyptian University in 1908[55] and some of the teachings of Luṭfī al-Sayyid on education.[56]

The most congenial feature of the New Sorbonne was undoubtedly the ascendancy positivists came to enjoy there, partly as a result of their alliance with the state. Almost all of Ṭāhā's teachers were positivists, given a sufficiently loose definition of the term. Thus Seignobos, Durkheim, Bouglé (who was Durkheim's follower and assistant), Alfred Croiset, Glotz, Lévi-Bruhl, Lanson and Aulard may be described as positivists in one sense or another. Ṭāhā, who was a committed positivist himself and had been longing to learn the doctrine at its source, must have felt at home in that intellectual environment, seeing that it fulfilled his deepest wishes. Without minimizing the role of Ṭāhā's undeniable gifts or that of Suzanne's support, we may say that this fact must account, partly, for his remarkable achievements at the Sorbonne.

The new knowledge offered at the Sorbonne was well received, for it either confirmed his convictions or was considered by him as an improvement on his path to modernism. We shall see in the sequel that Ṭāhā's development both in France and thereafter reflected in many ways the state of positivism as he found it at the time.

The Positivist field

At that time, positivism was already past its heyday. Earlier on, and during a period stretching back to the eighties of the last century, the doctrine had already experienced a late outburst of energy marked by the rise of its adherents to unprecedented pre-eminence, both in the academic world and public life, and also by the birth of several social disciplines as "scientific" subjects *sui generis*, including history, sociology and the history of literature. By 1914, the main heroes of the story had already given their best, and were weakened by external attacks, internal feuds and the outbreak of war. But they were still around at the Sorbonne to tell their story and to act out the few remaining chapters.

Writers on the period under consideration (1880–1914) are agreed that the prevailing intellectual climate was permeated by positivism, considered as a diffuse orthodoxy in which Comte's doctrine was mediated by various simplifications, popularizations[57] and, we may add, serious and fruitful revisions.

But what do we mean by positivism? In the present work the term has been, and will continue to be, used in a fairly loose sense according to well-established conventions, so as to cover a wide variety of thinkers. What binds these thinkers together is their faith in the ideals of scientific knowledge as exemplified by the natural sciences, knowledge, that is, which is based, to say the least, on the observation or establishment of facts as revealed to the senses. Given this minimal definition which we propose tentatively and provisionally, we may introduce a number of refinements and distinctions. Leaving aside for the moment the fact that the formula "observation *or* establishment of facts" involves a potential source of disagreement among positivists, we may note first that the proposed definition would only meet one of two requirements laid down by Auguste Comte for positive knowledge in the law of the three states. According to this law, positive knowledge, having been based on facts, must proceed to formulating general causal laws.[58]

Thinkers like Taine and Fustel de Coulange, whom we may describe as early positivists, diverged from the founder of the doctrine and would disagree among themselves. Taine, it might be said, is somewhat closer to Comte to the extent that he would not, like Fustel, be satisfied with the establishment of facts, postponing or dropping altogether the need to arrive at general laws. But Taine, unlike Comte, did not believe that it was possible in history to formulate laws in the manner of established sciences. Instead, as we have already seen, he proposed to explain historical facts in terms of a law-like triadic formula (*race, milieu,* and *moment*) about the mind of each nation, a proposal which carries Hegel's imprint.[59]

Coming now to the period which concerns us here (namely 1880–1914), a late period in the history of the doctrine, we are able to see, in retrospect, that the cleavage between early positivists over what to take from and what to leave out of Comte, heralded in a way what was to come later. For apart from orthodox Comteans who adhered strictly to the master's ideas, including his philosophy of history as embodied in the above-mentioned law,[60] we are able to distinguish two classes of revisionist positivists who rejected Comte's philosophy of history and developed new disciplines or forms of knowledge purporting to be purely factual or aspiring to make law-like generalizations.

The first to appear on the scene and to establish their discipline as an independent science are a class of historians, to be described henceforth as "scientific", "methodical" or "documentary". They flatly rejected Comte's second condition, arguing that history was a purely descriptive science confined to the establishment of facts through the critical investigation of documents. With Fustel de Coulange as their immediate forerunner, scientific historians launched their programme in 1876 with the establishment of the *Revue Historique*[61] and reached their zenith towards the end of the century, when they completed the professionalization, institutionalization and codification of their discipline. At that time they came to be represented by Langlois and Seignobos, who gave the methodology of scientific history its final shape.[62]

The second class of revisionist positivists to attain distinction were sociologists, namely Durkheim, who fathered sociology as a science *sui generis* and codified its methodology, and his followers. They had their hour of glory with the appointment of their leader to the chair of the "Science of Education" at the Sorbonne in 1902, his subsequent rise as a great professor and a powerful administrator[63] or a "patron" as Clark would say.[64] They in turn established their organ, *L'Année Sociologique*, in 1896. Compared with Langlois and Seignobos, Durkheim was closer to Comte, for he assumed that the new science of sociology could aspire to the same status as natural sciences, satisfying the two conditions set by Comte for positivity. And yet, Durkheim was not an orthodox Comtean, if only because he rejected Comte's philosophy of history.

Beside these two main classes of revisionist positivists, we may again distinguish a third class, which is limited to one member, namely Lanson, who established, single-handly, the history of literature as an independent subject, and developed for that purpose a synthetic methodology combining several strands of thought from different sources, including Taine, the scientific historians and Durkheim. Lanson was no orthodox positivist either, if only because he believed that there was in the history of literature an irreducible place for a subjective, non-scientific element.

Recently, however, some writers have questioned the appropriateness of applying the title "positivist" to scientific historians who, it is said, are only tenuously related to Comte and who, it may again be argued, drew inspiration from other sources in German historiography of the nineteenth century, especially Von Ranke[65] or from still much older traditions of philological or historical criticism going back as far as the early eighteenth century[66] or earlier.[67] Other scholars would even go as far as to claim that Seignobos was not much of a "positivist", even when positivism is broadly defined.[68] But while we may agree or disagree about the origins and development of scientific history, I think that the established conventions concerning the use of the term "positivist" may be maintained, provided of course that further refinements and distinctions are made. There is in fact some advantage to be gained from referring such different schools to Comte, if only because they all seem to operate within the conceptual space that he opened up and delimited for a new science of man, sociological in character and inherently historical. There is, therefore, a need to study such a variety of thinkers with reference to Comte, whether they agree with him, or react against him.

Such, in very rough terms, was the state of positivist thought as it presented itself at the turn of the century until the outbreak of the First World War. Given this background, we may now proceed to consider some of the main influences that shaped Ṭāhā's development beyond that point in time. Prior to his arrival in France, we may recall, he had advocated a very simplified version of Comte's law of the three states and an equally simplified version of Taine's systemic objectivism. He had also some elementary but active knowledge of codified scientific history as well as some rudimentary notions about Durkheim.[69] In France, he improved his knowledge of Comte and Taine, studying them in the original. But the strongest influences exerted upon him came from his three revisionist teachers, Seignobos, Durkheim and Lanson, who represented the rising disciplines of scientific history, sociology and history of literature, respectively. Thanks to their influence, he came to give up, while still in France, the Comtean philosophy of history as well as his Taineian objectivism. And for many years after his departure from France, the combined influence of the three masters continued to mark his thought.

We shall begin our discussion of these influences by considering those of them which converged towards agreement on certain issues or rallying points and tended on the whole to confirm and refine Ṭāhā's earlier convictions.

Positivist reformism

As already indicated, the three masters, together with other Sorbonne positivists, were allied to the Third Republic. They supported and helped to carry out the Republic's educational reforms, including the establishment of the Nouvelle Sorbonne; they contributed intellectually to the development of the republic's ideology and enjoyed in return the necessary political backing for their rise to prominence.

They were all progressive reformists, where reform implied stopping short of supporting revolutionary change. As pointed out by George Weisz, republicanism at the time covered a wide spectrum of political views ranging from conservative republicanism to moderate socialism but excluding those Catholics who were vociferous in opposing the secularization of education, revolutionary socialists along with a few unrepentant monarchists.[70]

Leaving aside republicanism as such, many elements in the picture so far outlined agreed with Ṭāhā's own political and ideological convictions as a follower of Luṭī al-Sayyid and a sympathiser with the *Umma* party. This is particularly true of meritorious elitism and the importance attached to the role of intellectuals. The progressive reformism of Ṭāhā's masters, with its concern for stability, moderation and gradual change, corresponded to some of his deepest inclinations and must have strengthened his further development in the same direction. In the course of a long career of involvement in politics, he changed his loyalties more than once, but remained throughout his life deeply committed to liberal democracy. At times, especially in the late 1940s, he spoke as a radical or as a socialist, but he always assumed that the type of reform he called for was to be realized by peaceful means and was to enhance the intellectual or spiritual side of life.

Towards the end of the third volume of *al-Ayyām* the author relates how, on his way back to Egypt after the end of his study mission in France, he too, in an age of historical upheavals and transformations, dreamt of initiating a revolution in Egypt. But the revolution he had in mind was to be carried out peacefully and under the leadership of the intelligentsia, according to the teachings of Saint-Simon as expounded by Durkheim.[71]

It is true that later on Ṭāhā Ḥusain, as he himself goes on to explain, came to doubt the ability of intellectuals to rise above politics,[72] but he never doubted their ability, or duty for that matter, to play a leading role in society; nor did he ever lose faith in ideas as a driving force in history or as an initiator of revolutions.[73]

As late as twenty-one years after his return to Egypt, he was to defend the record of the Third Republic, the republic of professors and teachers, as it used to be called, against its critics.[74]

The reformism of Ṭāhā's teachers at the Sorbonne contained, however, an element which was more or less novel for him, namely, the theoretical limits which reform should never overstep.

For it was in Paris, and through the teachers in question, that Ṭāhā acquired, most probably for the first time, the essentials of his knowledge of, and his objections to, Marxism. Positivist historians and sociologists were unanimous in condemning Marxism as an interpretation of history. Thus Seignobos criticized Marx's economic interpretation of history, according to which economic organization constituted the infrastructure of social life as a whole.[75] This interpretation, Seignobos affirmed, was based on the vague idea that man was an animal, and was led therefore to postulate a material cause for all human actions, whether individual or collective, and also for the whole organization and evolution of society.[76]

Seignobos also criticized the materialist interpretation of history by invoking observed facts concerning the disinterested motivations of great men. In this vein, he wrote that "the apostles and martyrs of all religions, of all sciences, of all politics have always been characterized by their indifference to the material pleasures of which economic life is made. Human beings [especially the great among them] do not act for the sole purpose of attaining material pleasures."[77]

Durkheim in turn conducted his own critique of the materialist conception of history, arguing, among other things, that it was contrary to observed facts on which sociologists and historians agreed. "Sociologists and historians", he wrote, "tend increasingly to come together in their common affirmation that religion is the most primitive of all social phenomena. It is from it that have emerged, through successive transformations, all the other collective manifestations of collective activity – law, morality, art, science, political forms, etc."[78]

Following in Durkheim's footsteps, Bouglé castigated the materialist philosophy of history for having found in economic determination the sole key to social becoming, in other words for maintaining that law, morals, religion and art were nothing but "superstructures" or epiphenomena of economics.[79] He would not deny the role of economic forces in determining social developments. But he would affirm nevertheless that the last word in this domain belongs to conscience, a force which can bravely challenge our most palpable economic interests.[80]

As for Ṭāhā Ḥusain, his first reaction to Marxism was evasive: the least said, the better. When in the early 1950s he confronted the then rising champions of socialist realism in Egypt, he pretended first that their theses were incomprehensible: " it is all Greek to me" as he would say.[81] After this first ploy, however, he engaged his opponents in a headlong clash, showing that he understood perfectly what was at issue, except that his understanding was based *grosso modo* on the teachings of his old positivist masters. His opponents, he argued, assumed that literature should reflect social situations and facts, which was tantamount to saying that it should portray misery, hunger and people's needs for the amenities of life.[82] "Man according to these gentlemen and also according to their teachers," writes Ṭāhā Ḥusain, "was created in order to eat and lead a comfortable life; all his work, effort, thought, reflection, feelings and emotions must be devoted to one sole thing, namely to make social life more convenient and to satisfy those of people's needs which related to their bodies only."[83] In another place, Ṭāhā Ḥusain points out that some intellectuals might understand the call for literature to be for the sake of life as meaning that "literature must be put in the service of a certain modern doctrine on politics, philosophy and sociology, to the effect that literature ought to be dedicated to the task of convincing ordinary men and their likes that life is nothing but matter and that the human spirit and related faculties such as the mind and the heart are no more than myths"[84]

It should be noted that Ṭāhā's position, as so far expressed, is closer to Seignobos than to Durkheim. While Durkheim and Bouglé confined their criticisms to economic materialism considered as a thesis to the effect that economics constituted the ultimate explanation of social life or history, Seignobos, followed by Ṭāhā, went a step further, interpreting the same doctrine as a crude form of materialism to the effect that the ultimate aim of social life was the satisfaction of the base needs of the human animal.[85]

However, Ṭāhā seems to have been impressed by what looked like a concordance between the three masters on the primacy of ideational and spiritual factors and on the altruistic motivation of great men. On this latter point we may consider two Durkheimian lines of thought which appear to have had an important impact on Ṭāhā, contributing substantially to his mature reflections on a wide-ranging set of problems revolving around the place of the artist in society.

In his address to the lycéens of Sens, Durkheim asks, "Is it true that a great man consumes without any possibility of return, what is the best in the nation?". To this, he replies by saying: "It would no doubt be this way if the man of genius, once created, cut himself off from society and shut himself up in a proud solitude. But, unfortunately, as great and as disdainful as he may be, he is no less a man and cannot easily do without his fellow men. He needs the sympathy, the respect, and the admiration of the very people whose inferiority he disdains. He must return to the masses which have remained behind; he must hold out his hand in order to be followed, must instruct in order to be understood. He thereby repays, a hundred times over, all that has been loaned him".[86] This is tantamount to saying that while a great man may be inclined towards solitude, self-sufficiency or egocentrism, he is bound in the final analysis to show solidarity with his fellow men, for as a social being he needs them (just as much as they need him).

This argument from the basic social needs of great men is adopted as it stands by Ṭāhā, especially when he writes: "The man of letters who takes up writing is always deluding himself, pretending that he is neither concerned with other people nor thinks of them, and that he only writes to please his mind, heart and taste ... But ... as soon as he begins to write, he feels the pressing need to be read. Such is his nature that he needs to write; such is his nature that he has to communicate with others ..."[87]

But Durkheim has another reply to the above-mentioned question, in which he tries to explain the altruism of (at least some) great men with reference to their moral function, for they are so formed as to incarnate the ideal. "... Humanity," we are told, "was not made to taste easy and vulgar pleasures forever. It is therefore necessary that an elite be formed to make humanity scorn this inferior life, to tear it from this mortal repose, to urge it to move forward. That ... is the purpose served by great men. They are not solely destined to be the crowning of the universe, at once grandiose and sterile. If theirs is the privilege to incarnate the ideal here on earth, it is in order to make it visible to all eyes in a palpable form; it is in order to make it understood and loved. If, therefore, there are those among them who do not deign to look down upon the rest of their fellow men, who busy themselves exclusively with the contemplation of their own grandeur, or who isolate themselves in the enjoyment of their superiority, let us condemn them without a second thought. But for the others – and this is the greater number – for those who give themselves entirely to the masses, for those whose sole concern is for sharing with them their minds and their hearts, for those who, in whatever century they may have lived ... for those ... may we have only words of admiration and love. Let us respectfully proclaim them the benefactors of humanity".[88]

According to this line of thought, it is society which generates the impulse to rise above material pleasures and educates some individuals in such a manner as to enable them to lead the way to what is higher. This argument is reflected in Ṭāhā's view, propounded in several works, on literature as a true guiding mirror (*mir'āh ṣādiqa nāṣiḥa*) or a mirror of conscience.[89] According to this view, good literature brings human beings face to face with their failings and shortcomings and by thus reflecting the true state of affairs, so to speak, also expresses the higher ideals of humanity. In portraying what is the case, a writer also leads the way to what ought to be, acting sometimes against the reluctance, inertia or positive hostility of society. Literature, Ṭāhā Ḥusain would say, "is by its very nature meant for life at its best, highest and most enduring ...; life as it concerns the minds and the hearts, things which neither suffer death nor decay".[90]

However, Durkheim's second argument from the moral function of great men is not accepted in its entirety; it is present, but it is modified and somewhat diluted, as Ṭāhā Ḥusain tends to gloss over Durkheim's insistence on society as the source of, and driving force behind, the urge for what is higher. Ṭāhā would rather say that literature is good and altruistic by its very nature, that the artist, who holds the mirror of conscience for all to see, does so freely and of his own accord. "A man of letters," writes Ṭāhā, "does not create his literature with a view to realizing one purpose or another ... Literature is an end in itself; and the man of letters writes because he has no choice but to do so ... This does not mean that literature is sterile or that a man of letters is egoistic by nature; but it means that reform, change and improvement ... naturally emanate from literature in the same way as light emanates from the sun and as fragrance emanates from the flower ..."[91]

In a nutshell, while Durkheim tends to stress the role of social determination in the quest for what is higher, Ṭāhā is rather inclined to emphasize the role of individual spontaneity and freedom.

Cartesian doubt

Scientific historians, Durkheimian sociologists and literary historians were all preoccupied by questions of method, something which was normal in a period exceptionally fertile in theoretical work devoted to the establishment and codification of new disciplines. To illustrate this abundance of methodological thought, we may mention some of the relevant publications which appeared at the time: Durkheim's *Les règles de la méthode sociologique (1895)*; Langlois and Seignobos' *Introduction aux études historiques* (1898); Seignobos' *La méthode historique appliquée aux sciences sociales* (1901) and Lanson's many statements concerning the question of method in the history of literature.

Ṭāhā, who had to read the above-mentioned works either as textbooks or as necessary tools for his research on Ibn Khaldūn and who had been concerned himself with questions of method since 1911, could not have failed to take note of, and derive satisfaction from, the phenomenon. There was, however, one negative aspect of the methodological investigation which attracted his attention most, because it was a point of general concordance among positivists and also because it corresponded to his own critical dispositions. By this I mean the agreement of almost all the parties concerned on the necessity of Cartesian doubt.

Langlois and Seignobos repeatedly warn against man's natural laxity and instinctive inclination to trust hearsay reports or anonymous and unguaranteed statements and documents. This natural bent of mind, we are told, has to be resisted as the first step in historical enquiry.[92] "Here as in every science," the two authors write, "the starting-point must be methodical doubt. All that has not been proved must be temporarily regarded as doubtful, no proposition is to be affirmed unless reason can be adduced in favour of its truth. Applied to statements contained in documents, methodical doubt becomes *methodical distrust*."[93]

Durkheim is no less insistent on the basically Cartesian character of his own methodology of sociology. Having laid down the first rule of method, namely, the need to consider social facts as "things", he expounds what he considers as a corollary, namely, that one must systematically discard all preconceptions. For him this rule stands in need of no special proof, as it necessarily follows from what has already been laid down, besides being at the basis of all scientific method.[94]

As the necessity of applying Cartesian doubt was also emphasized by Fustel de Coulange,[95] a main source of inspiration for all these authors, we may conclude that the turn of the century witnessed the emergence of a whole tradition of doubt affiliated to Descartes. It is with this tradition in mind that Ṭāhā Ḥusain in 1926 launched his theory concerning the spuriousness of most of pre-Islamic poetry with the following announcement. "I would like to say that in this type of enquiry I shall follow in the footsteps of modern practitioners of science and philosophy ... I shall adopt in the study of literature the philosophical method devised by Descartes for the pursuit of truth at the beginning of the modern age. Now everybody knows that the basic rule in this method stipulates that the investigator free himself of all prior knowledge and that he receive the object of enquiry with his mind having been emptied of everything that has been said about it."[96] And yet, strangely enough, the question of whether Ṭāhā's scepticism concerning the authenticity of pre-Islamic poetry was genuinely Cartesian has been the subject of continuous debate ever since the publication of his above-mentioned work. Several writers have questioned Ṭāhā's knowledge of Descartes and/or the appropriateness of applying Descartes' method to historical enquiries.[97] All these criticisms are, I think, misguided. Ṭāhā, as must be clear by now, drew on a solid tradition of historical and sociological affiliation to the father of modern philosophy.

Ṭāhā's positivist teachers at the Sorbonne were aware that Cartesian doubt had not been originally designed for the empirical study of man; they were also aware of Descartes' lack of faith in the very possibility of history as a science. They assumed nevertheless that the Cartesian method could, and must, be extended or adapted to that type of study. To be more precise, they assumed that it was necessary in any endeavour aiming at the establishment of a new discipline to begin by wiping the slate clean of all preconceptions of the subject at hand. According to Durkheim, Bacon's theories of the idols had the same significance as Descartes' methodological doubt.[98]

Both Langlois and Seignobos on the one hand and Durkheim on the other anticipate and answer objections concerning the extension of Cartesian methodical doubt to their respective subjects. Thus the authors of the *Introduction to the study of history* seem to suggest that Descartes, coming at a time when history still consisted in the reproduction of pre-existing narratives, must be excused for his failure to apply methodical doubt to the subject and for his consequent refusal to place it among the sciences.[99] By the same token, the two authors seem to imply that now that history has become, or is about to become, a rigorous science, the application of methodical doubt in historical enquiry would be most appropriate from a Cartesian point of view.

Durkheim is more precise still in showing how Descartes' method may be adapted to the empirical study of sociology. Just as Descartes stipulated that the first link takes precedence in the chain of scientific truths, he (i.e. Durkheim) would commence his own study of the religious phenomenon, or any human phenomenon for that matter, by going back to the most primitive form of the object concerned.[100] "To be sure," writes Durkheim, "it is out of question to base the science of religions on a notion elaborated in the Cartesian manner that is, a logical concept, pure possibility constructed solely by force of thought. What we must find is a concrete reality that historical and ethnographic observation alone can reveal to us".[101]

All this was familiar to Ṭāhā and was at the back of his mind when he announced his affiliation to Descartes in 1926. From this we should not conclude, however, that Ṭāhā Ḥusain, as suggested by some scholars, derived his scepticism concerning the authenticity of pre-Islamic poetry from Descartes' methodical doubt.[102] This is the kind of loose thinking which is based on no accurate knowledge of Ṭāhā's development. As we have already seen, the main source for Ṭāhā's scepticism is the observation, mainly derived from Nallino, that neither the language nor the religious content of what is known as pre-Islamic poetry tally with the mainly Ḥimyarite inscriptions recently discovered in Arabia. This observation, reiterated by Ṭāhā with a sense of puzzlement in 1911, was to become the hard core of his thought on the subject. In 1914, that is to say in "Ḥayāt al-ādāb", the puzzlement develops into serious doubt about the authenticity of some of the lore described as pre-Islamic poetry. This development, which is part of a general form of incredulity with regard to received traditions, is coupled with, and seems to be sharpened by, a new rudimentary awareness of positivist historical methodology and criticism. In 1915, while in Montpellier, Ṭāhā takes up the question, casting doubt on the historical character of pre-Islamic poets and on the traditional sources, whether oral or written, on the subject. At this stage more precise knowledge of Langlois and Seignobos' rules for historical criticism come into play.[103]

All this happens prior to any knowledge of Descartes. By the time that "Ḥayāt al-Khansā'" is written, Ṭāhā, we may say, is already in possession of almost all the main elements for his mature sceptical theory of 1926. In this theory he develops and refines his early substantial doubts concerning the above-mentioned discrepancies between pre-Islamic poetry and the conditions known to have prevailed in Arabia before the rise of Islam, using the newly mastered methodology laid down by Langlois and Seignobos for the criticism of sources. It is only at this stage that the Cartesian doubt is invoked, but we can now see that it only plays a secondary role; it cannot be said to be the source, or even *a* source, of Ṭāhā's scepticism, as it is drawn upon indirectly, that is to say insofar as it is adapted by Seignobos for historical purposes.

The only main ingredient of Ṭāhā's mature scepticism, which is still missing in the early writings and in "Ḥayāt al-Khansā'" is the thesis that, in contrast to pre-Islamic poetry, the Qur'ān, as the first written and most authentic document in Arab history, provides the most representative image of linguistic, religious and intellectual conditions in Arabia before the rise of Islam.

This thesis, which appeared only in 1926, seven years after Ṭāhā's return to Egypt, seems to have been derived from more than one source. First, it follows from acceptance of Seignobos' principle to the effect that only written documents are historical: as the Qur'ān is the first Arabic text to have been written down, it is also the first historical document in Arab history. A second possible source for the thesis in question seems to be Ṭāhā's teacher at the Collège de France, Paul Casanova. Apart from co-supervising Ṭāhā's dissertation on Ibn Khaldūn, Casanova gave two courses of lectures, both of which were attended by Ṭāhā: the first on Qur'ānic exegesis, while the second was intended for the general public.[104] Neither course was published, but thanks to some information given by Casanova himself and the testimony of Ṭāhā, we can form an idea about the nature and relevance of the first course, which alone concerns us here.

In his *Mohammed et la fin du monde*, Casanova considers this work as an introduction to a fuller and more ambitious exegesis which he hoped to provide in a few years. The proposed exegesis was to start from the conviction that the recension of the Qur'ān as it came down to posterity was no more than an unfaithful reproduction of Muḥammad's thought. By a rigorous application of modern criticism, carried out on the largest possible scale and with the utmost liberty of thought, Casanova proposed to edit, translate and comment upon, the Qur'ān in as independent a manner as possible from traditional Muslim exegesis and its imitations in the West.[105] The proposed edition of the Qur'ān, we may gather, was meant to establish what was thought to be the original authentic text.

This is the type of exegesis which Casanova was practising when he lectured to Ṭāhā and others at the Collège de France from 1916 onwards. Further information on Casanova's practice is given by Ṭāhā himself as he describes his master's scientific detachment and objectivity. Casanova, we are told, was such a fervent believer in Christianity that his faith verged on mysticism. "But as soon as he entered the lecture room ... he forgot everything about Christianity, Judaism and Islam, save the fact that their respective texts were to be subjected to philological study just as matter was to be investigated by scientists in their laboratories ..."[106] Further on, Ṭāhā indicates that Casanova would study the Qur'ānic text with an eye to its wording and meaning, while also investigating its history, relating it to the traditions of ancient Arabs and to those of the People of the Book (*ahl al-kitāb*) and seeking to ascertain its impact on Muslims when it was recited to them.[107]

From this we can gather that Casanova's methodology was Cartesian, inasmuch as he took care to set aside his religious and national convictions as he approached the object of study.[108] More importantly, we can see that this methodology was historical or positivist in that it applied to the Qur'ānic text the rules of internal and external criticism, as codified by Langlois and Seignobos, with a view to ascertaining what it meant and establishing the historical conditions under which it appeared.

Of all of Ṭāhā's masters, whether in Egypt or France, Casanova was the only one who applied the historical method so described to the Qur'ān. In view of all this, it would be fair to conclude that Seignobos' equation of what is written with what is historical and Casanova's practice of Qur'ānic exegesis (according to Seignobos' rules) were the main sources of inspiration for Ṭāhā's thesis that the Qur'ān, rather than pre-Islamic poetry, reflected or mirrored the life of the pre-Islamic Arabs. Given that this poetry was oral and therefore prehistorical and that the poets to whom it was attributed were legendary figures, it is only through a critical study of the Qur'ān, so the argument goes, that we could hope to establish the facts about Arab history before the rise of Islam.

In fact, Ṭāhā Ḥusain's *Fi'l-shi'r al-jāhilī* bears the imprint of Casanova's teachings in more than one respect. Thus, for instance, Ṭāhā's doubts concerning the authenticity of the poetry attributed to Umayya Ibn Abi'l-Ṣalt[109] echoes Casanova when he writes in connection with this poet that "All the work done by Muslim exegetes for supporting their arbitrary philology by citing poems alleged to be contemporaneous with the Qur'ān is suspect. A few verses may be authentic, but we have no criterion [for deciding which]. Should there be such a criterion, then it must be that all verses having a Qur'ānic character must have been altered or completely invented. But even this cannot be established".[110]

The Methodological crisis

Scientific historians and Durkheimian sociologists shared a common hostility to the philosophy of history, an attitude which had its roots in Comte's insistence on the need for strict adherence to perceptible facts, independently of all theological and metaphysical speculation. But Comte's law of the three states itself involved a general theory on the development of humanity or the progress of the human mind, which Comte's heirs in both schools did not fail to denounce as a speculative philosophy of history. Thus Langlois and Seignobos castigate thinkers who imagine themselves to have discovered, "the laws which have governed the development of humanity" and thus to have "raised history to the rank of a positive science".[111] In similar terms, Durkheim criticizes Comte's law, for it is meant to apply not to societies but to human society as such. As good positivists, the three thinkers would object to Comte's treatment of humanity or human society in general as if it were a concrete reality, when in fact it was no more than a "creation of reason", to use Durkheim's words.[112]

It is remarkable that news of the positivist hostility to the philosophy of history reached Ṭāhā while he was still a newcomer in Montpellier and that, on hearing the news, he hastened to denounce the method employed in philosophizing about history for not being based on sound principles.[113] Later, during the Paris period, he came to qualify this point of view, but his position on the subject remained basically the same. Thus, in his thesis on Ibn Khaldūn, he would not deny that the philosophy of history ever existed or that it had some grounds for existence, but he would insist on the need to have it clearly distinguished from science.[114] Ibn Khaldūn, Ṭāhā would say, produced philosophical theories on the laws of human development in general which are not sufficiently objective to be considered as scientific.[115] All this is a far cry from Ṭāhā's earlier position in "Ḥayāt al-ādāb", where Comte's philosophy of history is advocated, albeit in a simplified version, and where, generally speaking, there is no clear distinction between science and philosophy.

But let us go back to the concurrence already observed between scientific historians and Durkheimian sociologists on the need to adhere strictly to the facts of experience, according to Comte's injunction. This concurrence, we may now note, is somewhat ephemeral: if hard pressed, it would give way to the most profound disagreement between the two sides over the nature and knowability of the facts concerned. Earlier on we decided to postpone examination of this divergence through the employment of a compromise formula according to which, it has been said, historians and sociologists agreed on the necessity of observing *or* establishing the facts. But this formula itself can no longer hide the difference, and it is a very wide one, expressed by the "or". Now is the time, therefore, to face the most fundamental disagreement within the positivist camp, with Durkheim's holistic and realistic conception of social facts at the one end, and Langlois and Seignobos' conception of historical facts in terms of their methodological individualism at the opposite end.

For Durkheim, who, as we have just seen, rejects the concept of humanity or society in general, the true historical realities are particular tribes, nations and states[116] and, we may add, other collective phenomena such as particular groups, institutions as well as collective representations.[117] In other words, having excluded humanity or human society as a creation of reason, Durkheim assumes that the primary and most concrete facts for social enquiry are irreducibly collective phenomena. Society, he would say, is not the mere sum of individuals; while it cannot exist independently of these as "substrata" and while it arises from their association, it constitutes, once it is so formed, a system representing a specific reality which has its own characteristics.[118] The point would apply, *mutatis mutandi*, to all collective phenomena, for they are all wholes which involve or implicate individuals but are irreducible to their characteristics.

Durkheim's use of the term "substratum" for the designation of individuals gives the impression that he conceives of the relation between society and individuals in terms of the Aristotelian distinction between form and matter, in which the former term is the determining and therefore the more real factor. The impression is confirmed when Durkheim asserts: "It is the form of the [social] whole that determines that of the parts. Society does not find, ready-made in individual consciousnesses, the basis on which it rests; it makes them for itself."[119] Not only does society have a specific reality of its own; it also produces the individual. This latter, Durkheim would say, is the product of society, rather than its cause.

Having reduced the ontological status of individuals, Durkheim would also seek to ensure that social facts are knowable independently of them. Thus social facts are considered as natural phenomena which are by their very nature observable; they are, to use Durkheim's term, *things*, which means that they are external to, and exert constraint on, individuals. Collective representations, Durkheim would say, do not have as their causes certain states of consciousness in individuals and are not to be explained in terms of these states; collective representations have their causes in the conditions under which the body social as a whole exists and are to be explained only with reference to these conditions.[120]

Steven Lukes is right when he argues that Durkheim overstated his case against methodological individualists, claiming that social facts could only be explained in terms of other social facts, while he need only have claimed that these facts could not be wholly explained in terms of individual facts.[121] It should be recalled, however, that methodological individualists such as Langlois and Seignobos were no less relentless in waging war against collective phenomena.

Langlois and Seignobos admitted that historical facts present themselves in very different degrees of generality, from the highly general facts involving a whole people and lasting for centuries (institutions, customs, beliefs) down to the most transient actions of a single man.[122] But this is only an initial and provisional admission, to be followed by a series of eliminations and reductions with a view to restricting the range of primary historical facts to the lowest level of generality. Thus, for example, society is conceived of as the sum total of its members;[123] the comparative study of institutions is discouraged;[124] great transformations, it is assumed, can be explained with reference to small events and accidents.[125] In general, we are told, the "social fact" as recognized by certain sociologists, is a philosophical construction, not a historical fact.[126]

At times, Langlois and Seignobos seem to settle for a short list containing only three types of fact: (1) living things and material objects; (2) collective and individual actions of men and (3) psychic facts or motives and conceptions.[127] But Langlois and Seignobos would soon remove collective actions from the picture. The question of whether such actions are of the same nature as individual ones is, for Seignobos, a controversial issue in philosophy; methodologically speaking, or as far as the *observer* is concerned, there is only a sum of individual actions or words.[128]

With this reference to the "observer", we reach the nub of the matter, so to speak. In history, according to Langlois and Seignobos, the facts are not directly observed, but established by derivation from the critical analysis of documents.[129] As historians have no direct access to past events, they rely on the evidence supplied by the authors of documents, who observed these events. But, argues Langlois and Seignobos, these authors did not and could not have observed collective phenomena as these are not the type of thing that could be seen or heard. In other words, Langlois and Seignobos defined "observation" so strictly as to stand for sense-perception or sensory experience;[130] and it is on these grounds that they assume that collective phenomena are not among the basic data of observation or the primary types of historical facts. Anything apart from these data and the psychological facts which are supposed to explain individual actions and single events must be either a metaphysical hypostatization or a logical construction out of such data.[131] The phenomena mentioned above are such logical constructions the knowledge of which is derivative, that is to say, reached through synthesis or reconstruction, and hence less certain.

The antagonism between scientific historians and Durkheimian sociologists is at its strongest when Langlois and Seignobos argue for the psychological character of historical explanation and, what is still worse, the ultimately subjective nature of historical knowledge. On the first point, Langlois and Seignobos find it necessary to explain individual actions with reference to psychological facts, namely the motives of agents.[132] As for the second point, the two historiographers would say that historical knowledge is inevitably based on "imagining". For in trying to establish the facts as perceived by the authors of documents, historians only "imagine" what it was like for things to be so perceived.[133]

From this we can see how, starting from the Comtean concern for strict adherence to the facts of experience, the two major camps within positivism move in opposite directions, with scientific historians adopting a reductionist and subjectivist conception of historical facts.

Now at the time of his arrival in France, Ṭāhā dogmatically believed, following Taine, that the requirements of scientific history would be satisfied if it were based on a holistic and completely objectivist conception of history. By that same time, however, French positivism had outgrown both the Comtean and Taineian moulds and was in fact past its heyday; for in the very act of giving birth to different disciplines, it went into disintegration. What Ṭāhā found in 1915–1919 was no longer a homogeneous doctrine, if it ever had been one, but two main schools of thought diametrically opposed to each other, with each side furiously seeking to impose its hegemony or "imperialism" by annexing the opposite discipline.[134]

The polarization could not have escaped the attention of Ṭāhā, who, having studied under both Seignobos and Durkheim, must have read some of the criticisms that they exchanged, either implicitly or explicitly.[135] He was, anyway, duly informed of the methodological controversy ("*Methodenstreit*") involving the so-called "historicist historians" (i.e. advocates of factual, political history) and "sociologist historians" (i.e. advocates of history based on the study of economic, social and cultural facts) by Bouglé[136] and also by Langlois and Seignobos themselves.[137]

This polarization was the most salient feature of the positivist landscape; indeed it was the most predominant theme in positivist thought in general. The dichotomy between the individual and society assumed many forms, giving rise to a number of antinomies: methodological, ontological, moral and literary. In one such form, the issue concerned the role of (great) individuals in history, and was debated by many authors with whom Ṭāhā was familiar in Paris: for instance, Auguste Comte.[138]

Cournot,[139] Durkheim, Langlois and Seignobos, and Bouglé.[140] In moral terms, the issue took the form of a question concerning the altruism or egocentrism of great men.[141] Posed in the literary sphere, the problem concerned the role of individual genius or subjectivity in literary works. Faced with this multi-faceted debate, Ṭāhā Ḥusain did not take sides, but sought reconciliation, as we shall see in the next chapter.

Notes

1 Ṭāhā Ḥusain, *A Passage to France* (Leiden 1976), p. 75.
2 According to 'Abdurrahman Badawi (ed.), *Ilā Ṭāhā Ḥusain fī 'īd milādih al-sab'īn* (Cairo 1962), p. 12, Ṭāhā attended also a course on psychology.
3 His stay in Montpellier lasted about ten months from November 1914 till September 1915.
4 See Philippe Cardinal's preface to Taha Hussein's *Adib ou l'aventure occidentale*, tr. Amina and Moënis Taha-Hussein (Paris 1988), p. 11.
5 See interview with Suzanne Ṭāhā Ḥusain: "*Le Progrès* écoute : Suzanne Taha Hussein", *Le Progrès Egyptien*, 18 May 1980.
6 Cf. Ṭāhā Ḥusain, op. cit., p. 84.
7 During the period in question, he prepared his thesis on Abu'l-'Alā' for publication and contributed several articles to the literary weekly *al-Sufūr*. Ibid., p. 90.
8 Ibid., p. 89.
9 In *al-Sufūr*, 12 and 19 November 1915, respectively. To be referred to henceforth as "al-Khansā'" I and "al-Khansā'" II.
10 A pseudonym standing, I guess, for Mayy Ziyāda (1886–1941), the Palestinian-born and French-educated poetess and writer whose literary salon in Cairo was attended by many literary figures at the time, including Luṭfī al-Sayyid and Ṭāhā Ḥusain. See the latter, op. cit., pp. 28 ff. Admired by all and courted by some, al-Ānisa Mayy – as she was commonly called – was considered by Ṭāhā to embody the ideals of all the intellectual and moral attainments to which Oriental young ladies should aspire. See "al-Khansā'" I, *al-Sufūr*, 12 November 1915, pp. 2–3, p. 2.
11 The first to draw attention to the importance of this work is Muḥammad Abu'l Anwār. See his *al-Ḥiwār al-adabī ḥawl al-shi'r*, 2nd edn. (Cairo 1987), pp. 112–114.
12 "Al-Khansā'" II, p.2
13 Ṭāhā Ḥusain, op. cit., p. 3. He gives the French equivalent in the singular. Cf. idem., "al-Khansā'" II, *al-Sufūr*, 19 November, p. 2.
14 Ibid, p. 2.
15 See Ch.-V. Langlois and Ch. Seignobos, *Introduction to the study of history* (London 1912).
16 Ṭāhā Ḥusain, op. cit., p. 2.
17 See above, ch. IV, p. 84.

18 "Ḥayāt al-ādāb" I, *J*, 15 January 1914.
19 "Al-Khansā'" II, pp. 2–3
20 "Al-Khansā'" I, p. 3
21 Ibid
22 "Al-Khansā'" II, p. 3.
23 Ibid.
24 Ṭāhā assumed that Ibn Qutayba was the author of the work in question, but according to recent research, the work is apocryphal. See G. Lecomte, *EI*[2] art. "Ibn Ḳutayba".
25 "Al-Khansā'" I, p. 3. "His [i.e. Ibn Qutayba's] love for 'Alī's descendants impaired his mind or intellectual integrity".
26 Ibid.
27 Ibid.
28 Langlois and Seignobos, op. cit., pp. 71 ff.
29 Sulaymān al-Bustānī, *Iliyādhat Hūmirūs* (Beirut n.d.), vol. I, p. 120 ff. See also Albert Hourani, *Islam in European thought*, reprint (Cambridge 1993), p. 180.
30 See al-Bustānī, op. cit., pp. 57–58, where it is taken for granted that the *Iliad* is a reliable source on Greek history and geography and where Homer is treated as the first historian and geographer.
31 In France, the major representative of this current of thought was Renan, who maintained that works such as the Homeric poems and pre-Islamic traditions, though non-historical, were highly instructive concerning the social life prevailing at the time of their production. See Ernst Renan, *Histoire du peuple d'Israel, Oeuvres complètes,* ed. Henriette Psichari, vol. VI, p. 18. See also idem, *La vie de Jésus, Oeuvres complètes,* vol. IV, p. 76.
32 "Al-Khansā'" I, p. 3.
33 Ibid.
34 See above, ch. V, p. 122.
35 Ṭāhā Ḥusain, op. cit., p. 3.
36 Aḥmad al-Ṣāwī Muḥammad, "al-Ductūr Ṭāhā Ḥusain fī Barīs" (interview with Ṭāhā Ḥusain on his life in Paris), *al-Hilāl,* 1928, pp. 1181–1183, p. 1182.
37 Serialized in the Cairo weekly *Ākhir Sā'a,* 1955, the work was not published as the third volume of *al-Ayyām* until 1972.
38 *A Passage to France,* pp. 101–102.
39 Ibid., p. 109.
40 Ibid., pp. 87, 98, 107.
41 Ibid., p. 111.
42 See Berque's introduction to Taha Hussein, *Au delà du Nil* (Paris 1977), p. 15.
43 Cf. Arlette Tadié, "Le troisième *Livre des Jours*", *La Nouvelle Revue du Caire,* vol. I (1975), pp. 49–58, p. 56.
44 Cf. Leïla Louca, "Le discours autobiographique de Ṭāhā Ḥusayn selon la clôture du *Livre des Jours*", *Arabica,* vol. XXXIV (1992), pp. 246–357, p. 355.
45 Suzanne Ṭāhā Ḥusain, *Ma'ak* (Cairo 1979), p. 16.
46 Ibid., p. 17.

47 Aḥmad al-Ṣāwī Muḥammad, op. cit., pp. 1182–1183.
48 Ṭāhā Ḥusain, op. cit., p. 121. The work was published as *Etude analytique et critique de la philosophie sociale d'Ibn-Khaldoun* (Paris 1917).
49 Cachia's statement in his *Taha Husayn, his place in the Egyptian literary Renaissance* (London 1956), p. 55 to the effect that Ṭāhā Ḥusain obtained the *Doctorat d'Etat* is not true.
50 According to the regulations in force at the time, the granting of the Doctorate was conditional on passing an oral examination on two subjects. The subjects assigned for Ṭāhā were: (1) Sociology according to Auguste Comte and (2) Lawsuits brought against provincial governors, according to Pliny the Younger. See Ṭāhā Ḥusain, *A Passage to France,* p. 126.
51 Ibid., p. 128.
52 The only exception is Latin. Unless otherwise indicated, the information given in the list are derived from the third volume of *al-Ayyām* (*A Passage to France*).
53 See Ṭāhā Ḥusain's letter to Miftah Tahar in the latter's *Ṭāhā Ḥusayn: sa critique littéraire et ses sources françaises,* (Tunis 1976), p. 152.
54 See Fritz Ringer, *Fields of Knowledge. French academic culture in comparative perspective, 1890–1920* (Cambridge 1992), pp. 212 ff. Cf. T.N. Clark, *Prophets and patrons: The French university and the emergence of the social sciences* (Cambridge 1973), pp. 28–29 and 172–173. See also George Weisz, "The republican ideology and the social sciences; the Durkheimians and the history of social economy at the Sorbonne" in Philippe Besnard (ed.) *The Sociological domain. The Durkheimians and the founding of French sociology* (Cambridge 1983), pp. 90–119, p. 90.
55 See above, ch. III, p. 48 on the non-utilitarian aims of education according to advocates of the University.
56 See above, p. 47 on Luṭfī's elitism.
57 Ringer, op. cit., pp. 207 and 211.
58 See above, ch. V, p. 128. Cf. R.G. Collingwood, *The Idea of history* (Oxford 1994), pp. 126–127
59 On Taine's Hegelianism, see Gerard Delfau and Anne Roche, *Histoire/Littérature. Histoire et interpretation du fait littéraire* (Paris 1977), pp. 59–60. Ṭāhā Ḥusain himself was not unaware of Hegel's influence on Taine. See his "al-Faylasūf Taine" ("The Philosopher Taine"), *al-Jihād,* 1 March 1935, pp. 10–11, p. 10.
60 Guy Bourdé and Hervé Martin, *Les écoles historiques* (Paris 1989), pp. 205–206.
61 Ibid., pp. 182 ff.
62 Delfau and Roche, op. cit., pp. 71–72 and 77.
63 On Durkheim's influence at the Sorbonne, see Steven Lukes, *Emile Durkheim. His life and work* (Harmondsworth 1975), pp. 368 ff. and 372 ff.
64 Clark, op. cit., p. 98.
65 Bourdé and Martin, op. cit., p. 207. See also J. Erhard and G. Palmade, *L'Histoire* (Paris 1964), pp. 69–70.
66 Bourdé and Martin, op. cit., p. 128. Cf. Erhard and Palmade, op. cit., pp. 39 and 45.

67 For an outline of the history of historical criticism, see Marc Bloch, *The Historian's craft* (Manchester 1992), pp. 66 ff.
68 Ringer, op. cit., pp. 274–275.
69 Mainly derived from Massignon's *Muḥāḍarāt*, pp. 115–116 and 119–120. A possible contribution from Luṭfī al-Sayyid cannot be ruled out.
70 George Weisz, op. cit., p. 116.
71 *A Passage to France*, pp. 154–155.
72 Ibid., p. 156.
73 See for instance "Min mushkilāt adabinā al-ḥadīth", *Khiṣām wa-naqd* in *MK*, vol. XI, 1974, pp. 540–552, p. 551. Article first published in *al-Jumhūriyya*, 11 December 1953.
74 "Ṣar'ā al-ḥaḍāra" in *Fuṣūl fī 'l-adab wa'l-naqd* in *MK*, vol. V, 1973, pp. 534–551, pp. 546 ff. First published in three instalments in *al-Thaqāfa*, 9 July, 16 July and 10 August 1940, respectively.
75 Ch. Seignobos, *La Méthode historique appliqué aux sciences sociales* (Paris 1901), pp. 261 ff.
76 Ibid., p. 265.
77 Ibid., pp. 267–268.
78 See Durkheim's review of Antonio Labriola's, "Essais sur la conception matérialiste de l'histoire", *Revue philosophique*, 44 (1897), pp. 645–51, as reprinted in idem *The Rules of sociological method and selected texts on sociology and its method*, ed. Steven Lukes, reprint (London 1990), pp. 167–174, p. 173.
79 C. Bouglé, *Qu'est-ce que la sociologie* (Paris 1907), p. 27 ff.
80 Ibid., p. 29.
81 Ṭāhā Ḥusain, "Yūnānī fa-lā yuqra'" ("It is Greek, therefore incomprehensible") in *Khiṣām wa-naqd*, in *MK*, vol. XI, 1974, pp. 587–599.
82 Ibid., p. 592.
83 Ibid.
84 Ṭāhā Ḥusain, "al-Ḥayāt fī sabīl al-adab" in *Khiṣām wa-naqd*, in *MK*, vol. XI, 1974, pp. 600–613, p. 607.
85 But notice that Ṭāhā Ḥusain sometimes advocates more balanced views about communism. Thus in *Alwān* (*MK*, vol. VI, 1981, pp. 630–631), Ṭāhā sees the legitimacy of the communist socialist call for social justice, but argues that it is incompatible with another, no less legitimate requirement, namely freedom.
86 Durkheim, "Address to the Lycéens of Sens", in idem, *On Morality and society*, ed. Robert N. Bellah (Chicago 1973), pp. 25–33, p. 31.
87 Ṭāhā Ḥusain, *Khiṣām wa-naqd*, in *MK*, vol. XI, p. 540. See also idem, *Alwān* in *MK*, vol. VI, p. 661.
88 Durkheim, op. cit., pp. 33–34.
89 See for instance "Mir'āt al-gharība" in *Khiṣām wa naqd*, in *MK*, vol. XI, pp. 535–539, pp. 535 ff. See also Jābir 'Uṣfūr, *al-Marāyā al-mutajāwira. Dirāsa fī naqd Ṭāhā Ḥusain* (Cairo 1983), pp. 82 ff.
90 Ṭāhā Ḥusain, "al-Ḥayāt fī sabīl al-adab" op. cit., p. 606.
91 Idem, "al-Adab wa'l-ḥayāt ayḍan" in ibid., pp. 564–574, p. 565.
92 Langlois and Seignobos, op. cit., pp. 68, 69, 155 and 156.
93 Ibid., pp. 156–157. Italics in the original.

94 Durkheim, *The Rules of sociological method, etc.*, p. 72. "... It is necessary to begin by freeing the mind of every preconceived idea ... It is not from our prejudices, passions or habits that we should demand the elements of the definition which we must have; it is from the reality itself which we are going to define," ibid. Cf. idem, *The Elementary forms of religious life*, tr. Karen E. Fields (New York 1995), p. 38.

95 On this point, see Jane Herrick, *The Historical thought of Fustel de Coulanges* (Washington, D.C. 1954), pp. 20 ff.

96 Ṭāhā Ḥusain, *Fi'l-shi'r al-jāhilī*, p. 11.

97 See for instance Muḥammad Luṭfī Jum'a, *al-Shihāb al-rāṣid* (Cairo 1926), pp. 17 ff.; Muḥammad Aḥmad al-Ghamrāwī, *al-Naqd al-taḥlīlī li-kitāb Fi'l-adab al-jāhilī* (Beirut 1981), pp. 116 ff. and Jacques Berque, "Une affaire Dreyfus de la philologie arabe" in Jacques Berque and Jean Charnay (eds.) *Normes et valeurs dans l'Islam contemporain* (Paris 1966), pp. 267–285, p. 278. Al-Ghamrāwī's book was first published in 1929. See also Ṭāhā Ḥusain's satirical attack on two of his critics who questioned his knowledge of Descartes, in "Descartes" in *Min ba'īd*, in *MK*, vol. XII, 1974, pp. 209–225.

98 Durkheim, *The Rules of sociological method, etc.*, p. 72.

99 Langlois and Seignobos, op. cit., p. 156, n. 2.

100 Durkheim, *The Elementary forms of religious life*, p. 15.

101 Ibid., p. 16.

102 In his "Ṭāhā Ḥusain al-nāqid" ("Ṭāhā Ḥusain as a critic") in Ṭ*āhā Ḥusain kamā ya'rifuh kuttāb 'aṣrih* (Cairo n.d.), pp. 163–180, p. 169, Francisco Gabrieli writes that European orientalists think that the question of pre-Islamic poetry as treated by Ṭāhā Ḥusain was the first fruit of the Cartesian principles with which his thought was impregnated during his stay in Europe.

103 See above, p. 153.

104 Ṭāhā Ḥusain, "Paul Casanova" (obituary of Paul Casanova), *al-Siyāsa al-Usbū'iyya*, 27 March 1926, pp. 9–10, p. 9.

105 Paul Casanova, *Mohammad et la fin du monde. Notes complémentaires* I (Paris 1913), p. 162. See also ibid., n. 3.

106 Ṭāhā Ḥusain, op. cit., p. 9.

107 Ibid., pp. 9–10.

108 Ibid., p. 10.

109 *Fi'l-shi'r al-jāhilī*, pp. 82 ff. It may be noted, however, that Nallino (see his *Tārīkh*, pp. 93–94) was the first to draw Ṭāhā's attention to these doubts.

110 Casanova, *Mohammad et la fin du monde. Notes complémentaires* II (Paris 1924), p. 223.

111 Langlois and Seignobos, op. cit., pp. 1–2.

112 Durkheim, *On Morality and society*, p. 9.

113 See above, p. 155.

114 T. Hussein, *Etude analytique et critique de la philosophie sociale d'Ibn-Khaldoun*, p. 55.

115 Ibid., pp. 78–79.

116 Durkheim, *On Morality and society*, p. 9.

117 On Durkheim's *representations collectives*, see Steven Lukes, *Emile Durkheim. His life and work* (Harmondsworth 1975), pp. 6 ff.
118 Durkheim, *The Rules of sociological method. etc.*, p. 129.
119 Idem, *The Division of labour in society*, with an introduction by Lewis Coser, tr. W.D. Halls, reprint (London 1993), p. 287.
120 Idem, *The Rules of sociological method, etc.*, p. 131.
121 Steven Lukes, op. cit., p. 20.
122 Langlois and Seignobos, op. cit., pp. 212–213.
123 See for instance ibid., p. 239, where groups such as states and churches are said to be nothing but superficial unities composed of heterogeneous elements; and p. 242, where society, instead of being considered as a "real existence" having a structure and functions, is analysed in terms of individual men and their relations.
124 Ibid., pp. 290–291.
125 "It goes against the grain to admit that Cleopatra's nose may have made a difference to the Roman Empire. This repugnance is of metaphysical order ..." Ibid., p. 248.
126 Ibid., p. 218.
127 Ibid., pp. 217 ff.
128 Seignobos, *La méthode historique appliquée aux sciences sociales*, p. 107. Italics are mine.
129 Langlois and Seignobos, op. cit., p. 211.
130 See ibid., p. 218, where the two authors speak of "physical perception" and [sense] "impressions".
131 Such is Langlois and Seignobos' fear of the metaphysical dangers posed by abstract and general terms (e.g. "society", "the state", "humanity", "group" and even "evolution") that one is reminded of logical positivists.
132 Seignobos, op. cit., pp. 108–109.
133 Ibid., pp. 218, 219.
134 On Durkheim's attempt to assimilate history to sociology and Seignobos' counterattack, see Philippe Besnard "The Epistemological polemic: François Simiand", in idem (ed.), *The Sociological domain, etc.* (Cambridge 1983), pp. 248–261, p. 116.
135 See for instance the text of the famous debate between Durkheim and Seignobos on explanation in history and sociology (1908) in Durkheim, *The Rules of sociological method, etc.*, pp. 211–228.
136 Bouglé, op. cit., p. 57.
137 See above, p. ch. V, p. 125 and ibid., n. 22.
138 Auguste Comte, *Physique sociale. Cours de philosophie positive, leçons 46 à 60*, ed. Jean-Paul Enthoven (Paris 1975), pp. 106, 115.
139 A.A. Cournot, *Considérations sur la marche des idées et des événements dans les temps modernes, Oeuvre complètes*, vol. IV, ed. André Robinet (Paris 1973), pp. 15–16.
140 Bouglé, op. cit., Ch. III.
141 See above, pp. 167, 168 and 169.

CHAPTER VII

Reconciliations

In this final chapter, I propose to study a certain characteristic of Ṭāhā Ḥusain's thought which, while already present in his early writings and during the Paris period, subsequently became a prominent feature of his maturity. By this I mean the tendency to seek synthetic formulae[1] or reconciliations for antinomies resulting from his adoption of positivism.

In the early writings, the introduction of positivist modernism, methodically elaborated, entails critical implications for the Arab cultural heritage, giving rise to drastic revisions of Ṭāhā's received ideas as well as to dichotomies. Thus, for instance, the Arab contribution to history is reduced to the mere provision of materials for methodologies developed in the West. Worse still, this contribution is lumped together with Semitic and Oriental historigraphical traditions – as distinct from, and inferior to, Western counterparts. Again, miracles, having been excluded from the realm of history, are relegated to the realm of religion. But having reached these conclusions, Ṭāhā, by virtue of an almost instinctive reaction, would seek to heal, or simply patch up, the fractures. We have seen how his thesis on Abu'l-'Alā', the crowning point of his early writings, attempts to redress the balance in favour of al-Marṣafī's (neo-classical) linguistic approach, now considered indispensable for the study of Arabic literature and a necessary complement to (Western) historical methodology.

During Ṭāhā's years of study in France, further fractures emerged, sometimes within the positivist camp itself, calling for other forms of synthesis. In Montpellier, Ṭāhā hastened, under the direct or indirect influence of Lanson, to acknowledge, besides Taine's objectivism, a psychological factor with an irreducible part to play in the creative process. As he moved on to Paris, Ṭāhā discovered that rifts within positivism were numerous and more serious. While in Cairo, positivism seemed to be as homogeneous and solid a doctrine as the Taineian system;

in Paris it turned out to be ridden with a number of antinomies, involving a tug of war between objectivism (holism) and subjectivism (individualism).

Having already adopted Lanson's synthesis, Ṭāhā's faith in this solution was further confirmed in Paris, as he came to study under Lanson himself. But this literary form of reconciliation left the door open for other antinomies and other synthetic formulae. As we shall see shortly, Ṭāhā sought to unite Durkheim and Seignobos in a common, modernist front against Ibn Khaldūn, considered as an Oriental thinker. But this very solution aggravated, for Ṭāhā, the antinomy between East and West. Furthermore, during the same period, the antinomy of science versus religion, which had arisen in Cairo, was exacerbated as a result of Ṭāhā's improved knowledge of positivism and, more specifically, his adherence to Durkheim's sociology of religion.

Generally speaking, while some of the antinomies engendered by positivism emerged and inviteded some conciliatory efforts in Cairo, the full extent and range of these conflicts became clear only in Paris. From that point onward, Ṭāhā was to spend many years trying to find synthetic remedies for these rifts. As some of these remedies were only developed well after Ṭāhā's return to Cairo, the enquiry into a number of Ṭāhā's reconciliations has to go beyond the limits of his formal education at more than one point.

The Lansonian synthesis

Confronted with the positivist crisis, Ṭāhā realized that Lanson was the master to follow, being a man of reconciliation and synthesis in literary history. The call for synthesis was in the air,[2] but Lanson had the advantage of working in the field which interested Ṭāhā most.

In an oft-cited article, Lanson tries to reassure all parties, especially those lovers of literature who like to imagine that "the method" is a nightmare against whose mortifying tyranny they need to defend their pleasures and their intellectual appreciation (*forme d'esprit*).[3] In fact, however, these fears are unjustified, according to Lanson. Nor, he adds, would he seek to abolish any form of literary criticism.[4] On the contrary, it was part of his policy to try to incorporate the main contributions of his predecessors.[5]

The basic element in Lanson's method is a healthy and refreshing call for a return to the texts. It is works of literature themselves rather than summaries and textbooks which, so the argument goes, must be the focus of attention. Without reading the original texts for their own sake, literary history would be a sterile exercise leading back to medieval times when knowledge was confined to compendia (*sommes*), textbooks, glosses and commentaries.[6]

Having thus fixed the immediate object for study, Lanson develops a critical method combining three main approaches which, in his view, should together provide an exhaustive, balanced and adequate knowledge of literary works. First, to study literary texts as documents, using "the exact and positive" procedures of scientific history as established by Langlois and Seignobos:[7] knowledge of manuscripts, bibliography, chronology, biography, textual criticism and yet other disciplines, as and when required, as auxiliary sciences.[8]

Secondly, to endeavour to explain literary works by relating them to their determining conditions. Lanson speaks here of all endeavours which, through the application of "scientific methods", serve to connect our particular ideas and impressions into a synthetic form and thereby show the progress, growth and transformations of literature.[9] What he has in mind are the theoretical constructions of Taine and Brunetière: the former's theory on *race, milieu* and *moment* and the latter's theory on the evolution of literary *genres*.

But, argues Lanson, when all these means of "determining" literary works have been exhausted, there would still be a residue which none of these explanations can reach and none of these causes determines; and it is this unexplained and undetermined residue which constitutes the superior originality of the work and the literary individuality of the author. This irreducible residue, Lanson would say, is the proper object of literary history. There is, therefore, a need for a third kind of approach which involves the use of subjective faculties. Hence, thirdly, the need to approach literary texts subjectively or insofar as they are a source of aesthetic pleasure or an object for taste, with a view to grasping what is essentially and uniquely literary in them. Literature, Lanson would say, is not an object of knowledge; it is rather a matter of exercise, taste or pleasure; it is not something to be known or learnt, but to be practised, cultivated and loved.[10]

Under this last heading, Lanson would consider the case of Sainte-Beuve, which is a difficult one. On the one hand, he is one of the three or four men whom Lanson acknowledges as masters of literary criticism, for he established criticism on firm foundations by basing it on the biographical study of authors as living individuals.[11] On the other hand, Sainte-Beuve was a moralist who turned almost all literature into biography.[12] Instead of using biographies in order to explain literary works, he used literary works in order to construct biographies.[13] In view of this, Lanson would not advocate a simple return to Sainte-Beuve,[14] but would accommodate the latter's biographical approach, with the proviso that it should be used for the explanation of texts.

Also under the same heading, Lanson would consider the case of (Jules Lemaitre's) impressionism, which he considers to be perfectly irreproachable and legitimate if maintained within the proper limits. While he warns against impressionism when it masquerades as history or impersonal logic, Lanson would welcome the straightforward brand which expresses the reaction of a mind to a literary work.[15]

Thus, we may gather, Sainte-Beuve's biographical method as well as straightforward impressionism are to be used, within certain limits, in order to account for the irreducible element of individuality in literary works. Given this, Lanson's method would be complete, at least according to his programmatic pronouncements in his history of French literature. In other statements, however, the methodological issue is reopened as the above-mentioned element seems to remain recalcitrant, posing still further difficulties for Lanson. One such difficulty is that he would want to define original individualities which are by their very nature unique and incommensurable.[16]

Another difficulty is that the attempt to account for individuality, if adequately carried out, entails reference to what is general and universal. Individuals, however great or sublime, cannot, argues Lanson, be known in complete isolation from other things.[17] The most original writer is to a great extent a repository of preceding generations and a collector of contemporary movements.[18] To find him in his uniqueness we must separate from him all that mass of foreign materials.[19] But when this has been done the individual writer will have been known only potentially; to know his true quality and real "intensity", we have to see him as he acts on others and produces his effects, that is to say, to trace his influence on literary and social life. Hence, the need to study a whole range of general facts, genres, currents of ideas, conditions of taste and sensibility surrounding the great writer and masterpieces.[20]

Furthermore, what is most beautiful and greatest in individual genius is not the singularity that sets it apart, but rather its ability to sum up and symbolize in its very singularity the collective life of a period or a group; its ability, that is, to be representative. We must, therefore, try to apprehend the entire range of humanity, which is expressed through great writers.[21]

But by thus reopening the door of enquiry into the influence and representativeness of individual genius, Lanson adds a further component to his synthetic methodology, namely, a contribution from Durkheim, which exposes his thought still further to the antinomic tension between the individual and society.

Be that as it may, there can be no doubt that Lanson's methodological synthesis, as outlined above, had a lasting effect on Ṭāhā's mind. During the Montpellier period, Ṭāhā quickly acknowledged the inadequacy of Taineian objectivism and admitted the presence in literary works of an irreducible subjective residue. We shall see shortly that in his Paris dissertation on Ibn Khaldūn, Ṭāhā applied to the ancient historian a compound critical approach comprising two compartments, one based on Langlois and Seignobos, and the other based on Durkheim.

Some four years after his return to Egypt, Ṭāhā still maintained the Lansonian reconciliation, arguing for a comprehensive approach to criticism, which would combine Taine, Sainte-Beuve, Jules Lemaitre and others if need be.[22] The same catholicism of taste, if we call it that, was adopted in *Fi'l-adab al-jāhilī* (1927), where Ṭāhā called for a combination of two approaches to the history of literature, the one "scientific", represented by Sainte-Beuve, Taine, Brunetière, and the other "literary" or "artistic" based on the exercise of taste.[23]

It would be wrong, however, to assume that Ṭāhā's adherence to the Lansonian synthesis was strict and constant throughout his maturity. We shall see below that there came a time in the 1930s when the synthesis broke down as a result of Ṭāhā's adoption of unbridled impressionism. For the time being, we may examine the reasons for his loyalty to Lanson, as long as it lasted.

During the 1920s, Lanson must have appeared to Ṭāhā, the modernist, as the most modern of all historians of literature on account of his eclectic approach. Embracing as it did almost all that modern critical thought had to offer, and opening the doors wide to let in fresh air and light from all directions, this approach must have seemed to be most appropriate for the study and revival of Arabic literature.

And yet for all its flexibility, Lanson's scheme had, for Ṭāhā, the added merit of maintaining a hard core of positivist doctrine, involving "scientific" contributions from Taine, Brunetière and Seignobos. The space allocated to this strand of positivist thought was curtailed, but not abolished, by the admission of impressionism. The latter strand was accommodated, within limits, as a final residue; it was, in other words, admitted only when the whole range of scientific procedures had been exhausted.

Finally, Lanson's call for a return to the original texts uncluttered by "medieval" glosses, textbooks and commentaries must have been music to the ears of someone who had rebelled against Azhari scholasticism. More specifically, Lanson's insistence on the need to appreciate literary texts for their own sake, to "savour" them so to speak, must have reminded Ṭāhā of his old Azhari master al-Marṣafī, who was the first to draw his attention to the aesthetic aspects of literary texts. It may be said, in fact, that in being so loyal to his French master, Ṭāhā was only being faithful to himself. Had he not already advocated in *Tajdīd dhikrā Abi'l-'Alā'* the need to adopt a compound critical strategy involving a modern historical component and a linguistic component after the manner of al-Marṣafī? Given this early move in the right direction, all he needed to do was to stretch the boundaries of both components so as to accommodate all the best in modern critical thought and thus mobilize the maximum resources for the study of Arabic literature.

A Common front against Ibn Khaldūn

According to the author of the *Etude analytique et critique de la philosophie sociale d'Ibn-Khaldoun,* the ancient Arab historian, besides Abu'l-'Alā', was one of two exceptional men in the history of Arabic literature, who, each in his own way, made a unique and most remarkable contribution.[24] Having previously written his Cairo thesis on Abu'l-'Alā', Ṭāhā Ḥusain thought that it was most appropriate to devote his doctoral thesis in Paris to the study of the Arab historian. The latter work appears, therefore, to be a natural sequel to the earlier thesis. The problem is to understand in what sense.

According to Ahmed Abdesselem, the main objective of the Paris thesis was to revive the tradition of thought that Ṭāhā Ḥusain favoured most, namely the rationalist humanist current which ran from Aristotle to the French *philosophes* of the eighteenth century. As viewed by Ṭāhā Ḥusain, we are told, Ibn Khaldūn belonged to that current, which permeated universal thought and ensured progress from one century to another.[25] It is as if Ṭāhā Ḥusain, who had presented Abu'l-'Alā' as a universal figure within the tradition in question, wanted to render a similar service to Ibn Khaldūn. But to think along these lines would be to miss the whole point of the work under consideration.

The truth of the matter is that after his study on Abu'l-'Alā', Ṭāhā Ḥusain wanted not so much to portray Ibn Khaldūn as yet another rationalist thinker but to demonstrate that, contrary to what might appear to be the case, the Arab historian was an oriental[26], Muslim thinker of his time (the Middle Ages); a man who, in spite of his exceptional gifts and certain modern-like intuitions and inklings, was not to be classified among the moderns where it mattered most, that is to say, among scientific historians and sociologists. In this way, Ṭāhā sets out to refute several European scholars, such as Schultz, Gumplowicz and Von Kremer, who believed that the "medieval" thinker had anticipated the modern founders of scientific history and sociology. Contrary to these unqualified admirers of Ibn Khaldūn, Ṭāhā proposes, probably for the first time ever, to study the Arab historian within the limits of his medieval oriental world. Although Ibn Khaldūn fathered a highly original social philosophy, he was not, according to Ṭāhā, to be credited with the honour of having founded either history or sociology as a science well before the nineteenth century.

But if this is the main message of the work, why should it come as a natural sequel to Ṭāhā's thesis on Abu'l-'Alā'? Let us first draw attention to Ṭāhā's precocious familiarity with, and close reading of, Ibn Khaldūn. The early writings, starting with the series of articles on Zaydān (1911), abound in references, both implicit and explicit, to the Arab historian, especially the *Muqaddima*. Ṭāhā's reflections on the development of Arab society before and after the rise of Islam drew heavily on Ibn Khaldūn's teachings on the interplay between nomadism or the bedouin way of life (*al-badāwa*) and city-dwelling. Of even greater relevance still is the fact that Ibn Khaldūn served as a valid interlocutor in Ṭāhā's early discourse on modern historical methodology. Thus the young man's ambition to expound in a series of prelogomena (*muqaddimāt*) what was needed for literary history to be a science clearly evokes the Khaldūnian precedent of aspiring to establish history as a discipline *sui generis*. Again, Ṭāhā's early scientistic determinism which purported to be Taineian, contained, as we have already seen, a Khaldūnian strand.

It was, therefore, highly appropriate and judicious for the author of *Tajdīd dhikrā Abi'l-'Alā'* to choose Ibn Khaldūn as a subject for his Paris thesis. First of all, the choice was convenient for someone who wanted to achieve the maximum within the shortest possible time. It was partly due to this choice that he managed to write his thesis in the record time of under two years.[27] We shall see below with what admirable economy of energy and logical acuity he tackled the subject.

But the choice was not simply a matter of convenience; it was also, and in an important sense, logical and unavoidable. Ibn Khaldūn must have posed a serious problem for Ṭāhā. Being such a valid interlocutor with regrd to the modern scientific study of Arab literary history, an essentially or methodologically European product according to Ṭāhā, Ibn Khaldūn had a *prima facie* claim to "modernity"; and the question was bound to arise as to what extent this claim was justified. In fact, the question had already arisen and had been answered after a fashion in "Ḥayāt al-ādāb" (1914), where Ibn Khaldūn is criticized on more than one account from a positivist point of view. We shall see shortly how these criticisms were taken up and developed in the Paris thesis. But it should be clear by now that Ibn Khaldūn constituted a serious challenge for the young modernist or the budding positivist, and had to be confronted for a final settling of accounts.

Concerning the modernity of Ibn Khaldūn, the author of the Paris thesis gives a finely shaded, but potentially misleading, answer. He goes out of his way to stress time and time again Ibn Khaldūn's remarkable originality and to give him the credit for many pioneering and apparently modern innovations. Thus Ibn Khaldūn is said to be the first among Muslims to have written in an almost modern form the history of their literary and intellectual development;[28] his achievement in this sphere was all the more remarkable in that he treated science as a social phenomenon.[29] His views on education, Ṭāhā affirms, can compare with those of Herbert Spencer[30] and Pestalozzi.[31] As far as history is concerned, Ibn Khaldūn was the first historian not only in the Islamic world but also in ancient and medieval times, to have viewed history globally, and to have devised a method for examining the historical facts as well as an auxiliary discipline which helped make these facts comprehensible.[32] It happens ever so often that Ibn Khaldūn's ideas remind us of some of the great minds in political philosophy, such as Aristotle, Machiavelli and Montesquieu. At times, the Arab historian even surpasses the first two thinkers.[33] He was after all the first to free politics from religious considerations and to give it a more scientific form, steering it away from practical ends.[34] On the question of the Caliphate, Ṭāhā, drawing on an insight of Paul Casanova, argues that Ibn Khaldūn was the first Muslim to express personal and impartial views, secular ideas so to speak, on a subject which had hitherto been of a purely religious character.[35] Ṭāhā also detects close parallels between Ibn Khaldūn and Cournot.[36]

All this is very well, but it should not divert attention from the main thrust of Ṭāhā's thought. In two successive chapters, namely II and III, he criticizes Ibn Khaldūn's claims to modernity on two accounts, first as a founder of scientific history and then as a practitioner of scientific sociology. On both accounts, the performance of the Arab historian is judged according to criteria laid down by Ṭāhā's masters at the Sorbonne: Seignobos for history and Durkheim (mainly) for sociology. It is they who are supposed to be the ultimate authority on what should count as scientific in history and sociology, respectively.

Beginning with history then, the main target is Ibn Khaldūn's aim of establishing a reliable method for ensuring the comprehensibility and accuracy of history through the establishment of truth concerning past occurrences and the clear exposition of the deeper laws governing social mechanisms. The main criticism levelled against this enterprise, so defined, is that it pertains to the philosophy of history, and not to [scientific] history according to "modern historians" or "modern schools" [of historiographical thought].[37] For these, so the argument goes, history is essentially a study of the material traces left by past events; a modern historian is required to discover and examine these traces and thereby establish the events they point to, all in a methodical and precise manner.

As for Ibn Khaldūn, it never occurred to him to study such traces; instead, he, like Vico, chose to reflect upon the facts themselves and thus to derive general laws concerning the course of events and social life.[38] For Ibn Khaldūn, the rules governing the examination and verification of reported events can be reduced to a single rule, namely, to ascertain, in a purely speculative fashion, whether such an event is possible in itself, does not contradict social laws or is in harmony with what is the case at the time and place of its occurrence.[39]

The point about Ibn Khaldūn's failure to realize that history is essentially the study of the material traces of past events is just a generalized version of Ṭāhā's earlier criticism, made in "Ḥayāt al-ādāb", concerning Ibn Khaldūn's exclusive concern with oral traditions and consequent neglect of written documents.[40]

Having made his first criticism of Ibn Khaldūn, Ṭāhā adds that the Arab historian never intended to change the nature of historical enquiry. History remained for him, as for his predecessors, a narration of events pertaining to an age or a race, except that he rightly believed that to relate events intelligently, it was not enough to adduce the bare facts; rather the story should be based on knowledge concerning "the general conditions of regions, races and periods". But, contends Ṭāhā, this type of knowledge is not provided by history itself as conceived of by Ibn Khaldūn; it is rather the proper subject of another enquiry which, though auxiliary to history, is considered as a discipline *sui generis*, concerned with human association (*al-'umrān*).[41]

Those who believed that Ibn Khaldūn intended to establish history as a science were, according to Ṭāhā, misled by his use of the Arabic word *'ilm* which had been mistranslated as "science", when in fact it meant no more than "knowledge".[42]

Furthermore, continues Ṭāhā, one only needs to consider Ibn Khaldūn's practice as a historian to realize that he did not achieve the aims attributed to him. For, while in the *Muqaddima* he seems to be about to revolutionize the study of history, he proceeds in his *History* as an Arab narrator of the common and usual type, who relates events indiscriminately and uncritically.[43]

Following his refutation of Ibn Khaldūn's claim to be the founder of scientific history, Ṭāhā proceeds to consider whether his *'ilm al-'umrān* (science, or to be more precise according to Ṭāhā, knowledge of human association) could be equated with scientific sociology, in other words to consider whether in founding the discipline in question, Ibn Khaldūn had anticipated modern sociology. Here again, Ṭāhā gives a negative answer, supported by several arguments derived in the main from Durkheim.

Ibn Khaldūn is criticized for having taken into account one social form, namely the organized state (*sha'b* or *umma*), studying its development and transformations in history. He did not realize the importance of other social forms, namely particular groups within Islamic political society, for instance the Sūfī orders of whose existence he was well aware.[44]

In fact, Ṭāhā would say, Ibn Khaldūn's overriding concern was historical rather than sociological; though convinced that his study of society constituted a discipline *sui generis*, he conducted it not for its own sake but for the sake of history and for history as an account of political events. This is why he approached society in its external political form, i.e. the state, and studied this form in a most elementary fashion. His interest in the nomadic tribe stemmed from his belief that it was the origin of all empires.[45]

At a more fundamental level, Ibn Khaldūn is said to have had no clear conception of society as distinct from his conception of the individual; he did not realize that society had a reality of its own independently of that of its members; he based his study of society on the study of individuals, and, particularly, on data already furnished by theological and metaphysical studies of the human soul; thus to study this soul was for Ibn Khaldūn a matter of applying to it the laws of individual psychology.[46] Even the development of the state was assimilated to that of the individual.[47]

It is obvious that all these criticisms are based on Durkheim's views on the ontological and methodological primacy of society (as a whole and not the mere sum of its members) and on his hostility to the introduction of psychological factors in sociological explanation.

However, in a final criticism levelled against the speculative character of Ibn Khaldūn's methodology, Ṭāhā develops some of his own objections previously made in "Ḥayāt al-ādāb" concerning Ibn Khaldūn's recourse to the supernatural in historical explanation. This methodology, we are told, purports to base its demonstrations on experience, and yields fruitful results as long as it adheres to this base. At times, however, Ibn Khaldūn abandons his experimental method for a theological or metaphysical manner of explanation. This happens for instance when he seeks to explain the sweeping victories of the nascent Islamic state over Persia and Byzantium by invoking miraculous intervention.[48] On more than one occasion, he draws his proofs from metaphysics. Thus all that he has to say on the human soul and its mode of perception is pure metaphysics.[49]

In conclusion, Ṭāhā affirms that Ibn Khaldūn made some highly original and profound sociological insights, but his merit would be diminished in no way if it was said that the *Muqaddima* offered a kind of groping for sociology rather than sociology itself.[50] For Ṭāhā, Ibn Khaldūn was a social philosopher but not a sociologist.

Now Ṭāhā's argumentation against Ibn Khaldūn is ingeniously economic. Taking his premises from his Sorbonne masters, he mounts his attack on two fronts, one for history and one for sociology, spotting the weak points in the Khaldūnian system (e.g. the failure to consider history as the study of the material traces of the past: the problematic relationship between history and sociology;[51] the appeal to theological and metaphysical explanation) and making use of his own earlier findings. Nothing is wasted and no efforts are squandered. Once the target has been set, Ibn Khaldūn is caught between the hammer of documentary history and the anvil of positivist sociology.

And yet one cannot help feeling that there is something basically wrong with Ṭāhā's dialectically skilful procedure, if only because Ibn Khaldūn, thus trapped, is not allowed to present his case for what it is worth. Indeed, he is treated "analytically", where analysis means being considered piecemeal, according to external criteria and in such a way as to be necessarily vulnerable. Ibn Khaldūn's science of human association (*'ilm al-'umrān*) is first refused a hearing in the historical compartment on the ground that it is supposed to constitute a discipline *sui generis*, and is consequently relegated to the sociological compartment only to be condemned there for its alleged shortcomings from a Durkheimian point of view.

In this criticism, carried out in the name of modernity, Ṭāhā speaks with two voices, depending on which side of the fence he is standing on, and with no regard for consistency. Thus, where he is under the influence of Langlois and Seignobos, he criticizes Ibn Khaldūn for reflecting on the nature of facts themselves, this being condemned as philosophical speculation. He does not take into consideration that Durkheim himself had also reflected on social facts, and that he had been castigated on that account by methodological individualists who accused him of ontologizing.

Moving to the sociological compartment, Ṭāhā himself implicitly condones Durkheim's theses concerning the primacy and holistic nature of society.

From this latter side of the fence, he would also criticize Ibn Khaldūn for his exclusive concern with political history; a point which is debatable, but the least that can be said is that it ignores the fact that Langlois and Seignobos, the paragons of modernity in history, favour political history over sociologically oriented history.[52]

The Croisets

Ṭāhā's classical education in France is such an interesting subject as to deserve a whole chapter, to say the least. For reasons of convenience, however, we shall limit the enquiry to certain aspects of this education, which had a bearing on two questions. The first concerns Ṭāhā's views on pre-Islamic poetry and will be dealt with immediately, while the second concerns Ṭāhā's mature humanism which will be the subject of the following section. Luckily, considerations of convenience derive some support from the fact that Ṭāhā's production in the classical sphere as such did not occupy an important place in his total output. The bulk of this production was completed within the six years (1919–1925) following his return to Egypt, a period during which he taught ancient history at the Egyptian National University. In 1925, when this establishment became (the state) University of Cairo, Ṭāhā was appointed professor of Arabic literature; and from that point onward, his interest in the classical sphere as such was limited and occasional. In fact, almost all of Ṭāhā's work in this area was carried out not for its own sake, as a mere scholarly exercise so to speak, but with an eye to subjects close at home. In other words, Ṭāhā's knowledge of Graeco-Roman history and literature was used for the analogies and contrasts it could offer in a comparative study of Arabic literature, or for the light it might throw on Egypt's identity and place in universal culture.

With regard to the first question mentioned above, we may consider how Ṭāhā uses knowledge gained from Alfred and Maurice Croiset's *Histoire de la littérature grecque* in the study of pre-Islamic poetry. Whether or not Ṭāhā had read this work when he wrote "Ḥayāt al-Khansā'",[53] we know that it served as a textbook for his study of the history of Greek literature under Alfred

Croiset at the Sorbonne; we equally know that it subsequently became a major reference for Ṭāhā's writings on Greek literature and history. One aspect of the work which must have appealed to him is that the authors, like Lanson, opted for a synthetic approach to the subject, which combined, according to them, the main methodological insights of Taine, Brunetière and Sainte-Beuve – together with an emphasis on the role of subjective taste.[54]

Traces of the Croisets' influence are to be found in Ṭāhā's *Qādat al-fikr* (1925), especially in the chapter devoted to Homer. But it is in Ṭāhā's work on pre-Islamic poetry (1926) that the Croisets come to play their most prominent role. Their discussion of the Homeric question and its various ramifications serve as a primary source for substantiating Ṭāhā's claim that poetic forgery is a universal phenomenon to be found not only in Arab culture but also in ancient Greek and other cultures. By the same token, the Croisets' work is a rich source of materials for the many parallels that Ṭāhā draws between Homeric Greece and pre-Islamic Arabia. More specifically, the Croisets' views on the unity, composition, authorship and transmission of the *Iliad* constitutes a model which Ṭāhā copies, to what extent we shall see shortly, in his corresponding views on pre-Islamic poetry.

How close was Ṭāhā's imitation of the Croisets? Miftah Tahar, who compiled an impressive list of the points of concordance between the Croisets and Ṭāhā, tends, I think, to be misleading.[55] By being too analytical, and confining himself to the mere enumeration of such points, he creates the impression that the Croisets' influence was of fundamental importance, when in fact it was not.

It should be noted first that despite agreement between the two sides it does not always follow that Ṭāhā derived the view concerned from the authors of *L'histoire de la littérature grecque.* Thus Ṭāhā's thesis concerning the temporal priority of poetry over prose, a conviction that he shares with the Croisets, can be traced back to an earlier source, namely Nallino[56].

More importantly, Ṭāhā's procedure diverges at certain points from that of the Croisets. Unlike them, he never tries to differentiate within the work criticized between a hard core of early or authentic elements and later accretions and interpolations. This is clearly recognized by Miftah Tahar,[57] but he draws from the fact no critical conclusions: he does not realize that the divergence in question is of a fundamental nature, that in comparison with it all of Ṭāhā's borrowings from, and imitations of, the Croisets appear to be relatively minor, playing as it were a logically supportive role in Ṭāhā's case against pre-Islamic poetry.

The existence of this divergence suggests that Ṭāhā's radical scepticism concerning the authenticity of pre-Islamic poetry was based on some other principles. What principles these are is not difficult to ascertain.

We may recall that in "Ḥayāt al-Khansā'" (1915), Ṭāhā held certain views which were reminiscent of the Croisets, whether or not he had read them, while maintaining others under the clear influence of Langlois and Seignobos. In the former case, he believed that there was something to be gained from the study of orally transmitted, pre-historical or legendary poetry; while in the latter case he argued that the main written sources on al-Khansā', which were compiled two centuries after the rise of Islam, were bound to prove unreliable when critically examined. The rules of procedure according to which this examination was to be carried out were derived partly from Langlois and Seignobos and partly from the Islamic methodology of *al-jarḥ wa'l-ta'dīl*.[58]

However, by 1926, when he had studied the Croisets' work and perfected his knowledge of Langlois and Seignobos, Ṭāhā was completely converted to the latters' position. He came to the conclusion that the study of oral or legendary traditions could yield no useful results.[59] He also questioned the motives and reliability of post-Islamic transmission and records of pre-Islamic poetry,[60] according to what Langlois and Seignobos described as the negative internal criticism of the good faith and accuracy of authors.[61] With this development, Ṭāhā's views came to be constructed mainly according to the critical principles prescribed by Langlois and Seignobos.

It follows from this that Ṭāhā Ḥusain did not derive his theory of pre-Islamic poetry from the Croisets or from other Hellenists, for that matter.[62] This theory had a long history which may be now outlined as follows. It all started in Cairo (1911) with the observation, made mainly under the influence of Nallino, that neither the language (form) nor the religious content of the so-called pre-Islamic poetry corresponded to recently discovered, mainly Ḥimyarite, inscriptions. It was also in Cairo (1914), and under the same influence, that Ṭāhā questioned the motives and reliability of post-Islamic transmitters of that poetry. In Montpellier (1915) he identified the rudiments of the methodology he needed to develop his doubts, namely (1) the general principle that oral traditions are necessarily pre-historical and legendary; (2) the assumption that the critical study of pre-historical, legendary poetry could yield useful results for historical research; (3) elementary rules of textual criticism; and (4) elementary rules for the character criticism of the main written sources on pre-Islamic poetry.

This rudimentary methodology was of a mixed character. The general principle (1) could be easily traced back to Langlois and Seignobos. The assumption (2) might or might not have come from the Croisets. The set of rules (3) must have come from the same source as the general principle (1). The set of rules (4) were of Islamic origin.

In 1926, the above-mentioned observation was developed into two major arguments, one to the effect that the language of pre-Islamic poetry did not reflect the linguistic conditions prevailing in Arabia before the rise of Islam,[63] and the other to the effect that the content of that poetry did not reflect the religious, intellectual or social conditions in ancient Arabia.[64] At the same time, the scientific methodology adopted to back up these arguments, thus far based on mere observations, was derived not from the Croisets but from Langlois and Seignobos. Thus, while maintaining the general principle (1), Ṭāhā rejected the assumption (2). In this fashion, he was able to place on firmer ground the thesis that the true image of life in ancient Arabia could not be sought in (orally transmitted) pre-Islamic poetry, as well as the correlate thesis to the effect that the image in question could only be sought in the Qur'ān.[65] Implicit in the general principle mentioned above, this latter thesis was explicitly formulated thanks, partly, to the influence of Casanova's practice of Qur'ānic criticism.[66]

Finally, Ṭāhā's fully fledged criticism of the post-Islamic transmission and sources of pre-Islamic poetry,[67] though originally inspired by Nallino, was carried out in full awareness of Langlois and Seignobos' codified, negative criticism of the faith and accuracy of authors.

Given this, we can see that Ṭāhā had at his disposal all the essential elements for the construction of his theory of pre-Islamic poetry well before 1926. To be more precise, the theory in question, already embryonic during the Montpellier period, was virtually complete and ready for formulation in Paris. Further contributions were added either at this latter stage or afterwards, but they could not have been essential. It is in this sense that

Ṭāhā's imitations of the Croisets' model of Homeric criticism, though extensive, played only a supportive role.

This long history of Ṭāhā's views on pre-Islamic poetry shows, moreover, the falsity of the accusation, frequently levelled against him, that he plagiarized Margoliouth's "The Origins of Arabic poetry".[68] Given his development and the logic of his argument, the author of *Fi'l-shi'r al-jāhilī* did not need the support of the British orientalist. If, for the sake of argument, we assume, what Ṭāhā Ḥusain himself denied, that he had access to Margoliouth's work before or while formulating his theory, then the most that can be said is that this work played the role of a catalyst.[69] Any correspondence between the two authors may be, therefore, attributed to reliance on common sources and exposure to the same influences. Margoliouth himself was sufficiently perceptive and fair to concede as much.[70]

Hellenic humanism

By "Hellenic humanism" I mean Ṭāhā Ḥusain's vision of a universal culture originating in ancient Greece and encompassing Egypt as well as the rest of the Near East. This vision came into existence during the Cairo period under the influence of Luṭfī al-Sayyid and some of Ṭāhā's teachers at the Egyptian University, especially Santillana and Massignon. Some of Ṭāhā's early writings incorporated such influences into an embryonic form of humanism, exemplified by scattered insights concerning, for instance, the importance of the Greek contribution to 'Abbāsid culture, the Aristotelian affiliation of Abu'l-'Alā' and also his wide-ranging interests and universal significance.

But Ṭāhā's humanism took on a definitely Hellenic character as a result of his classical studies at the Sorbonne, namely the history of Greek literature (under Alfred Croiset), Greek history (under Gustave Glotz), Roman history (under Gustave Bloch) and Byzantine history (under Charles Diehl). The teachings of these masters, together with possible further readings, led Ṭāhā to the view that Ancient Greece had played a central and active role in unifying the world and creating a universal culture. These were the sources from which Ṭāhā derived sufficient knowledge for substantiating and elaborating his humanism in the series of works which he published between 1919 and 1925 in his capacity as professor of ancient history.[71]

However, the urge to evolve a rounded humanist vision of world culture did not simply come from those sources; it seems to have stemmed from Ṭāhā's preoccupation with Egypt's identity and destiny in a world which he himself had divided into East and West. In his thesis on Ibn Khaldūn, he, as a zealous modernist, had set the Arab historian apart as an oriental thinker who did not fit within the mainstream of Western thought running from ancient Greece to modern Europe. This dichotomy between Western civilization, with its ancient Greek roots, and a radically different, recalcitrant, Orient, is as old as Thucydides and must, we may assume, have been promoted, in one form or another, by Ṭāhā's teachers of classics and possibly by further readings, during the same period.

But the dichotomy became problematic, or antinomic, only to Ṭāhā, who was also an oriental Egyptian. For if it is true that there is such a wide or unbridgeable gulf between the East and the West, how would it be possible to modernize Egypt and to revive Arab culture? Given this challenge, we can understand why as soon as he was back home he set out to solve the problem in the above-mentioned series of works. Constituting almost the bulk of his production in the classical sphere, assuming at times a scholarly form (translation and commentary) and written with an eye to the needs of Egyptian undergraduates (with no background in the field concerned), these works were primarily addressed to the urgent task, namely to show that the gulf was bridgeable. To achieve this aim, the works in question were meant to highlight for the Egyptian audience both the spread and the eternal relevance of Greek culture.

In *Ālihat al-Yūnān* ("The Greek deities"), which is an elementary study of Greek religion, Ṭāhā assumes, no doubt under the influence of Fustel de Coulanges, the primacy of religion in Greek life. Thus the whole of Greek literature (with the exception of history and philosophy) as well as Greek moral codes and plastic arts are said to be offshoots (*āthār*) of the Greek religious phenomenon.[72] It is also under the same influence that Ṭāhā assumes that the ancient Aryans had two religions; the one was domestic, based on the cult of the dead and that of the sacred fire, while the other was public inducing people to study the nature of things and to hold them as sacred.[73]

Being a summary of Ṭāhā's first course of lectures during the academic year 1919–1920, *Ālihat al-Yūnān* contains little of substance, but its importance lies in its being Ṭāhā's first attempt to marshal his recently acquired knowledge with a view to tackling the above-mentioned issue. His approach to Greek religion is evolutionary, by which he means that it changed for the better or progressed (*al-ruqiyy* or *al-irtiqā'*). He would, he suggests, study Greek religion as it evolved with the evolution of Greek civilization, a movement which, we gather, involved the achievement of a higher level of refinement. "These deities," writes Ṭāhā, "were originally gods of war and combat, but they grew civilized little by little, finally becoming gods of civilization and security".[74]

With the achievement of this refinement, Greek religion came to exert a beneficial influence beyond its proper domain: while it helped to unify the Greeks into a single commonwealth,[75] some Greek gods so evolved as to exert a considerable influence on philosophy and literature.[76] Such was the importance of that influence, we are again told, that some philosophers believed that the higher principles of Christianity were the fruit of Greek philosophy.[77]

These developments were not, however, accidental. Ṭāhā assumes that the Greeks had a natural capacity for civilization (*isti'dād al-sha'b al-Yūnānī li'l-ḥaḍāra*); and under this title he devotes what could have been a whole lecture to the subject.[78] The most important aspect of this natural drive for improvement is Greek rationalism. "It is a well-known fact," says Ṭāhā, "that as soon as the Greek nation came to be aware of its own existence and of having a mind of its own, it became attached to intellectual life, giving it priority over everything else."[79]

It is through such observations that Ṭāhā tries to convey the message that the Greek mind, having naturally evolved towards a more refined conception of the gods and a more rational view of the world, influenced, and became relevant to, the rest of the world. The message is clearly stated in the preface, where Ṭāhā stresses the need for Egyptians to study the Greek legacy as an indispensable means of understanding the modern world and modernizing their own culture. The study of Greek history, he maintains, receives little attention and is even derided, when in fact it should be a matter of national concern. "Knowledge of our own history", he writes, "depends on knowing the Greeks with whom we have entertained close relations, literary as well as political, for the last twenty-five centuries. Our modern progress depends on studying this history, for it means that we take what suits us from modern civilization, which is Greek first and foremost."[80]

For Egyptians to understand their own history and to gain access to modernity, they must therefore study the Greek heritage. This is the moral of the story related in *Ālihat al-Yūnān.* Two main reasons are given in justification: that Greek culture, far from being alien to Egypt, has always been close to it; and that modern (European) civilization is essentially Greek. In subsequent works in the series, Ṭāhā amplifies and develops these arguments.

In his introduction to *Niẓām al-Athīniyyīn li- Arisṭuṭālīs,* which is a translation of Aristotle's *The Athenian Constitution,* Ṭāhā introduces for the first time what amounts to a major theme, namely the Hellenization of the ancient world by Alexander. Drawing mainly on Glotz, Ṭāhā shows how Alexander, having destroyed the power of Greece and Persia, sought to build on the ruins of both empires a new Hellenic, or to be more precise Hellenistic, dominion in which East and West were united. The Greek nation, thus reborn, endeavoured to reduce the intellectual distance between the two sides, imposing upon them a single mode of conception and thought.[81]

In *Qādat al-fikr* ("Leading figures in human thought"), the last work produced by Ṭāhā as professor of ancient history, the theme is developed into a general account of the progress of the Greek mind towards universality or, in other words, the Hellenization of the human mind. The inspiration here is partly Comtean[82] inasmuch as the account in question concerns the development of the human mind and the final triumph of rationalism and science. But Ṭāhā's view of history diverges from Comte's law of the three states in more than one way. First, the former view is offered as a mere description of what happened in history, and not as a general law prescribing for each and every culture the path it must follow. Secondly, instead of Comte's three stages, Ṭāhā reckons that the human mind has gone through five ages, three of which are characterized by one predominant activity and are represented by one or more major figures. Thus we have a first age of (epic) poetry represented by Homer, followed by a philosophical age represented by Socrates, Plato and Aristotle. Then comes the age of political leadership, in which the major figures are Alexander and Julius Caesar. The fourth age (the Middle Ages), which is seen as predominantly religious, is not associated with any such figures; while the fifth, and final, stage (modern times) is protrayed as involving a diversity of activities (and, presumably, a great number of leaders).

It would seem, therefore, that the author of *Qādat al-fikr* draws inspiration from yet another source; namely Durkheim. Ṭāhā's leading figures are reminiscent of the latter's "benefactors of humanity", that is to say, great men who, while being the product of their society, come to represent and lead it forward as they incarnate its higher ideals. It is probably with this in mind that Ṭāhā inaugurates his work by raising the issue of society versus (great) individuals, and opts for a compromise solution. Great individuals, we are told, are influenced by society and are in fact social phenomena, but they in turn exert an influence on society.[83]

Be that as it may, the main problem for the author of *Qādat al-fikr* is, as has already been mentioned, the Hellenization or unification of the world. Alexander, and Julius Caesar for that matter, are considered not only as great conquerors (or empire-builders), but also as major figures in human thought; for while the former unified the ancient world towards the east, the latter unified it towards the west, under the banner of Greek culture. Alexander, in particular, is said to have made it possible for Greek literature and philosophy "to permeate the inner depths of the Orient, to influence the minds of Orientals and to impose upon them that Greek character (*al-ṣibgha al-Yūnāniyya*) which previously had been designed to be a universal and immortal character of the human mind as a whole."[84]

Though imposed by the force of arms, this character was, according to Ṭāhā, primarily philosophical and scientific. Forged originally by Greek philosophy in the fifth century B.C., it reached its highest and most influential form with Aristotle, who set out, consciously, to systematize ancient knowledge and to provide an exhaustive account covering the laws of human thought and expression as well as of public and private life.[85] These laws, argues Ṭāhā, are immutable and suitable for man *qua* man and not insofar as he is Eastern or Western, ancient or modern.[86] Aristotle, according to Ṭāhā, represented, at the intellectual level, the new Greek nation and world unity created by Alexander; it was he who reflected, in the realm of thought, the drive to make the Greek mind universal and chart for humanity the way to further progress.[87] More specifically, he is thought to be an empiricist or even a positivist philosopher who was attached to perceptible, indubitable reality (*al-wāqi' al-muḥass al-ladhī lā shakka fīh).*[88] Again, we are told that Aristotle was the forerunner of Auguste Comte, because he was the first to establish the unity of the world and the unity of philosophy (human knowledge) as well as being the first pioneer as far as sociology is concerned.[89]

From this, it would appear that by "the Greek character" Ṭāhā means rationalism and what he takes to be its extension in modern times, namely empirical science. The same character also stands for the Greek love of freedom. In ancient times, we are told, the human mind assumed two conflicting forms; the one was purely Greek, characterized by rationalism and attachment to freedom, whether political or individual, while the other was Oriental, dominated by the religious spirit and absolute, holy monarchy.[90] It was partly due to its intrinsic excellence and universal aspirations that the former type of mind, finally, and after numerous setbacks, gained ascendance and still dominates human life. The second type of mind has been defeated several times and is laying down its arms in complete surrender.[91]

Such was Ṭāhā Ḥusain's Hellenic humanism as expressed in 1919–1925. It rested, as we have just seen, on Ṭāhā's assumptions concerning the exemplary character of Greek thought and its triumphant unification of the world, sometimes through conquest, against a recalcitrant Orient attached to religion and political tyranny.

This was not, however, Ṭāhā's final resolution of the conflict between East and West. In *Mustaqbal al-thaqāfa fī Miṣr* (1938), as if irked by the feeling that his humanism, as hitherto formulated, was one-sided in favour of the West and laid too much emphasis on the use of force, Ṭāhā reopens the issue in an attempt to provide a more harmonious account of the intellectual unity of the world, with Egypt occupying a more prominent place.

In this new attempt, the polarization between the East and the West is still maintained, except that the East is now restricted to the Far East.[92] There are now two distinctly different and bitterly antagonistic cultures on the earth; the one in Europe, and the other in the Far East. Given this, the fundamental question is whether Egypt is of the East or the West.[93] We may note here that Egypt, described as ancient and eternal,[94] is assumed, somewhat in the manner of Luṭfī al-Sayyid, to possess an identity of its own, over and above its Arab-Islamic history. With Egypt thus detached from its Arab-Islamic background, the stage is set for the relocation of Egyptian culture in a new mapping of the world. Ṭāhā's answer to the above-mentioned question is that Egypt is part of the Near East, and is, therefore, closer to the West or is even part of Europe. Having relocated Egypt in the Near East, Ṭāhā would regroup the whole region, together with ancient Greece and Rome as well as modern Europe, within the Mediterranean basin or within the Mediterranean family of cultures.

To justify this new mapping of the world, Ṭāhā would point out to the long-standing close ties between Egypt and the Near Eastern countries on the one hand and the Aegean-Greek cultures on the other. Similar contacts, he would say, cannot be said to have prevailed between Egypt and the Far East.[95] Ṭāhā would also argue for the essential cultural homogeneity of the Western and Near Eastern members of the Mediterranean family. Drawing on Paul Valéry, who analysed the European mind in terms of (1) Greek civilization (with its literature, philosophy and art), (2) Roman civilization (with its political institutions and jurisprudence) and (3) Christianity,[96] Ṭāhā maintains that Islamic culture has an essentially similar constitution.

The fact that in this latter case Islam replaces Christianity does not, according to Ṭāhā, change in any significant way the basic affinity between the two sides, as both religions have the same (Near Eastern) origins, share the same fundamental tenets and have had similar relations with Greek philosophy. Ṭāhā would even go a step further, suggesting that the inclusion of religion in the equation does not alter the essential characteristics in either case, whether that of the European mind or of Islamic civilization. "If it is true," writes Ṭāhā, "that Christianity did not transform the European mind or eliminate either its inherited Hellenism or Mediterranean qualities, it must be equally true that Islam did not change the Egyptian mind or the mind of the people who embraced it and who were influenced by the Mediterranean Sea".[97]

Thus while the West, with its cult of reason and science, was previously set against the East with its religions and prophecies, there is now a common ground on which both Europe and the Near East stand, sharing essentially the same heritage, which is a mixture of reason and spirit. The author of *Mustaqbal al-thaqāfa fī Miṣr* denies that the spiritualist East with which some Europeans are fascinated is the Near East. The spiritualist East is the Far East, whereas the Near East was the cradle of the mind. This same area was also the source of the revealed religions adopted by Europeans and (Near) Easterners alike.[98] To identify the Near East with spiritualism is just as absurd as to identify Europe with materialism,[99] or with reason for that matter.

In this fashion, Ṭāhā finally resolves the East-West antinomy. In the final reconciliation between Europe and the Near East, there is no conqueror or conquered; nor is there a monopoly on either side of rationalism or spiritualism. Instead, there is a centuries old give-and-take of all sorts, through which an essential homogeneity of outlook has been created. To emphasize this point, somewhat dramatically, Ṭāhā affirms that Egypt has always been part of Europe as far as intellectual or cultural life is concerned.[100]

The Logic of the heart

The final reconciliation between Europe and the Near East, as established in *Mustaqbal al-thaqāfa fī Miṣr,* implies that the author of this work has also resolved another conflict, namely that between reason (science) and religion (Islam in particular). Thus Islam is seen to coexist with Greek and Roman components within Near Eastern culture, just as Christianity is seen to coexist with the same components within European culture. Ṭāhā makes the point explicit when he argues that an equilibrium between civilization and religion can be, and in fact has been, established. This, we are told, has happened in Christian Europe, when honest Europeans realized that the conflict was not between religion and civilization as such but between representatives of both sides. The equilibrium is all the easier to reach in the case of Islam, a religion which knows no clergy. Furthermore, the Muslim Arabs showed the way, having had no qualms in adopting the driving forces in Persian and Greek civilization.[101]

Now this kind of reconciliation is in turn the final stage in a long, torturous process of thought on the dispute between reason (science) and religion (faith). At the early stages of this process Ṭāhā assumed that the dispute was basic and, in a sense, insoluble. Let us therefore consider this line of development.

The problem first arose in Cairo, in 1914, as part of Ṭāhā's early positivism. At the time, we may recall, he decided that miracles must be excluded from the realm of (scientific) history and relegated to religious disciplines. In his thesis on Abu'l-'Alā', Ṭāhā went a step further, suggesting that religion as such might be assigned to the realm of sentiment or emotion.[102] From this point onward there arose an idea on which Ṭāhā Ḥusain was to insist for the rest of his life, namely the need for a separation of science and religion, with each having its proper place in the life of man. But what does it mean for these two forces to be separated?

It was only in the 1920s that the question began to occupy Ṭāhā's attention. In 1923, he suggested that religion served a psychological purpose, giving individuals a comforting refuge and a sense of security in moments of great danger.[103] He also wondered wistfully whether man could ever be able to combine the two forces of reason and faith, opposed to each other as they are.[104] From this we may gather that the separation of science and religion should ideally lead to a situation where they are combined in a state of equilibrium, where each, while occupying its proper place, counterbalances and complements the other.

Now I shall show in what follows that this ideal is impossible to achieve on Ṭāhā's positivist premises, and, equally, that he was to realize this only in the course of time, when he had abandoned his positivism. But let us consider first his views on the opposition between science and religion. In 1926, he believed that this opposition was fundamental and inevitable. It is true, he argued, that politics played a part in exacerbating relations between scientists and philosophers on the one hand and men of religion on the other, but politics could not be held responsible for the dispute between science (reason) and religion as such.[105]

There were, according to Ṭāhā, three reasons why this dispute was fundamental and inevitable. First, religion makes assertions about, and demands belief in, such matters as God's existence and prophecy, which science can neither prove nor disprove. Secondly, the divergence between the two sides does not stop at these fundamental matters of faith, but extends to specific questions relating to cosmology, astronomy, geology and embryology. Thirdly, and more seriously still, is the fact that science seeks to subject religion itself to critical investigation, treating it as a natural, social phenomenon like language, law and custom. As an illustration, Ṭāhā cites the example of Durkheim who maintained that [through religion] society worshipped and deified itself.[106]

For all these reasons, Ṭāhā rejected as futile all attempts, whether philosophical (al-Ghazālī and Ibn Rushd) or exegetic

(Muḥammad 'Abduh and his followers), to demonstrate the basic harmony of science and religion.[107] To resolve the conflict between the two, Ṭāhā suggests that each be assigned to a separate sphere of competence according to its necessity in human nature. Each one of us, he maintains, carries within oneself two "personalities", the one rational (critical, analytical and constantly revising its findings), while the other is affective, religious, aspiring for higher ideals and searching for the security of faith. One only needs to look into oneself to see the two "personalities" living side by side. Ṭāhā would also cite the example of scientists, scholars and clergymen who managed to combine the two forces. Pasteur, for instance, was a fervent and conscientious Christian; so were the many Christian clergymen who were distinguished scientists, including geologists, natural scientists and even philologists who subjected the Bible to analysis and criticism.[108] He could also have cited the already familiar example of Casanova who, while a fervent Christian, forgot all about his faith on entering the lecture room to engage in the critical study of religious texts.

But none of this is very helpful, as it reiterates the same idea concerning the need to separate, and yet combine, the two forces. Even the examples cited are not very informative, as Ṭāhā does not explain precisely how these scientists and scholars achieved that equilibrium. At times he even suggests that he has no answer to give.[109]

This lack of clarity seems to stem from the fact that Ṭāhā does not draw the logical conclusions of his own premises; while he has an answer to the question at hand, which is hinted at or implied by what has been said so far, he gives the impression that the answer was still to be found. Being committed as he was to the positivist premise that science had the monopoly over the realm of facts, he was also committed to the idea that religious statements purporting to be about the course of nature or history were in reality normative, symbolical, allegorical statements serving a purely moral and/or psychological function.

To separate religion from science by linking religion to human needs and values, was, therefore, the best that Ṭāhā could offer, as a good positivist, by way of establishing some sort of equilibrium between the two sides. But it is obvious that this solution settles the conflict in favour of science. Ṭāhā's presentation of the claims and counterclaims of each side in such spheres as cosmology, astronomy and so forth, is misleading to the extent that it gives the impression that the issue is still open, when in fact it has been logically closed. For there to be peace between science and religion, the latter had to relinquish all claims to the provision of knowledge about nature, and to base its case solely on its affective and/or moral necessity.

Furthermore, Ṭāhā, as a positivist, was also committed to the scientific endeavour of treating religion itself as a social phenomenon like any other. In his account of the reasons why science and religion are necessarily antagonistic, he speaks of this endeavour as if he were a neutral observer, when in fact he subscribes to it. Thus in his thesis on Ibn Khaldūn, he criticizes the latter for failing to treat religion as a social phenomenon. Ibn Khaldūn, as we are told, took a step in the right direction when he treated prophecy as a natural phenomenon having its source in the human mind, but he still assumed that it was independent of society. "Had he", writes Ṭāhā, "expounded his theory [of religion] impartially, leaving aside his own faith for a moment as the moderns are apt to do, and avoiding naive exaggerations, he would have occupied a place among so many modern philosophers who have explained the origin of religious ideas [with reference to society]."[110]

Among the "modern philosophers" in question, Ṭāhā must have counted Durkheim in the first place, who, as Ṭāhā has just pointed out, sought to explain religion with reference to its social function, namely the natural impulse to establish the group as an object of veneration over and above individuals. Further evidence to show that Ṭāhā actually subscribed to the Durkheimean point of view is to be found in Ṭāhā's book on pre-Islamic poetry, where he cast doubt on the historical veracity of the religious accounts of Ibrāhīm (Abraham) and Ismā'īl (Ishmael). The mere fact that they were mentioned in the Qur'ān, we are told, was not sufficient proof of their historical reality. More specifically, the story about Ismā'īl's migration to Mecca and being the father of 'Adnānī Arabs was treated as a legend or myth (*usṭūra)* designed to establish a physical link between the Arabs and the Jews.[111] As rightly remarked by Jacques Berque, Ṭāhā considers the story concerning the Abrahamic descent of the Arabs as an etiological legend in a manner reminiscent of Durkheim.[112]

Thus as long as Ṭāhā was committed to the positivist conception of science, his attempt to strike a balance between reason and faith was bound to be in the interests of the former. The latter had to relinquish its claims to the realm of facts and to be reduced to a fact like any other. This I think was Ṭāhā's position in Paris and throughout the 1920s. His statements on the need to separate science and religion, the necessity of religion or even on the desirability of reaching a state of equilibrium between the two forces were, in spite of appearances, perfectly compatible with the above-mentioned conception. They were also in line with a well-established tradition of positivist thought, according to which some form of religion was indispensable to human life, provided of course that it was secular. As examples of this tradition, we may cite Comte's religion of humanity, Renan's cult of science and Durkheim's cult of the individual human person.

It was only in the 1930s, and beginning with his work *'Alā hāmish al-Sīra* II ("On the Margin of the Prophet's biography") (1937), that Ṭāhā's position on the subject underwent a drastic change. There he laid greater emphasis on the necessity of faith and on the need to strike a balance between it and reason. Thus the wise old monk, Callicrates, who is the spokesman of the author, has the following to say to the Greek youth who was in search of truth:[113] "I believe, my son, that your soul (*nafs*) has instincts just as your body has, and that the instincts of the soul, like those of the body, do not originate in the mind and do not derive from it, but originate in one's nature and derive from one's constitution. And the need of the soul for faith, my son, is like the need of the body for food and drink."[114]

At first glance it seems that statements such as these, similar to Ṭāhā's corresponding views in the 1920s, carry nothing new, and that the proposed compromise between reason and faith is for all practical purposes biased in favour of the former. According to Cachia, the compromise in question exists only in words. "Religious faith", he writes, "is acknowledged, but only as a satisfaction of an emotional need. Reason is yet to retain the entire direction of human action".[115] There, I think, Cachia is mistaken, for he does not realize that the proposition that religion satisfies an emotional need or has an affective nature, now acquires a new sense which goes against the positivist assumption that the realm of facts is the exclusive domain of science (or reason). "The mind", says again Callicrates, "has been so deluded by its vanity as to strive for the imposition of its laws on nature ... But these laws cannot cover everything. Nature is still free and unbound, still greater, broader and wider in range than the mind's dominion. There are events which continue to occur and which the mind can neither deny nor explain nor subsume under its laws ..."[116]

Ṭāhā, we may note, is not suggesting that there are in nature such unobservable events as defy rational explanation; the events he has in mind are observable, but they are, and will always be, inaccessible to such an explanation. To illustrate his point, Callicrates cites the case of miracles attributed to Jesus Christ. "The mind", he argues, "cannot explain how the dead were brought back to life, how the blind were made to see or how the lepers were cured; and yet all these happenings did occur and were witnessed by all and sundry."[117] As Ṭāhā was to say later, such events, which cannot be subjected to scientific rigour, relate to faith and not to reason.[118] This is surely far removed from the exclusion of miracles from history in "Ḥayāt al-ādāb" and is worlds away from Ṭāhā's scolding of Ibn Khaldūn for having admitted the possibility of miraculous intervention into the normal, causally-determined, course of events.

There is now something drastically new by comparison with Ṭāhā's standpoint in the 1920s. Faith, according to Callicrates' argument, receives an independent place not only in the emotional or moral life of man, but also in observable nature itself: the world of facts, formerly assumed to be the monopoly of reason, is now divided between rational knowledge and faith.

To be completely sure that Callicrates' statements express Ṭāhā's point of view, we may refer to *Mir'āt al-Islām* ("The Mirror of Islam")[119] (1959), where Ṭāhā, speaking directly and straightforwardly, reiterates more or less the same ideas. "Religion", he writes, "originates in God's knowledge, which is limitless, whereas modern science, like classical science (*al-'ilm al-qadīm*) is limited."[120]

The main difference here, apart from replacing unbounded nature by God's limitless knowledge, is that Ṭāhā makes a point of extending his argument about the limitedness of human knowledge to modern, empirical science. In this way, we are left in no doubt that positivism has been totally abandoned.

What was it that made Ṭāhā take this final and drastic step? A satisfactory answer to this question is not possible without detailed knowledge of Ṭāhā's spiritual life in the 1930s. There is, however, one thing that is certain, and should already be obvious, namely that he then came to believe in the possibility of miracles. In

Mir'āt al-Islām the point is made with reference to the Qur'ān, on the miraculous character of which the work provides a whole chapter,chapter 2. "The most distinctive character of the Qur'ān, we are told, is that those who read it, or listen to it being recited, without believing in it lie to themselves; for their hearts are reduced to submission and their tastes are satisfied, but their minds show opposition and denial. They, therefore, contradict themselves, exhibiting disbelief while hiding their consent."[121]

Notice how Ṭāhā, even so late in life, still believes that the conflict between reason and faith is bound to arise – even, or to be more precise especially, in the face of the Qur'ān. This Book, Ṭāhā now suggests, brings into the open and accentuates the self-contradiction of those who show disbelief in it when they are in fact deeply contented. This suggestion in turn implies another, to the effect that it is the contented heart which is right, whereas resistant, sceptic reason is wrong, or, as it were, unreasonable.

That this is actually Ṭāhā's point of view is further confirmed by what he has to say about the need to accept the authority of the Qur'ān without questioning. To do so, he assumes, it is not enough to be overwhelmed by the Book's eloquence or aesthetic qualities, powerful and inimitable as they are;[122] it is also necessary to accept the following implications: (1) that the Qur'ān comes in its entirety from God (*min 'ind Allāh*);[123] (2) that the authenticity of the Qur'ānic text, as transmitted and recorded by the early Muslims, is beyond doubt;[124] and (3) that this text is to be accepted and understood in the same way as the Prophet and his companions would have done: simply and without forcing or contriving.[125]

If it is true that Ṭāhā came to believe in the possibility of miracles in the 1930s, then we may assume that he did so on the authority of the Qur'ān. For according to *Mir'āt al-islām* at any rate, the acceptance, without questioning, of the Qur'ānic miracle is at the basis of belief in all other miracles as related by the Book and as understood by early Muslims.

In this fashion, Ṭāhā Ḥusain found his final solution to the conflict between science and religion. During the 1920s, he called for striking a balance between the two sides, but due to his positivist convictions the compromise he proposed was in actual fact nominal. In the 1930s, however, he suggested a new and real compromise involving the curtailment of the scope of science. I believe that this compromise was at the back of Ṭāhā's mind when he maintained in *Mustaqbal al-thaqāfa fī Miṣr* that religion (whether Islam or Christianity) could coexist peacefully with philosophy and science within Mediterranean culture. It was with this compromise in mind that he could affirm what he had denied in the 1920s, namely that the quarrel between science and religion was simply fomented by men on both sides and exploited by politics.

Needless to say, Ṭāhā's final reconciliation of science and religion involved tacit adherence to Ibn Khaldūn, the very thinker whom Ṭāhā had begun by criticizing in favour of a more modern, and specifically positivist, outlook. But what is truly remarkable is that this drastic reversal was due to an act of faith in the Qur'ān, the very Book with which Ṭāhā's educational journey started.

Positivism dying hard

Ṭāhā's attempt to resolve the above-mentioned antinomies through the adoption of synthetic formulae brought to his thought a relative degree of stability. This is particularly clear with regard to the East-West dichotomy and the science-religion debate, where the balance struck in the late 1930s seems to have been more or less maintained ever after.

The situation is less clear with regard to the Lansonian synthesis of objective and subjective factors in literary history. This synthesis, established during Ṭāhā's stay in France and consolidated in the 1920s, was the first form of reconciliation to be reached. The stability thereby achieved did not, however, survive the period in question. While other antinomies in other spheres found their final solution in the late 1930s, it was precisely during this period, that the objective-subjective issue was re-opened. It was then that Ṭāhā's critical thought verged on a form of unbridled impressionism which was hardly reconcilable with any significant reference to an external object.

This is to be seen most clearly in the epilogue of Ṭāhā's *Ma' al-Mutanabbī* (1936), where he argued that a work of literary criticism could never provide a faithful biography of the poet concerned, as it depicted no more than brief and disconnected moments in the life of the critic himself, during which he occupied himself with equally brief and disconnected moments in the life of the poet.[126] It is true that he went on to affirm that he had no doubt that a literary work referred to something; but he could not tell whether this thing was the poet's soul or something else.[127] That Ṭāhā's thought took a new, predominantly subjectivist, turn is confirmed by further evidence. Thus, in his review of al-'Aqqād's *Raj'at Abi'l-'Alā'* ("*The Return of Abu'l-'Alā'*"), he argued that most literary historians believed that they could portray historical figures, when in fact they portrayed nothing but themselves. In their attempt to resuscitate such figures, literary historians, wrote Ṭāhā, depended almost exclusively on evidence and indications from which they derived their reconstructions by imagination.[128] Later on, in *Ma' Abi'l-'Alā' fī sijnih* (1939) Ṭāhā maintained that literary history, like political history, was a subject riddled with doubt and uncertainty.[129]

All these indications go to show that the Lansonian synthesis broke down. But looking now more closely at Ṭāhā's unbridled impressionism we can detect in it not only the influence of Jules Lemaitre but also that of Seignobos' subjectivism.[130] The fact that Ṭāhā's doubts concerning the objectivity of history were expressed in connection with Abu'l-'Alā' is highly significant, as it goes to show that these doubts were made in self-criticism, that, in other words, Ṭāhā rejected in the 1930s his own early objectivism, as advocated in his thesis on Abu'l-'Alā' (1914).

In the 1940s and early 1950s, while at the height of his maturity, Ṭāhā still showed some measure of faithfulness to Lanson, when he shifted the emphasis to a Durkheim-like concern with the social role and representativeness of writers, with all the ensuing antinomies between the individual and society. But we have already seen how in his treatment of this theme Ṭāhā was inclined to emphasize the part played by individual spontaneity and freedom.[131] Here again we can detect the influence of Seignobos. In view of all this, we may say that starting from 1936 onward, Ṭāhā abandoned his early objectivism as well as his attempts of the 1920s to maintain a Lansonian balance between objective and subjective factors. During that late period, which was to last till the end of his life, he tended to be closer to Jules Lemaitre and Seignobos. It is true that he continued to practise objective criticism[132] and to make objectivist-like statements, speaking of writers as the product and mirror of society.[133] But objectivism, so practised and expressed, seems to be a residue of Ṭāhā's early positivism, which died hard: it is now dissociated from determinism and outshone by other tendencies pulling in the direction of individualism and subjectivism. Nor would Ṭāhā, during this late period, bother about synthesis: both objectivist and subjectivist forces are still at work, with the latter having the upper hand; but no attempt is made to strike a balance between the two sides. So it looks as if Ṭāhā's statement in *Ma' al-Mutanabbī* that literary works had a referent the nature of which he did not know, was an expression of helplessness or theoretical fatigue. Following that outburst, no more attempts were made to maintain positivism, even in a revised form.

It would appear, therefore, that the late 1930s saw the collapse of Ṭāhā's positivism. This is true whether the reconciliation achieved continued to hold as was the case for the East-West dichotomy and the science-religion debate, or broke down as was the case for the objective-subjective antinomy. It should be noted, moreover, that even in the first two cases, the accomplished stability was only relative and in comparison with the state of theoretical flux reigning in the sphere of (literary) history. Otherwise, the solution offered for the above-mentioned dichotomy in *Mustaqbal al-thaqāfa fī Miṣr* was not totally free from tension, as it contained a latent tug of war between the need to assert Egyptian identity and the equally strong drive to integrate Egypt within the mainstream of European culture.

As for the "final" reconciliation of science and faith in *Mir'āt al-Islām*, I have no doubt that it expressed Ṭāhā's genuine belief (at the time), satisfied him and gave him a measure of serenity. But his argument, based as it was on an act of will, a leap into faith after the fashion of Kierkegaard, or a wager such as that of Pascal or Abu'l-'Alā',[134] is, in the nature of the case, a precarious affair.

Notes

1 According to Ibrāhīm Amīn Ghāli, "Trois penseurs égyptiens", *La Nouvelle Revue du Caire*, vol. I (1975), pp. 219–239, p. 238, the quest for such formulae is a common characteristic among *al-Nahḍa* thinkers. While this may be true in general, Ṭāhā's case has its own specific features.

2 See Guy Bourdé and Hervé Martin, *Les écoles historiques* (Paris 1983), p. 217.

3 G. Lanson, "La méthode de l'histoire littéraire", in idem, *Essais de méthode, de critique et d'histoire*, ed. Henri Peyre (Paris 1965), pp. 31–55, pp. 31–32.

4 Ibid., p. 32.

5 "... I have never worried about being original or making discoveries; on the contrary, there was nothing I would like more, generally

speaking, than to have encountered the same ideas as the majority of my contemporaries on reading the same works." Lanson, *Histoire de la littérature française* (Paris 1951), Avant-propos, p. x.

6 Ibid., p. vi.
7 Ibid., p. vii. See also idem, op. cit., p. 33.
8 Ibid., pp. 43–44.
9 *Histoire de la littérature française*, p. vii.
10 Ibid., p. viii.
11 *Méthodes de l'histoire littéraire & Hommes et livres* (Geneva 1979), Avant-propos, p. vii.
12 Ibid.
13 Ibid., p. viii.
14 Idem, "La méthode de l'histoire littéraire", p. 32.
15 Ibid.
16 Ibid., p. 35.
17 Ibid.
18 Ibid.
19 Ibid., p. 36.
20 Ibid.
21 Ibid., pp. 36–37.
22 "Al-Qudamā' wa'l-muḥdathūn", in *Ḥadīth al-Arbi'ā'* II, *MK*, vol. II, 2nd edn., 1974, pp. 372, 373, 384. Article first published in *al-Siyāsa*, 31 January 1923.
23 Ṭāhā Ḥusain, *Fi'l-adab al-jāhilī*, in *MK*, vol. V, 1973, pp. 45 ff. Notice how in the same context Ṭāhā refers to the works of Langlois and Seignobos (ibid., p. 48, n. 2) and stresses the need to apply the critical procedures of scientific history, such as the discovery, interpretation and editing of literary texts (ibid., p. 52).
24 See Ṭāhā Ḥusain's preface to his *Falsafat Ibn Khaldūn al-ijtimā'iyya* (the Arabic translation of Ṭāhā Ḥusain's thesis on Ibn Khaldūn), tr. Muḥammad 'Abd'Allah 'Inān in *MK*, vol. VIII, 2nd edn., 1975, p. 9. The original French version of this preface has not been published.
25 Ahmed Abdesselem, *Ibn Khaldun et ses lecteurs* (Paris 1983), p. 51.
26 See T. Hussein, *Etude analytique et critique de la philosophie sociale d'Ibn-Khaldoun* (Paris 1917), p. 134, where Ibn Khaldūn is said to be basically oriental (*foncièrement oriental*) in spite of his occasional, striking similarities with some of the great minds of ancient and modern times.
27 Work on the thesis could not have been started before Ṭāhā's arrival in Paris, early in 1916. On the other hand, we know for a fact that the thesis was published in 1917.
28 T. Hussein, op. cit., p. 201.
29 Ibid., p. 203.
30 Ibid., p. 207.
31 Ibid., p. 210.
32 Ibid., p. 39. The discipline meant is sociology, which Ṭāhā considers, in Ibn Khaldūn's case, to be no more than a subsidiary science.
33 Ibid., p. 65.
34 Ibid.

35 Ibid., p. 163. Cf. Casanova *Mohammed et la fin du monde. Notes complémentaires* II (Paris 1924), p. 179.
36 Op cit., p. 160.
37 Ibid., p. 32. Notice that at this point (ibid., n. 1) Ṭāhā Ḥusain refers to Seignobos' *Introduction aux études historiques.*
38 Ibid., pp. 32–33.
39 Ibid., p. 33.
40 See above, ch. IV, p. 91.
41 Ibid., p. 34.
42 Ibid., p. 36.
43 Ibid., pp. 37–38.
44 Ibid., pp. 68–69. See also ibid. for Ṭāhā's explicit reference to Durkheim. For the latter's views on the importance of particular groups within political society, see his preface to the second edition of his *The Division of labour in society*, with an introduction by Lewis Coser, tr. W.D. Halls, reprint (London 1993).
45 Ibid., pp. 69–70.
46 Ibid., p. 70. See also p. 71.
47 Ibid.
48 Ibid., pp. 72–73.
49 Ibid., p. 73.
50 Ibid., p. 74.
51 The problem may be stated as follows: Ibn Khaldūn assumes that for history to be a truly critical discipline, it needs to be based on knowledge of the facts of human association. But how can we gain this kind of knowledge? Ibn Khaldūn would say that it can only be gained through history. But, argues Ṭāhā (ibid., p. 56), this is tantamount to a vicious circle.
52 On the debate between advocates of political history (i.e. history as a narrative of individual and transient acts of rulers) and advocates of history of civilization (i.e. history as an account of what is collective, general and durable), Langlois and Seignobos would not, they say, take sides: both kinds of history, they affirm, are necessary. See their *Introduction to the study of history* (London 1912), pp. 237–238. But committed as they are to methodological individualism (i.e. a history of individual acts and motives), the two authors are, logically, biased in favour of political history.
53 See above, ch. VI, pp. 154–155.
54 Alfred and Maurice Croiset, *Histoire de la littérature grecque*, vol. I (Paris 1887), pp. II ff.
55 *Ṭāhā Ḥusayn, sa critique littéraire et ses sources françaises* (Tunis 1976), pp. 96 ff.
56 Nallino, *Tārikh*, pp. 68, 95.
57 Miftah Tahar, op. cit., p. 109.
58 See above, p. 154.
59 "I have", writes Ṭāhā Ḥusain, "hardly any doubt that what has remained of the authentic pre-Islamic literature is very little, does not represent or prove anything and is not reliable for extracting the true literary picture of this pre-Islamic era." *Fi'l-shi'r al-jāhilī* (Cairo 1926), p. 7.

60 See ibid., pp. 42 ff.
61 For Langlois and Seignobos' views on this type of criticism, see their op. cit., ch. VII. It may be noted that at this stage Ṭāhā no longer refers to the Islamic *al-jarḥ wa'l-ta'dīl.* It is also important to note that it was Nallino who opened for Ṭāhā the negative enquiry into the motives and reliability of Muslim transmitters of pre-Islamic poetry. See above, ch. III, p. 91.
62 The case for a Hellenist source has been made by Miftah Tahar, op. cit., pp. 87–88; Jābir 'Uṣfūr, *al-Marāyā al-mutajāwira. Dirāsa fī naqd Ṭāhā Ḥusain* (Cairo 1983), pp. 251 ff.; and Ahmed Etman, "al-Ādāb al-Ūrubbiyy al-qadīma (al-Adab al-Yūnānī wa'l adab al-Lātīnī)", in 'Abd al-Mun'im Tallīma (ed.), *Ṭāhā Ḥusain, mi'at 'āmm min al-nuhūḍ al-'Arabī, Fikr,* No. 14 (Cairo 1989), pp. 225–276, p. 251 and pp. 253–254.
63 Ṭāhā Ḥusain, *Fi'l-shi'r al-jāhilī* (Cairo 1926), pp. 24 ff.
64 Ibid., pp. 5 ff.
65 Ibid.
66 See above, pp. 173, 174 and 175.
67 Op. cit., p. 42 ff.
68 *JRAS,* 1925, pp. 417–449.
69 In a letter to Miftah Tahar (op. cit., pp. 150–151, p. 151), Ṭāhā Ḥusain affirmed that he had not read Margoliouth's study until a year after the publication of his own work.
70 See Margoliouth's notice on *Fi'l-adab al-jāhilī* (revised edn. of *Fi'l-shi'r al-jāhilī*) in *JRAS,* 1927, pp. 902–904, pp. 902–903.
71 Arranged chronologically, these works are as follows: *Ṣuḥuf mukhtāra min al-shi'r al-tamthīlī al-Yūnāni* ("Selected pages from Greek dramatic poetry") (Cairo 1919); *Ālihat al-Yūnān* (Cairo 1919); *Niẓām al-Athīniyyīn li- Arisṭuṭālīs* (Cairo 1921); *Qādat al-fikr* (Cairo 1925).
72 *Ālihat al-Yūnān,* p. 51.
73 Ibid., p. 52. For the corresponding distinction in Fustel de Coulanges, see his *The Ancient city* (Baltimore-London 1980), pp. 112, 113, 114.
74 Op. cit., p. 57.
75 Ibid., p. 87.
76 Ibid., p. 70.
77 Ibid.
78 Ibid.
79 Ibid., p. 5.
80 Ibid., pp. 5–6.
81 *Niẓām al-Athīniyyīn,* in *MK,* vol. VIII, 2nd edn. 1975, p. 306. Cf. Gustave Glotz, *Alexandre et l'Hellénisation du monde antique* (Paris 1938), pp. 243 ff.
82 Cf. Kamāl Qulta, *Ṭāhā Ḥusain wa-athar al-thaqāfa al-Faransiyya fī adabih* (Cairo 1973), pp. 103 ff.
83 *Qādat al-fikr,* in *MK,* vol. VIII, 2nd edn., 1975, pp. 189 ff.
84 Ibid., p. 266.
85 Ibid., p. 257.
86 Ibid., p. 258.
87 *Niẓām al-Athīniyyīn,* pp. 306, 319.
88 Ibid., p. 266.

89 Ibid., pp. 314 ff.
90 Op. cit., p. 207.
91 Ibid., p. 206.
92 "It seems to me," writes Ṭāhā, "that there are two distinctly different and bitterly antagonistic cultures on the earth. Both have existed since time immemorial, the one in Europe, the other in the Far East." Taha Hussein, *The Future of culture in Egypt,* tr. Sidney Glazer (Washington, D.C. 1954), p. 3.
93 Ibid., p. 3.
94 Ibid., p. 2.
95 Ibid., pp. 3–4.
96 Ibid., p. 10.
97 Ibid., p. 7.
98 Ibid., pp. 21–22.
99 Ibid., p. 21.
100 Ibid., p. 9.
101 Ibid., p. 18.
102 "It should be noted", writes Ṭāhā, "that the transition of religion from simplicity to complexity and from strength to weakness, is natural in all religions and in all creeds deriving from sentiment (*al-'āṭifa*) and affective life (*al-wijdān*). *Tajdīd dhikrā Abi'l-'Alā', MK,* vol. X, 1974, p. 78, n. 1.
103 "Fi'l-safīna", in *Min ba'īd,* in *MK,* vol. XII, 1974, pp. 13–20, pp. 16–17.
104 Cf. Cachia, *Taha Husayn, his place in the Egyptian literary renaissance* (London 1956), p. 80.
105 "Bayn al-'ilm wa'l-dīn" in *Min ba'īd, MK,* vol. XII, pp. 151–182, pp. 169 ff. First published as a series of articles in the monthly *al-Ḥadīth,* February-May 1927. See also idem, "al-'Ilm wa'l-dīn", *al-Siyāsa al-Usbū'iyya,* 17 July 1926, p. 5.
106 Ibid.
107 Ibid.
108 Ibid.
109 Ibid.
110 *Etude analytique et critique de la philosophie sociale d'Ibn-Khaldoun,* p. 100.
111 *Fi'l-shi'r al-jāhilī,* pp. 26.27. Cf. Taha Hussein, "Tendences religieuses dans la littérature égyptienne d'aujourd'hui", *Cahiers du Sud,* 1947, pp. 235–241, p. 238, where he lists some of the conclusions reached in the aforementioned work. In this work, he argues, he questioned certain beliefs which did not touch religion, although they were mentioned in the Qur'ān and the Prophet's traditions.
112 Jacques Berque, "Une affaire Dreyfus de la philologie arabe" in *Normes et valeurs dans l'islam contemporain,* ed. idem and Jean-Paul Charnay (Paris 1966), p. 274. For Durkheim's views on legends of origins, see his *The Elementary forms of religious life,* tr. Karen E. Fields. (New York 1995), 375 ff. It should be noted, however, that Ṭāhā's views on the above-mentioned story were not directly derived from Durkheim. They were derived most probably from Renan, who made similar statements in his "Maḥomet et les origines de

l'Islamisme", in *Oeuvres complètes*, ed. Henriette Psichary (Paris 1947–1961), vol. VII, pp. 168–220, p. 208.

113 I owe this point to Cachia, op. cit., p. 79.

114 *'Alā hāmish al-Sīra* II, in *MK*, vol. III, 1981, p. 212. As translated by Cachia (op. cit. p. 81), with one minor modification: I read "soul" where he reads "spirit".

115 Ibid., p. 81.

116 Ṭāhā Ḥusain, op. cit., p. 213 and 221.

117 Ibid., pp. 213–214.

118 "Tendences religieuses de la littérature Egyptienne d'aujourd'hui", p. 239.

119 The last in a long series of works which Ṭāhā Ḥusain devoted to Islamic subjects, starting from 1933, when he published *'Alā hāmish al-Sīra* I.

120 *Mir'āt al-Islām* in *MK*, Vol. VII, 1975, p. 344.

121 Ibid., p. 244.

122 On this aspect of the Qu'rānic miraculousness, see ibid., pp. 225–226 and 243–244.

123 Ibid., p. 272.

124 Ibid., pp. 246–247.

125 Ibid., p. 343. In this connection, Ṭāhā (ibid., pp. 336 ff.) addresses the familiar strictures to all endeavours, whether philosophical or exegetic, ancient or modern, which, putting too much confidence in reason, have aspired in vain to grasp God's essence and attributes. Surprisingly, even Abu'l-'Alā' comes in for criticism along the same lines. (see ibid., p. 354).

126 *Ma' al-Mutanabbī*, *MK*, vol. VI, 1981, pp. 380–381.

127 Ibid., p. 382. Cf. David Semah, *Four Egyptian literary critics* (Leiden 1974), p. 136.

128 "*Raj'at Abi'l-'Alā' li'l-Ustādh al-'Aqqād*" in *Fuṣūl fi'l-adab wa'l-naqd*, in *MK*, vol. V, 1973, pp. 357–362, p. 358. Article first published in *al-Thaqāfa*, 17 January 1937.

129 *Ma' Abi'l-'Alā' fī sijnih*, in *MK*, vol. X, 1974, p. 322.

130 See above, ch. VI, pp. 178–179.

131 See above, p. 169.

132 This can be seen even in *Ma' al-Mutanabbī*, where Ṭāhā describes in detail the political and social conditions surrounding the poet and his work.

133 See for instance Ṭāhā Ḥusain, "The Writer in the world today" in *The Artist in modern society; essays and statements collected by Unesco* (Paris 1954), pp. 69–81, p. 81. See also "Ma' udabā'inā al-mu'āṣirīn", in *Fuṣūl fi'l-adab wa'l-naqd*, in *MK*, vol. V, 1973, pp. 339–346, pp. 339 ff. Article first published in *al-Thaqāfa*, 3 January 1939. Cf. Jābir 'Uṣfūr, op. cit., p. 79, where he quotes from this article. But I disagree with him where he maintains (ibid.) that the mirror analogy is necessarily associated with social determinism.

134 Abu'l-'Alā' states the matter as follows: The astrologer and physician, both of them, / Deny the resurrection of the body. / "Oh, get ye gone! said I; if your belief / Be true, then I lose nothing; or if mine,

/ 'Tis upon you perdition falls, not me." As translated by R.A. Nicholson in his *Studies in Islamic poetry*, reprint (Cambridge 1969), p. 185. Notice that Ṭāhā was aware of a Abu'l-'Alā''s wager. See his *Tajdīd dhikrā Abi'l-'Alā'*, p. 300. He was also informed of the concordance between Pascal and Abu'l-'Alā' by Massignon. See the latter's *Muḥāḍarāt*, pp. 154–155. Notice again that Massignon cites the two authors in a discussion concerning the conflict between reason and revelation (or faith).

Conclusion

The story of Ṭāhā's life started with that primordial awareness of confinement and the correlate drive to break out of the barriers into the world. From that point onward, Ṭāhā's journey involved a number of "breakthroughs" – in the strict sense of the world.

It was at the Azhar, and under the influence of Muḥammad 'Abduh and Sayyid 'Alī al-Marṣafī, that he discovered literature and literary freedom. Thanks to that discovery he managed to break out of Azhari scholasticism and the Azhar altogether. With this step taken, the door was open for the reception of modern, secular forms of knowledge at the Egyptian university, the development of his positivist modernism and, finally, the formation of his humanism.

There are many lessons to be learnt from Ṭāhā's journey thus described. But let us confine ourselves to the main conclusions concerning Ṭāhā's attempt to synthesize his two cultures in modernist and humanist terms.

Aḥmad Luṭfī al-Sayyid had a crucial rule to play in the progress of Ṭāhā's thought along these lines. It was he who taught Ṭāhā that Egypt had an "eternal" identity underlying and reaching beyond its Arab and Islamic affiliations. It was again "the teacher of the generation" who taught the young Azhari rebel that modern science and the fruits of Western civilization could, or should, be received without inhibition and for their own sake. Initiating the young man into Greek philosophy (especially Aristotle's practical philosophy) and to positivism, Luṭfī was the first to suggest to Ṭāhā the idea of a balanced synthesis (*mizāj mu'tadil*) of the two cultures. Ṭāhā was not to realize this ideal to his own satisfaction until 1938, when he expounded his mature, Mediterranean – oriented humanism.

But Luṭfī's teachings lacked a historical framework and methodology. The "discovery of history" was made at the Egyptian University, thanks in the main to Ṭāhā's orientalist teachers.

Nallino taught him how to study Arabic literature historically, that is to say, with reference to social and environmental conditions. As these conditions were not organized into any system, Nallino taught Ṭāhā an open-ended form of objectivism, which was mildly positivist. But Nallino introduced Ṭāhā to yet another current of thought in the positivist tradition, namely "scientific" historical methodology and criticism – again in a mild and diffuse form. It was Massignon, as a critic of this tradition, who unwittingly initiated Ṭāhā into tough- minded positivism, including, systemic objectivism as well as historical methodology and radical criticism as codified by Langlois and Seignobos.

Arriving in France, at the source of positivist thought, Ṭāhā inaugurated a new phase in the history of his involvement with positivism. The doctrine as he found it at the time was at its twilight, having given birth to several social disciplines and in the process disintegrated mainly into two warring schools: the scientific historians who advocated an individualist, subjectivist methodology and Durkheimian sociologists who defended, no less relentlessly, methodological holism and objectivism. Characterized by the full discovery of positivist antinomies, the new phase also witnessed Ṭāhā's now conscious and more or less systematic attempt to heal or to patch up the rifts through a set of synthetic formulae or reconciliations.

The discovery of history was the biggest and most decisive breakthrough in Ṭāhā's intellectual life. One may say that the Ṭāhā we know was born at that point in time, 1911, when he started to introduce this discipline as a subject *sui generis.* It was then that he, the polemicist and pugnacious practitioner of verbal criticism, raised the question of method in literary criticism and history as such. While seeking the answer in the teachings of his European masters, he set out to rethink the whole in an orderly fashion and with an eye to the history of Arabic literature. It was through this enquiry that Ṭāhā outlined the programme of his future work, committing himself, in writing, to tough-minded positivism, with its main components, namely Taine's systemic objectivism and Seignobos' "scientific" history and radical historical criticism. This form of positivism, which by-passed both Nallino and Massignon, anticipated Ṭāhā's education in France and was to occupy him, in one way or another, for the rest of his life.

Ṭāhā's conciliatory efforts in turn were to continue for a long time. But here we may draw a further distinction, as his thought on the subject underwent yet another important change. Initially, that is to say during the period covering both his study years in France and the 1920s, Ṭāhā sought to attenuate his positivism by adding further elements which, however important, were assumed not to affect the hard core. Thus, in the literary sphere, Ṭāhā, following Lanson, admitted Sainte-Beuve's psychologism and Jules Lemaitre's impressionism, provided that they were subjected to certain limits. During the same period, Ṭāhā also assumed that Seignobos' scientific history and Durkheim's sociology were perfectly compatible and could be unified in a common, modernist front against Ibn Khaldūn.

Something similar can be said about Ṭāhā's solutions to the East-West antinomy and to the science-religion dispute in the 1920s. In both cases, the proposed solution involved only a nominal concession to the case of spirituality and faith (as opposed to Western rationalism and science). With regard to the antinomy in question, the world was said to have been united under the banner of Greek culture. As for the science – religion dispute, faith was said to have an affective and moral necessity: a proposition which implied that science had total mastery over the realm of facts.

In all these attempts at reconciliation, the synthesis aimed at was meant to preserve the integrity and supremacy of the positivist core. It is true that these attempts, which reflected the disintegration of positivism at its twilight, implied that the doctrine had lost its original purity, but they did not, as far as Ṭāhā was concerned, involve any major concession to the newly introduced elements or any drastic revision of the doctrine.

In the 1930s, however, Ṭāhā's search for synthetic formulae involved precisely such a revision and amounted in fact to the total collapse of his positivism. Thus in the literary sphere, Ṭāhā's unbridled impressionism exceeded the limits of Lanson's synthesis. It is true that he hastened to curb the overflow, arguing that he was certain that literary works reflected something or had an objective referent. But he did not know what sort of thing this referent was or else he identified it with disparate moments in the life of the author. From that point onward the subjective components gained the upper hand; occasional objectivist statements were only signs that his positivism was dying hard.

During the same period, Ṭāhā made real concessions to faith (in the science – religion dispute) and to the (Near) East (in the East-West dichotomy).

This account of Ṭāhā's development from 1911 onward is much more complex and, I hope, truer to the facts than other previous accounts. They all fail to do justice to Ṭāhā's long involvement with positivism, as they neglect his early development in Cairo and can hardly come to grips with the French period. This criticism applies even to Miftah Tahar, who studied the French influences on Ṭāhā Ḥusain, but did so in a purely analytical manner.

Further criticisms can be addressed to other scholars, such as Pierre Cachia, David Semah and Jābir 'Uṣfūr, who tried to account for the evolution of Ṭāhā's critical thought. The first two tend to think that this evolution proceeded, in a linear fashion, from an objectivist (scientific) phase to a subjectivist (impressionist) phase. In opposition to both of them, Jābir 'Uṣfūr offers a structural account based on an extensive analysis of Ṭāhā's central idea, namely that literary works were reflections or mirrors (of something external). According to this analysis, Ṭāhā used the metaphor in several senses, with literature reflecting at times objective (social) reality, while reflecting at other times the psychology of the author or the universal ideals of humanity. The problem, argues Jābir 'Uṣfūr, is that Ṭāhā, having failed to integrate these senses in a dialectical form of unity, left them in a state of juxtaposition[1]. And as this eclectic structure is recurrent throughout Ṭāhā's career as a critic, Jābir 'Uṣfūr is inclined to think that Ṭāhā's critical views underwent no (essential) change.

Both accounts of Ṭāhā's evolution are, I think, untenable because they simplify the facts in one way or another. The truth seems to be more complex than either, since it is a combination of both. There was indeed a pattern or structure to Ṭāhā's critical thought, but this structure itself so evolved as to let subjectivism have the upper hand. Given this, we can distinguish three main phases within Ṭāhā's development. During the first phase of Ṭāhā's commitment to positivism, the balance is definitely in favour of "scientific", objectivist criticism. At the time, Ṭāhā's thought becomes increasingly scientistic and stringent, moving as we have just seen, from open – ended objectivism to systemic objectivism. He, it is true, admits that the process of creation involves also psychological factors, but these are treated as an extension of objective conditions. It is also true that his writing (especially on Abu'l-'Alā'), involves a streak of subjectivism, but this early impressionism is embryonic, undeveloped and almost unconscious. It enters the scene as an after-thought and is expressed in purely lyrical terms without any theoretical underpinnings, save an implicit adherence to al-Marṣafī's idea of criticism as an exercise of taste. At this stage, there is no question of literary works reflecting moments in the author's life.

During a second period, stretching from 1917 to the late 1920s, the pattern above-mentioned recurs, except that it now assumes the form of a conscious, more balanced and more stable synthesis. Subjective factors, now admitted as an irreducible force in the act of creation, are assumed to coexist with objective ones, with each side counterbalancing and limiting the other. This is the period of Lanson's synthesis, by means of which Ṭāhā seeks to attenuate his tough-minded positivism (or systemic objectivism) without making any major concessions on matters of substance.

Finally, in 1936, Ṭāhā's critical thought enters a third phase in which subjectivism gains the upper hand. This is the time when Ṭāhā's impressionism breaks out of the Lansonian synthesis, reducing the objective referent to something I do – not – know – what – unless it is disparate moments in the author's life. During this period, which was to last till the end of Ṭāhā's life, he would from time to time make objectivist-like statements and even practice objectivist criticism, but these are outshone by other impressionist statements and practices. It appears that the impressionist outburst and expression of helplessness in 1936, were the signs of theoretical fatigue. From that point onward, Ṭāhā would not seek any synthesis: both objectivist and subjectivist forces are still at work, but no attempt is made to reconcile them. Hence, the idea of Ṭāhā's positivism dying hard.

Let it be admitted, therefore, that Ṭāhā's critical thought was always many-sided or eclectic. We must bear in mind, however, that this eclecticism assumed different forms.

First, in the early period, the accent was laid on objective factors, while the element of subjectivity was latent and given expression almost surreptitiously; then, in the middle period, some sort of balance, after the fashion of Lanosn, was found and maintained for a while; and, finally, a period of theoretical flux in which the balance was tipped in favour of subjective factors.

Far from being changeless, as Jābir 'Uṣfūr is inclined to think, the structure in question evolved according to the influences at work and Ṭāhā's own concerns. The early Tainean objectivism suited his youthful zeal for rigour and his drive to establish direct links with

France; the balance of the middle period, the only time when the conflicting forces were "juxtaposed", reflected the twilight of positivism and the consequent search for reform. The final stage, characterized by the theoretical flux and the predominance of subjectivism, corresponded to the influence of Jules Lemaitre and Seignobos. The eclectic structure cannot explain anything, as it stands itself in need of explanation: it can only be understood with reference to the development of Ṭāhā's commitment to positivism.

Having considered Ṭāhā's development with special reference to his critical thought, we may now try and evaluate his performance in general, as a modernist and a humanist. With regard to the former subject, we may begin by highlighting the positive aspects of Ṭāhā's thought. While he derived his premises and guiding principles from his teachers, he did so critically, where criticism means analysis, reconstruction and adaptation. For instance, he relied heavily on Nallino, but he did not receive the latter's teachings as a final body of doctrine. Instead, he set out, in an orderly fashion, to articulate and generalize the otherwise implicit or diffuse assumptions concerning matters of method. It was in this way that he sought to introduce the history of Arabic literature as a subject *sui generis*.

Through this endeavour, he secured for himself a prominent place in modern Arab thought as the advocate of a unique form of modernism, based on the appropriation of scientific methods and procedures. In this respect, he differed from such modernists as Shiblī Shumayyil and Salāma Mūsā, who simply promoted the cause of science and popularized scientific knowledge. Like them, he assumed that this knowledge had to be imported, but he laid the emphasis on possessing the necessary rules and procedures of research.

Limiting himself to the task of mastering imported methodologies, he was able to devote his energy to the actual study of Arabic literature. This he did with admirable virtuosity and on an unprecedented scale. His lack of interest in theoretical matters beyond the minimum required by this task and his indifference to theoretical purity enabled him to be dynamic and exuberant, multiplying experiments and forays in different directions. The resulting achievement is outstanding as far as Arab culture is concerned. Through the process of methodological appropriation and experimentation, Ṭāhā created the modern history of Arabic Literature as a discipline.[2] By the same token, he may be counted as the first Arab in modern times to have raised the question of method in history to the level of theoretical awareness.[3] In this connection, Ṭāhā's early "Ḥayāt al-ādāb", however half-baked, stands as a unique landmark, both in Ṭāhā's career and in modern Arab thought. As it sets out to do for literary history what Ibn Khaldūn had done for history as such, expounding the first principles of the discipline concerned in a series of prolegomena, "Ḥayāt al-ādāb" comes nearest to a historical discourse on method. This is not a mean accomplishment if we bear in mind that Ṭāhā's knowledge on the subject at the time was elementary and that he had no knowledge of Descartes. It is true that, as we shall see shortly, his task was tremendously facilitated by Ibn Khaldūn, but it is to Ṭāhā's credit that he was the first Arab in modern times to read the *Muqaddima* from a methodological point of view.[4]

His quest for what is fundamental and his drive for the sources of positivism are reminiscent of Fritz Ringer's definition of modernism as a self-conscious mastery of an intellectual tradition, involving a process of *clarification* or an *emergence toward clarity*.[5] Adapting the definition to Ṭāhā's case, we may say that Ṭāhā, instead of reproducing what he learnt about positivism, sought to master the doctrine as a methodological tool.

And yet for all its merits, Ṭāhā's modernism is bound to be theoretically disappointing, precisely because of its total dependence on imported methodologies, the validity of which is never questioned. Having decided that historical methodologies are to be sought mainly in French positivism, Ṭāhā's contribution to the subject is limited to reproducing, in succession, the alternative solutions offered by the doctrine (i.e. tough-minded objectivism, Lanson's synthesis and extreme subjectivism) and reliving its demise. When, in 1936, he reaches the end of the road, having found out that none of the tried solutions was satisfactory, he would not seize the opportunity to announce the collapse of his positivism and to highlight thereby the need for a new methodological departure. Apart from a perfunctory expression of theoretical fatigue, Ṭāhā went on to act as if nothing had happened. But it is only by dwelling on such moments of crisis and taking the full measure of the deadlock involved, that the human mind makes its great breakthroughs.

But the worst aspect of Ṭāhā's modernism is that it does less than full justice to the Arab culture which it seeks to revive. The assumption that scientific methodologies are a purely Western product goes hand in hand with the idea that the best that Arab culture can do is to provide imported methodologies with an object of study and a source of materials. Established as early as 1911, this unfair distribution of roles was later consolidated by other views, such as Ṭāhā's sweeping criticism of traditional Arab and Semitic historiographies. It is true that these views were attenuated, if not abandoned, in the 1930s at the time of Ṭāhā's final reconciliation of the East and the West. But even this more balanced view did not, I think, fully succeed in rectifying the damage.

The main, and most obvious, victim of Ṭāhā's modernism is Ibn Khaldūn, towards whom Ṭāhā maintained a systematically ambivalent attitude. Criticized in the early writings for having confined his attention to oral reports, the Arab historian is later (in the Paris thesis) excluded from among the founders and practitioners of scientific history and sociology. And yet there can be no doubt that Ibn Khaldūn played a fundamental role in the development of what Ṭāhā presented as the scientific or modern study of the history of Arabic literature. Take, for instance, the first move in this enterprise, namely the decision to give up explanation with reference to political chronology for explanation in terms of deeper social and environmental factors. Consider again the assumption that the prevailing "morals" occupy a prominent place among these factors, or the more general assumption that all of these factors are to be studied within a context or a framework constituted by a whole way of life, whether it is bedouin or sedentary. All these principles come from Ibn Khaldūn.

They came also from Nallino, but he was only a transmitter inasmuch as he taught Ṭāhā a history of Arabic literature constructed according to these same principles. At this point we need to make an important clarification concerning Nallino's sources. Some of these principles, for instance the need to reach beyond political chronology for deeper, social factors have their roots in the Western tradition. We have already shown how Nallino's history took sides in the long-standing European debate over history of civilization versus political history, opting for the former. We have also spoken of Nallino's history as a form of (mild) positivism. All this is true, but we must now add that some of these principles were of mixed origin, deriving from Western sources and also from Ibn Khaldūn, with the latter playing a supportive role, providing thereby the Italian orientalist with further confirmation of his European acquisitions.

There was, however, one particular principle which went into the making of Nallino's project and which could only have been derived from the Arab historian. By this I mean the assumption concerning the need to refer ultimately to the way of life of the people concerned, whether it is bedouin or sedentary. This assumption, which is characteristically Khaldūnian, constituted the backbone of Nallino's study of Arabic poets and Arabic amorous poetry (*ghazal*) according to their nomadic or urban background. This study could not have been conducted without Ibn Khaldūn's detailed analyses of Arab society, revolving as they did around the interplay of desert-dwelling and sedentariness, with all that goes with the two ways of life by way of environmental, economic, political, moral and intellectual conditions. Having chosen to study the history of Arabic literature as a history of Arab civilization, Nallino found in the *Maqaddima* the indispensable key to Arab society. To put the point in other terms, it was Ibn Khaldūn, rather than Durkheim or any other European source for that matter, who unlocked this society for Nallino and Ṭāhā for that matter.

Now Ibn Khaldūn was no literary historian, but some of the methodological principles he laid down for history informed in a substantial way the history of Arabic literature as initiated by Nallino and as introduced and generalized by Ṭāhā Ḥusain. Both can be criticized for their ambivalence towards the Arab historian, since they both failed to acknowledge their substantial debt to him. The ambivalence in Ṭāhā's case is all the more glaring in view of the fact that, by studying under Nallino and closely reading Ibn Khaldūn at the same time, he was in the best possible position to perceive the latter's contribution to the scientific study of Arabic literature.

Having failed to see this in his early writings, Ṭāhā missed in Paris yet another opportunity to rectify the injustice committed against Ibn Khaldūn. While multiplying the examples which went to show how the Arab historian anticipated modern thinkers in various spheres, Ṭāhā used all his ingenuity to demonstrate that Ibn Khaldūn was neither modern nor scientific where it mattered most, that is to say, in relation to history and sociology. Had it not been for his zeal as a modernist and as a positivist, some of these very examples could have led him to the opposite conclusion. Take, for instance, the correspondence he noted between Ibn Khaldūn and Cournot (1801–1877). According to him, the former had clearly remarked that the origin of all forms of government should be sought in the way of life of the people who constitute them. The latter, on the other hand, wrote that: "It is the way of life, whether it is nomadic or sedentary, rural or urban, which characterizes them (i.e. political institutions). The transition from one way of life to another is in fact the efficient cause of the mutations they undergo".[6]

Another, noted correspondence between the two thinkers concerns what they both take to be the law governing the rise and decline of all civilizations. In this connection, Cournot is reported to have written the following.[7]

"The most ancient philosophers noticed the law and set out to explain it. They told us how every institution becomes corrupted and perish, to be replaced by another, likewise fated to become corrupted and perishes. The inevitable excesses of absolute power make people want freedom; freedom is followed by licence, and the most unbearable excesses of licence make people seek their salvation in the sacrifice of their freedom. The aristocracy shrinks and becomes concentrated, until people forget the services rendered by the older generation and notice only the vices or the pride of its descendants: and then it perishes under the wrath of the populace or the oppression of a tyrant. Heroes found dynasties, and their successors, spoilt by flattery and worn out by the pleasures that stem from position and power, organize their decline and ruin. Peoples are no more exempt from *this fateful law* than their leaders: their courage and frugality give them victory, and the fruits of victory accustom them to luxury and sap their courage. The power that rose up when everybody's efforts needed to be united against a common enemy became, by its very success and the pride that stems therefrom, the common enemy against which all efforts join together. The ardour which a nation brought to possible enterprises is replaced by the lassitude and resignation to new conditions that tend to make the enterprises chimerical. Great empires arise, swallowing up the small states around them one after the other; and when this task of agglomeration has taken place, another process starts in the reverse direction: the drawbacks of centralization make themselves felt, the scourge of continually repeated small wars is followed by the scourge of proconsular harassment and oppressive taxation; patriotism and warlike spirit become debilitated; the leader's hand can no longer subdue hostilities from without or rebellions from within; and great masses break away, only to become fragmented in their turn, until division is pressed to its extreme point and another process of rebuilding begins".[8]

As justly noted by Ṭāhā Ḥusain, the close resemblances between the Arab historian and the French thinker are striking.[9] But he then fails to draw the right conclusions. It is obvious, first, that these resemblances could not have been a mere coincidence. All that has been said so far concerning the dependence of political institutions on the way of life (whether it is nomadic or sedentary, rural or urban); the law governing the rise and fall of states (centralization of power inevitably followed by disintegration) ; the corrosive effects of absolute power, excessive luxury and overtaxation; the ineluctable fate of frugal founding fathers being succeeded by spoilt, pleasure – seeking descendants; the disintegration of [tribal] solidarity and so forth – all this is pure Khaldūnian vintage. That Cournot attributes these views to "ancient philosophers" is sheer mystification which should not have passed unnoticed by Ṭāhā Ḥusain.

But what is more important than Cournot's plagiarism, for that is the proper word for it, is the fact, equally unnoticed by Ṭāhā Ḥusain, that the views in question are of fundamental necessity for Cournot's whole enterprise. He proposes to provide a philosophy of history, which, like that of Comte's, accounts for the progress of the human mind through the different forms of knowledge or sciences, but which endeavours to avoid the pitfalls of speculation. A philosophy of history, that is, which is *aetiological*, i.e. concerned with the causes and reasons of events, rather than *teleological*, i.e. concerned with the allegedly final ends of human progress.[10] In order to carry out his aetological enquiry, Cournot finds it necessary to identify, within historical reality, an essential order of facts, relating to the "nature of things" and subject to necessary laws – as distinct from what is fortuitous, accidental and superficial[11]. But this distinction turns out to be characteristically Khaldūnian, when expressed in concrete terms.

Following the Arab historian, Cournot equates what is accidental with the political order of things while equating what is essential with the sociological order. One is, therefore, reminded of Ibn Khaldūn's criticism of his predecessors who, according to him, had missed the "inner meaning" or "substance" of history, being content, in one way or another, with history as a superficial story devoid of understanding and explanation; as mere "information about political events, dynasties and occurrences of the remote past".[12] What Cournot understands by "the natures of things" is no other than Ibn Khaldūn's *waqāʾiʿ* (the facts) or *ṭabāʾiʿ* (natures) of *al-ʿumrān* (human association).

Surprisingly enough, Cournot puts forward these views within the framework of the first of eight "prolegomena", on his proposed philosophy of history or historical aetiology.[13]

Another conclusion which Ṭāhā Ḥusain should have drawn from his comparison between Ibn Khaldūn and Cournot is that the former's teachings, so incorporated in the latter's philosophy of history, are so close to what he regard as scientific, if only because they are so close to positivist sociology. It is on these grounds that Durkheim's follower Bouglé, who introduced Ṭāhā to Cournot,[14] was on the whole sympathetic to the latter's philosophy of history[15] and thought it fit to use Cournot's insights to support the Durkheimian side in the debate concerning political history versus history of civilization (or sociologically – based history).[16]

Durkheim himself would have shown the same sympathy for Cournot's ideas and, by implication, for Ibn Khaldūn's. He would have, in other words, approved the following theses of the Arab historian: (1) That historical reports must be verified according to whether they correspond, or fail to correspond, to reality ("the nature of things"). (2) That this reality is not political but sociological, constituting a distinct category of facts. (3) That sociological facts, having their own specific nature, are subject to necessary laws and are to be studied by a science *sui generis*.

By the logic of Durkheim's thought, Ibn Khaldūn's philosophy of history is scientific or signals the emergence of sociology as a science, inasmuch as it embodies the above-listed theses. "Science", writes Durkheim, "appears only when the mind, setting aside all practical concerns, approaches things with the sole end of representing them, when no longer hurried by the exigencies of life, it can take its time and surround itself with all possible precautions against all unreasonable suggestions. But this dissociation of theory from practice always assumes a relatively advanced mentality. For to arrive at the study of facts only with a view to knowing what they are, one must come to understand that they are of one definite sort and not another; that is to say, that they have a constant mode of existence, a nature from which necessary relationships are derived. In other words, one must have arrived at the notion of laws . . ."[17]

To sum up this discussion on Ibn Khaldūn, we may say that some of his fundamental ideas found their way, anonymously, into Nallino's history of Arabic literature and Cournot's aetiological philosophy of history, and in this latter guise found favour with Bouglé, because they agreed, in more than one way, with what was regarded as scientific and positivist. That Ṭāhā Ḥusain failed to see this was due to the fact that he was an arch-positivist with divided loyalties. Had he been whole-heartedly Durkheimian, like Bouglé, he would have seen the relevance of Ibn Khaldūn to modern scientific thought. But then he was also under the influence of Seignobos, for whom all philosophies of history and all theoretical generalizations smacked of metaphysical speculation. Instead of highlighting the positive aspects of Ibn Khaldūn's thought, Ṭāhā read the Arab historian selectively, with a view to picking out what was negative, according to each positivist master, considered separately. Being thus determined to seek methodologies only in the West and failing, consequently, to do justice to Ibn Khaldūn, Ṭāhā's modernism is inadequate as a means of reviving the theoretical potential of Arab culture.

As for Ṭāhā's humanism, it suffers from a similar drawback, which is not surprising in view of the fact that it is closely connected to his modernism. First, Ṭāhā's humanism is an extension of his modernism inasmuch as it adds to Western culture its classical (Graeco-Roman) dimension. Secondly, Ṭāhā's humanism, considered as an affirmation of the unity of the world and the universality of certain values, is an attempt to heal, or patch up, the rifts engendered by modernism between East and West. Thirdly, by thus emphasizing what is in common between the two, the attempt in question is meant to give some satisfaction to the side to be modernized and to promote the cause of modernization. Given these close relations, we can see that Ṭāhā's humanism fails, in its own way, to do justice to Arab culture.

This is particularly true of Ṭāhā's humanism of the early 1920s (the period 1919–1925), based as it was on a simplistic and one-sided view of the East-West relations. The unity of the world was assumed to have been imposed, sometimes through conquest, by a rationalist, freedom – loving Europe on an Orient dominated by religion and political tyranny. This latter part of the world, so the argument went, had no choice but to lay down its arms and accept, happily, this domination. Ṭāhā himself came to see the shortcomings of this point of view and tried to redress the balance in the late thirties.

His *Mustaqbal al-thaqāfā fī Miṣr* (1938) depicts the unity of the world in terms of a millenarian give-and-take across the Mediterranean between Europe on the one hand and Egypt together with Near Eastern civilizations on the other. It is to this later and more refined version of Ṭāhā's humanism that our comments will henceforth be addressed.

Ṭāhā is right when he highlights the fact that the relations linking Near Eastern countries with Europe have always been closer than those entertained with the Far East. He is also right when he, following Valéry, stresses the points in common between the two sides of the Mediterranean. It might even be argued that Egypt's Mediterranean and Near Eastern orientations will retain paramount importance in the future. While it would be true to say that Egypt can, or should, now explore new horizons eastward, establishing closer contacts with Asian countries like India, China and Japan, it would be no less true to say that Egypt's pre-occupation with Europe and the Near East should remain dominant, if only for historical and geopolitical reasons.

But having admitted all this, one need not go the whole way with Ṭāhā, glossing, as he does, over divergences and conflicts between the two sides of the Mediterranean. The admittedly perennial and close contacts with Europe have never obliterated all specific differences or antagonisms. Nor can the existence of these contacts, together with the important points in common, serve as a guarantee that harmony will prevail in the future. Sects within the same religious creed, political parties sharing the same ideology, schools of thought working for the same ends, are known for their ferocious feuds over fine points of detail or questions of emphasis. Fratricidal wars are sometimes the worst and most cruel forms of conflict.

The components which Ṭāhā finds that Western culture and Near Eastern cultures have in common create the illusion of harmony and unity, precisely because they are reached by a process of reductive analysis abstracting from historical conditions. Considered in context, these very components will be found to have been the subject of different, sometimes conflicting, interpretations.

By overstressing what is common and minimizing the differences between the two sides, Ṭāhā leaves in practice little room for the assertion of Egypt's identity. Although the affirmation of this "eternal" identity constitutes the first step in his (later) humanism, the subsequent steps, including the claim that Egypt has always been part of Europe, tend to nullify that affirmation. One gets the impression that the first step is taken mainly with a view to dissociating Egypt from her Arab-Islamic background, in order for it to be easily relocated in Europe.

It could be argued that this impression is false and that Ṭāhā's main concern is not so much to annex Egypt to the West, but simply to emphasize the need for Egypt to pursue such desirable goals as rationalism, democracy and even religious faith (reconciled with reason).[18] But even when the point has been so restated, we should always bear in mind that the pursuit of these common ideals need not rule out the possibility, or even the desirability, of disagreement and conflict. Without leaving such a margin for difference, one does not see how Egypt can assert its identity.

As a historian, Ṭāhā Ḥusain could not have been unaware of the long-standing and ever-renewed conflicts over dominance in the Mediterranean. Nor was he oblivious of the fact that Egypt needed to defend her own interests in the face of the West's continued ambitious designs in the area. But acknowledgement of these facts was not built into his humanist vision, being as it was too intellectual and too idealistic as to reflect the complexities of history and the entanglements of ideas with considerations of power. Thus, for instance, he loved France so much as to forget that it was not the modern extension, or incarnation, of ancient Greece. And although he was well-informed about the French imperialist wars under the Third Republic,[19] he assumed that French thought of that period could be completely dissociated from those manifestations of power.

His simplistic views were partly conditioned by the political circumstances in which *Mustaqbal al-thaqāfa fī Miṣr* was written. The signing of the Anglo-Egyptian treaty (1936) and the Montreux Convention (1937) signalled for the politically moderate Ṭāhā the beginning of a new era, in which Egypt could hope to be received in the community of independent, civilized nations.[20] He was not aware of the imminent dangers to which Egypt and the Near East were to be exposed as a result of other forms of foreign intervention and domination. It was only later, following the creation of the state of Israel in 1948 and the subsequent tripartite aggression against Egypt in 1956, that the picture grew clearer and uglier. At the moment, the idea of Mediterranean culture, now being revived by the stronger party, is receiving considerable backing in the West; but there is a feeling in the Arab world that it is only a sugar coating for the bitter pill.

The Arab attitude to Western culture should be now more realistic and more critical. While it is indispensable for Egypt and the Arab World to be receptive to Western science and culture, they should entertain no illusions about there being a basic harmony with Europe. All the issues involved in such a cultural dialogue will have to be fought out, bearing in mind that nothing could be taken on trust. Everything, including rationalism and scientific methodologies, should be open to debate as a matter of principle. Criteria concerning what is to count as rational or scientific have only relative stability and validity; Western rationalism and humanism are known to have their limitations and dark side. The Arab world will not be truly modernized until it has managed to partake in the production of knowledge and the necessary tools for its acquisition, mobilizing in the process all the relevant resources provided by its heritage and imposing its own character.

To this, Ṭāhā would reply by saying that the pursuit of such ambitions should be preceded by a period of apprenticeship, during which Egypt must be content with mastering Western methodologies. But this reasonable, gradualist approach, although unavoidable in practice, cannot be accepted as a long-term programme of modernization, let alone as a theory for the unity of the world. This is all the more true in view of the fact that the younger generations of Arab intellectuals, including those of them who are in favour of an intensified cultural dialogue with Europe, take a more critical stance towards the West and are aware that imported methodologies cannot be accepted at their face value or assembled in a purely eclectic fashion.

Notes

1 Hence the metaphor used in the title of Jābir 'Uṣfūr's work *al-Marāyā al-mutajāwira* ("Juxtaposed mirrors").

2 Nallino is certainly the forerunner, but it was Ṭāhā Ḥusain who, apart from articulating the methodological principles, extended the enquiry to all periods of Arab history.

3 In his book *The Writing of history in nineteenth-century Egypt. A Study in national transformation* (Cairo 1983), Jack A. Crabbs, Jr. traces the rise of Western – like historiography in authors like Muṣṭafā Kāmil (see p. 159). But none of these authors held a sustained discourse on matters of method.

4 Nineteenth-century Arab readers of *The Muqaddima* studied Ibn Khaldūn in a selective manner, for the practical lessons he could provide on the rise and fall of civilizations, moral questions and matters of reform. Cf. Fahmī Jad'ān, *Usus al-taqaddum 'ind mufakkirī al-Islām fi'l-'ālam al-'Arabī al-ḥadīth*, 2nd edn. (Beirut 1981), p. 93. See also Ahmed Abdesselem, *Ibn Khaldun et ses lecteurs* (Paris 1983), ch. III.

5 *Fields of Knowledge* (Cambridge 1992), p. 8. Italics in the original.

6 T. Hussein, *Etude analytique et critique de la philosophie sociale d'Ibn-Khaldoun* (Paris 1917), p. 160. For the quotation from Cournot, see his *Traité de l'enchaînement des idées fondamentales dans les sciences et dans l'histoire, Oeuvres complètes,* Vol. III, ed. Nelly Bruyère (Paris 1982), p. 407.

7 The quotation as given here is slightly longer than the version provided by Ṭāhā Ḥusain.

8 T. Hussein, op. cit., pp. 160–161. For the quotation, see Cournot, op. cit., pp. 480–481. Italics in the original.

9 T. Hussein, op. cit., p. 159.

10 A.A. Cournot, *Considérations sur la marche des idées et des événements dans les temps modernes, Oeuvres complètes,* vol. IV, ed. André Robinet (Paris 1973), p. 18.

11 Ibid., p. 13.

12 *The Muqaddima. An Introduction to history*, tr. Franz Rosenthal (London 1986),vol. I, p. 6.

13 Cournot, *Considerations . . .*, p. 10 ff.

14 Ṭāhā's quotations from Cournot are taken from Bouglé. See the latter's *Qu'est-ce que la sociologie* (Paris 1907), pp. 90–91 and 93.

15 Ibid., p. 82 ff.

16 Ibid., p. 57.

17 "Sociology in France in the nineteenth century", in Emile Durkheim, *On Morality and society*, ed. Robert N. Bellah (Chicago 1973), pp. 3–22, p. 5.

18 For a sympathetic and insightful reading of Ṭāhā Ḥusain's humanism along these lines, See Bahā' Ṭāhir," *Naḥnu wa'l Gharb fī adab Ṭāhā Ḥusain*", in *Abnā' Rifā'a* (Cairo 1993), pp. 86–149.

19 See his "Ṣar'ā al-ḥaḍāra" in *Fuṣūl fi'l-adab wa'l-naqd,* vol. V, pp. 534–551, p. 547.

20 Taha Hussein *The Future of culture in Egypt,* tr. Sidney Glazer (Washington, D.C. 1954), p. VII.

Bibliography

The following abbreviations are used for the very frequently cited works:

*EI*² = *Encyclopaedia of Islam*, new edn.
H = *al-Hidāya* (Cairo)
J = al-Jarīda (Cairo)
MK = *al-Majmū'a al-Kāmila li-mu'allafāt al-Ductūr Ṭāhā Ḥusain*, [*The Complete works of Dr Ṭāhā Ḥusain*], Beirut: Dār al-Kitāb al-Lubnānī.

Works by Ṭāhā Ḥusain

(A) In Arabic

(Most of Ṭāhā Ḥusain's works have been referred to as they appear in *MK*, which is far from complete as the title would suggest. The following listing systematically gives information on first editions in chronological order. Where the edition used is different, further information is given, wherever applicable, on the volume concerned in *MK*).

Ṭāhā Ḥusain, "Al-Naqd ḥaqīqatuh atharuh fi'l-umam shurūṭuh wa-maḍārr al-ghuluww fīh, *al-Bayān*, 1911 (precise date uncertain), pp. 377–383.
——, "Naqd ṣāḥib *al-Hilāl*" I, *H*, June-July 1911, pp. 447–462.
——, "Naqd ṣāḥib *al-Hilāl*" II, *H*, August-September 1911, pp. 601–623.
——, "Radd 'alā radd", ibid., pp. 632–639.
——, "Naqd ṣāḥib *al-Hilāl*" III, *H*, October-November 1911, pp. 812–830.
——, "Hal tastaridd al-lugha majdahā al-qadīm?", ibid., pp. 761–803.
——, "Ḥayāt al-ādāb" I, *J*, 15 January 1914
——, "Ḥayāt al-ādāb" II, *J*, 19 January 1914
——, "Ḥayāt al-ādāb" III, *J*, 21 January 1914
——, "Ḥayāt al-ādāb" IV, *J*, 26 January 1914
——, "Ḥayāt al-ādāb" V, *J*, 29 January 1914
——, "Ḥayāt al-ādāb" VII, *J*, 7 February 1914
——, "Ḥayāt al-ādāb" VIII, *J*, 28 February 1914*
——, "Shu'arā'unā wa'l-rithā'", *J*, 10 February 1914
——, *Dhikrā Abi'l-'Alā'* (Cairo 1915) 3rd edn. as *Tajdīd dhikrā Abi'l-'Alā'* (Cairo 1930); *MK*, vol. X, 1974.

* "Ḥayāt al-ādāb" VI never published

——, "Ḥayāt al-Khansā'" I, *al-Sufūr,* 12 Nov. 1915, pp. 2–3
——, "Ḥayāt al-Khansā'" II, *al-Sufūr,* 19 Nov. 1915, pp. 2–3
——, *Ālihat al-Yunān* ed. Muḥammad Ḥusain Jabra (Cairo 1919)
——, *Niẓām al-Athīniyyīn li-Arisṭuṭālīs*(Cairo 1921); *MK,* vol. VIII, 2nd edn. 1975.
——, "Al-Qudamā' wa'l-muḥdathūn; Abū Nuwās", *al-Siyāsa,* 23 January 1923; in *Ḥadīth al-Arbi'ā',* in *MK,* vol. II, 2nd edn., 1974, pp. 361–370.
——, "Al-Qudamā' wa'l-muḥdathūn", *al-Siyāsa,* 31 January 1923; in *Ḥadīth al-Arbi'ā',* in vol. II, *MK,* vol. II, 2nd edn., 1974, pp. 371–377.
——, *Qādat al-fikr* (Cairo 1925); *MK,* vol. VIII, 2nd edn. 1975.
——, *Ḥadīth al-Arbi'ā'* I (Cairo 1925).
——, *Ḥadīth al-Arbi'ā'* II (Cairo 1926).
——, *Ḥadīth al-Arbi'ā'* III (Cairo 1945).
All reprinted in *MK,* vol. II, 2nd edn. 1974.
——, *Fi'l-shi'r al-jāhilī* (Cairo 1926).
——, *Fi'l-adab al-jāhilī* (Cairo 1927); *MK,* vol. V, 1973.
——, "Paul Casanova", *al-Siyāsa al-Usbū'iyya,* 27 March 1926, pp. 9–10.
——, "Al-'ilm wa' l-dīn", *al-Siyāsa al-Usbū'iyya,* 17 July 1926
——, "Bayn al-'ilm wa'l-dīn", series of articles in *al-Ḥadīth,* February–May 1927; reprinted in *Min ba'īd,* in *MK,* vol. XII, 1974, pp. 151–182.
——, *Al-Ayyām* I (Cairo 1929).
——, *Al-Ayyām* II (Cairo 1940).
——, *Al -Ayyām* III (Beirut 1967).
All reprinted in *MK,* vol. I, 1980.
——, *'Alā hāmish al-Sīra* I (Cairo 1933).
——, *'Alā hāmish al-Sīra* II (Cairo 1937).
——, *'Alā hāmish al-Sīra* III (Cairo 1938).
All reprinted in *MK,* vol. III, 1981.
——, *Ḥāfiẓ wa Shawqī* (Cairo 1933); *MK,* vol. XII, 1974.
——, *Fi'l-ṣayf* (Cairo 1933); reprint (Beirut 1981).
——, "Muḥammad 'Abduh", *al-Wādī,* 11 July 1934.
——, "Al-Faylasūf Taine", *al-Jiḥād,* 1 March 1935, pp. 10–11.
——, *Min ba'īd* (Cairo 1935); *MK,* XII, 1974.
——, "Fi'l-safīna" in *Min ba'īd,* in *MK,* XII, pp. 13–20.
——, "Fi'l-ṭarīq" in ibid., pp. 107–115.
——, *Adīb* (Cairo 1935); in ibid.
——, *Ma' al-Mutanabbī,* 2 vols. (Cairo 1936); *MK,* vol. VI, 1981.
——, *Mustaqbal al-thaqāfa fī Miṣr* (Cairo 1938); *MK,* vol.IX, 1973.
——, *Ma' Abi'l-'Alā' fī sijnih* (Cairo 1939), *MK,* vol. X, 1974.
——, "Ma' udabā'inā al-mu'āṣirīn", *al-Thaqāfa,* 3 and 17 January 1939; in *Fuṣūl fi'l-adab wa'l-naqd,* in *MK,* vol.V, 1973, pp. 339–346.
——, "*Raj'at Abi'l-'Alā'* li'l-Ustādh 'Abbās Maḥmūd al-'Aqqād", *al-Thaqāfa,* 17 January 1939; in *Fuṣūl fi'l-adab wa'l-naqd,* in *MK,* vol. V, pp. 356–362.
——, "Ṣar'ā al-ḥaḍāra", series of three articles, *al-Thaqāfa,* 9, 16 July and 6 August 1940, respectively; in *Fuṣūl fi'l-adab wa'l-naqd,* in *MK,* vol. V, pp. 535–551.
——, "*Kitāb al-Siyāsa* li-Arisṭuṭālīs, tarjamat Aḥmad Luṭfī al-Sayyid", *al-Kātib al-Miṣrī,* December 1947; in *Kutub wa-mu'allifūn,* in *MK,* vol. XVI, 1981, pp. 334–340.

——, "Min mushkilāt adabinā al-ḥadīth", *al-Jumhūriyya,* 11 December 1953; in *Khiṣām wa-naqd, MK,* vol. XI, 1974, pp. 540–552.
——, "Al-Adab wa'l-ḥayāt", *al-Jumhūriyya,* 18 December 1953; in *Khiṣām wa-naqd,* in *MK,* vol. XI, pp. 553–563.
——, "Al-Adab wa'l-ḥayāt ayḍan", *al-Jumhūriyya,* 25 December 1953; in *Khiṣām wa-naqd,* in *MK,* vol. XI, 564–574.
——, "Al-Ḥayāt fī sabīl al-adab", in ibid., pp. 600–613.
——, "Yunānī fa-lā yuqrā'", *al-Jumhūriyya,* 5 March 1954; in *Khiṣām wa-naqd,* in *MK,* vol. XI, pp. 587–599.
——, *Khiṣām wa-naqd* (Beirut 1955); *MK,* vol. XI, 1974.
——, "Mir'āt al-gharība" in Ibid., pp. 535–539.
——, *Aḥādīth* (Beirut 1957); *MK,* vol. XII, 1974.
——, "Musṭafā 'Abd al-Rāziq kamā 'araftuh", preface to *Min Āthār Musṭafā 'Abd al-Rāziq, ed. 'Alī 'Abd al-Rāziq* (Cairo 1957); in *Kutub wa-mu'allifūn,* in *MK,* vol. XVI, 1981, pp. 43–51.
——, "Enno Littmann", *al-Majalla,* December 1958, pp. 11–14.
——, *Mir'āt al-Islām* (Cairo 1959); *MK,* Vol. VII, 1975.
——, "Fī dars al-adab wa-tārīkhih", *al-Adab,* April, 1959, pp. 12–14.
——, "Ustādhī wa-ṣadīqī Louis Massignon", in *Dhikrā: Louis Massignon* (Cairo 1963)- pp. 27–30.
——, "Al-Marḥūm al-Ustādh Aḥmad Luṭfī al-Sayyid", *Majallat Majma' al-Lugha al-'Arabiyya,* XVIII (1965), pp. 113–116.
——, *Kutub wa-mu'allifūn* (Beirut 1980); *MK,* vol. XVI, 1981.
——, *Adabunā al-ḥadīth mā lahū wa-mā 'alayh,* in ibid.

(B) In French

T. Hussein, *Etude analytique et critique de la philosophie sociale d'Ibn-Khaldoun* (Paris 1917).
——, "De l'emploi dans le Coran du pronom personnel de la troisième personne comme démonstratif. Mémoire présenté au XVIIe Congrès d'Orientalistes" (Paris 1928).
——, "La grande figure du Cheikh Mohammed Abdo", *Effort,* June 1934, pp. 3–5.
——, "La renaissance poétique de l'Irak au IIe siècle de l'Hégire, *Bulletin de l'Institut d'Egypte,* XXXIV (1941–1942), pp. 99–106.
——, "Tendances religieuses de la littérature Egyptienne d'aujourd'hui", *Cahiers du Sud,* 1947, pp. 235–241.
——, "L'écrivain dans la société moderne", in *L'artiste dans la société contemporaine; témoignages recueillis par l'Unesco* (Conférence internationale des artistes, Venise, 22–28 septembre 1952) (Paris: UNESCO 1954).
——, A letter to Miftah Tahar in his *Ṭāhā Ḥusayn, sa critique littéraire et ses sources françaises* (Tunis 1976), pp. 150–151.

(C) Translations, summaries and reports

Ṭāhā Ḥusain, *Falsafat Ibn Khaldūn al-ijtimā'iyya* (Arabic translation of *Etude analytique et critique de la philosophie sociale d'Ibn-Khaldoun*), tr.

Muḥammad 'Abd' Allah 'Inān (Cairo 1925); reprinted in *MK*, vol. VIII, 2nd edn., 1975.
Taha Hussein, *An Egyptian childhood* (translation of *al-Ayyām* I), tr. E.H. Paxton (London 1981). 1st edn. (London 1932).
Ṭāhā Ḥusain *The Stream of days* (translation of *al-Ayyām* II), tr. Hilary Wayment, 2nd edn. (London 1948). 1st edn. (London 1942).
——, *A Passage to France* (translation of *al-Ayyām* III), tr. Kenneth Cragg (Leiden 1976).
Taha Hussein, *Le livre des jours* (translation of *al-Ayyām* I and II), tr. Jean Lecerf and Gaston Wiet (Paris 1947).
——, *La traversée intérieure* (translation of *Al-Ayyam* III), tr. Guy Rocheblave (Paris 1992).
——, "The Writer in the world today" (translation of "L'ecrivain dans la société moderne"), in *The Artist in modern society; essays and statements collected by UNESCO* (International Conference of Artists, Venice, 22–28 September 1952) (Paris: UNESCO 1954).
——, *Au délà du Nil* (selections), ed. Jacques Berque (Paris 1977).
——, *Adib ou l'aventure occidentale*(translation of *Adib*), tr. Amina and Moënis Taha-Hussein (Paris 1988).
Taha Hussein *The Future of culture in Egypt* (translation of *Mustaqbal al-thaqāfa fī Miṣr*), tr. Sidney Glazer (Washington D.C. 1954).
——, *Min al-shāṭi' al-ākhar* (Arabic translation of a collection of writings, originally in French), ed. and tr. Abdelrashid Elsadik Mahmoudi (Beirut 1990).
Ṭāhā Ḥusein, "Una conferenza di Ṭāhā Husein su I. Guidi, C.A. Nallino, D. Santillana e altri orientalisti Italiani che insegnarono in Egitto", [summary of a lecture delivered in French, in Cairo, 19 February 1948], *Oriente Moderno*, XXVIII (1948), pp. 103–107.
——, "Visita a Rome di Taha Husein Bey" (report on a speech, delivered in French, in Rome, 15 May 1950, on "What is classical Arabic?"), in *Oriente Moderno*, XXX (1950), pp. 100–101.

Works on Ṭāhā Ḥusain and related subjects

Abdesselem, Ahmed, *Ibn Khaldun et ses lecteurs* (Paris 1983).
'Abduh, Muḥammad, *al-Islām dīn al-'ilm wa'l-madaniyya*, ed. 'Ātif al- 'Irāqī (Cairo 1987).
——, *Risālat al-tawḥīd* (Cairo: Dār al-Sha'b n.d.).
——, *The Theology of Unity* (English version of *Risālat al-tawḥīd*), tr. Isḥāq Mus'ad and Kenneth Cragg (London 1966).
Abu'l Anwār, Muḥammad, *al-Ḥiwār al-adabī ḥawl al-shi'r*, 2nd edn. (Cairo 1987).
Ahmed, Jamal Mohammed, *The Intellectual origins of Egyptian nationalism*, reprint (Oxford 1968).
Amīn, 'Uthmān, *Rā'id al-fikr al-Miṣrī al-Imām Muḥammad 'Abduh* (Cairo 1965)
Badawi,'Abdurrahman, (ed.), *Ilā Ṭāhā Ḥusain fī 'īd milādih al-sab'īn* (Cairo 1962).
——, *Mawsū'at al-mustashriqīn* (Beirut 1984).

Berque, Jacques, "Une affaire Dreyfus de la philologie arabe" in Jacques Berque and Jean Charnay (eds.) *Normes et valeurs dans l'Islam contemporain* (Paris 1966), pp. 266–285.

——, (ed.), *Au delà du Nil* (Paris 1977).

Besnard, Philippe (ed.), *The Sociological domain. The Durkheimians and the founding of French sociology* (Cambridge 1983).

——, "The Epistemological polemic: François Simiand", in ibid, pp. 248–261.

Bloch, Marc, *The Historian's craft* (Manchester 1992).

Bouglé, C., *Qu'est-ce que la sociologie* (Paris 1907).

Bourdé, Guy and Martin, Hervé, *Les écoles historiques* (Paris 1989).

Būḥasan, Aḥmad, *al-Khiṭāb al-naqdī 'ind Ṭāhā Ḥusain* (Beirut 1985).

Al-Bustānī, Sulaymān, *Ilyādhat Humirūs*, 2 vols. (Beirut n.d.).

Cachia, Pierre, *Taha Husayn, his place in the Egyptian literary renaissance* (London 1956).

Casanova, Paul, *Mohammad et la fin du monde* (Paris 1911).

——, *Mohammad et la fin du monde, Notes complémentaires* I (Paris 1913).

——, *Mohammad et la fin du monde, Notes complémentaires* II, (Paris 1924).

Cassirer, Ernst, *The Problem of knowledge. Philosophy, science and history since Hegel* (New Haven-London 1969).

Clark, T.N., *Prophets and patrons: The French university and the emergence of the social sciences* (Cambridge 1973).

Collingwood, R.G., *The Idea of history* (Oxford 1994).

Comte, Auguste, *Introduction to positive philosophy*, ed. Frederick Ferré (Indianapolis 1988).

——, *Physique sociale. Cours de philosophie positive, leçons 46 à 60*, ed. Jean-Paul Enthoven (Paris 1975).

Cournot, A.A., *Considérations sur la marche des idées et des événements dans les temps modernes, Oeuvre complètes*, vol. IV, ed. André Robinet (Paris 1973).

——, *Traité de l'enchaînement des idées fondamentales dans les sciences et dans l'histoire, Oeuvres complètes*, vol. III, ed. Nelly Bruyère (Paris 1982).

Crabbs, Jack Jr., *The Writing of history in nineteenth-century Egypt. A Study in national transformation* (Cairo 1983).

Croiset, Alfred and Maurice, *Histoire de la littérature grecque*, 5 vols. (Paris 1887–1899).

de Coulanges, Numa Denis Fustel, *The Ancient city*, with a forward by Arnaldo Momigliano and S.C. Humphreys (Baltimore-London 1991).

de Smedt, S.J., P. Ch. *Principes de la critique historique* (Liège-Paris 1883).

Delanoue, Gilbert, *Moralistes et politiques musulmans dans l'Egypte du XIXe siècle*, 2 vols. (Paris-Cairo 1982).

Delfau, Gerard and Roche, Anne, *Histoire/Littérature; Histoire et interprétation du fait littéraire* (Paris 1977).

Destrenau, C. and Moncelon, J., *Massignon* (Paris 1994).

Diderot, *Lettre sur les aveugles*, in *Oeuvres philosophiques*, ed. Paul Vernière (Paris 1964).

Diyāb, 'Abd al-Ḥayy, *al-Turāth al-naqdī qabl madrasat al-jīl al-jadīd* (Cairo 1968).

Durkheim, Emile, *On Morality and Society*, ed. Robert N. Bellah (Chicago 1973).

——, "Address to the Lycéens of Sens", in ibid, pp. 25–33.
——, "Sociology in France in the nineteenth century", in ibid, p. 3–22.
——, *Socialism and Saint-Simon,* tr. Charlotte Sattler, ed. Alvin Goulder (London 1959).
——, *The Division of labour in society,* with an introduction by Lewis Coser, tr. W.D. Halls, reprint (London 1993).
——, *The Elementary forms of religious life,* tr. Karen E. Fields (New York 1995).
——, *The Rules of sociological method and selected texts on sociology and its method,* ed. Steven Lukes, reprint (London 1990).
——, Review of Antonio Labriola's, "Essais sur la conception matérialiste de l'histoire" in ibid, pp. 167–174.
Al-Dusūqī, 'Abd al-'Azīz- *Taṭawwur al-naqd al-'Arabī al ḥadīth fi Miṣr* (Cairo 1977).
Ehrard, J. et Palmade, G., *L'Histoire* (Paris 1964).
Etman, Ahmed, "al-Ādāb al-Ūrubbiya al-qadīma (al-Adab al-Yūnānī wa'l adab al-Lātīnī), in 'Abd al-Mun'im Tallīma (ed.),*Ṭāhā Ḥusain, mi'at 'āmm min al-nuhūḍ al-'Arabī, Fikr,* No. 14 (Cairo 1989).
Fakkar, Rouchdi, *Aux origines des relations culturelles contemporaines entre la France et le monde arabe* (Paris 1973).
Al-Faqī, Muḥammad Kāmil, *al-Azhar wa-atharuh fi'l-nahḍa al-adabiyya al-ḥadītha* (Cairo 1965).
Al-Fārābī, *Kitāb al-Alfāẓ al-mustakhdama fi'l-manṭiq,* ed. Muhsin Mahdi (Beirut 1968).
——, *Kitāb al-Ḥurūf,* ed. Muhsin Mahdi (Beirut 1970).
Gabrieli, F., *EI^2* art. "Adab".
——, "Ṭāhā Ḥusain al-nāqid", in *Ṭāhā Ḥusain kamā ya'rifuh kuttāb 'aṣrih* (Cairo n.d.), pp. 163–180.
Gardet, L., *EI^2*, art. "Kasb".
Ghālī, Ibrāhīm Amīn, "Trois penseurs égyptiens", *La Nouvelle Revue du Caire,* vol. I (1975), pp. 219–239.
Al-Ghamrāwī , Muḥammad Aḥmad, *al-Naqd al-taḥlīlī li-kitāb Fi'l-adab al-jāhilī* (Beirut 1981).
Al-Ghazālī, *Iḥyā' 'ulūm al-dīn,* ed. Badawī Ṭabāna, 4 vols. (Cairo 1957).
Glotz, Gustave, *Alexandre et l'Hellénisation du monde antique* (Paris 1938).
Guidi, Ignazio, *Muḥaḍarāt fī adabiyyāt al-jughrāfiya wa'l-tārīkh wa'l-lughāt 'ind al-'Arab,* in *Majallat al-Jāmi'a al-Miṣriyya* (Cairo n.d.).
Haykal, Muḥammad Ḥusain, *Mudhakkirāt fī al-siyāsa al-Miṣriyya,* 3 vols. (Cairo 1990).
——, *Tarājim Miṣriyya wa-Gharbiyya* (Cairo 1980).
Herrick, Jane, *The Historical thought of Fustel de Coulanges* (Washington, D.C. 1954).
Al-Ḥimṣī, Qusṭākī, *Manhal al-wurrād fī 'ilm al-intiqād,* 3 vols. (Cairo 1907).
Hourani, Albert, *Arabic thought in the liberal age, 1798–1939* (Cambridge 1984).
——, *Islam in European thought,* reprint (Cambridge 1993).
Ibn Khaldūn, *The Muqaddima. An Introduction to history,* tr. Franz Rosenthal, 3 vols. (London 1986).
Ibrāhīm, Samiya Ḥasan, *al-Jāmi'a al-Ahliyya bayn al-nash'a wa'l-taṭawwur* (Cairo 1985).

Jad'ān, Fahmī, *Usus al-taqaddum 'ind mufakkirī al-Islām fi'l-'Ālam al-'Arabī al-ḥadith*, 2nd edn (Beirut 1981).
Al-Jamī'ī,'Abd al-Mun'im al-Dusūqī *al-Jāmi'a al-Miṣriyya wa'l-mujtama', 1908–1940* (Cairo 1983).
Jāwīsh, 'Abd al-'Azīz, *al-Islām dīn al-fiṭra wa'l-ḥurriyya* (Cairo 1983).
Jum'a, Muḥammad Luṭfī, *al-Shihāb al-rāṣid* (Cairo 1926).
Al-Jumaynī,'Umar Miqdād, "Malāmiḥ min al-ru'ya al-tārīkhiyya 'ind Ṭāhā Ḥusain", *al-Ḥayāt al-Thaqāfiyya*, No. 55, 1990, pp. 25–32.
Al-Jūndī, Anwar, "Ṣafaḥāt majhūla min ḥayāt Ṭāhā Ḥusain, 1908–1916", in *Ṭāhā Ḥusain kamā ya'rifuh kuttāb 'aṣrih* (Cairo n.d.), pp. 43–62.
——, *'Abd al-'Azīz Jāwīsh, min ruwwād al-tarbiya wa'l-ṣiḥāfa wa'l-ijtimā'* (Cairo 1965).
al-Kāshif, Muḥammad Ṣādiq, *Ṭāhā Ḥusain baṣīran* (Cairo 1986).
Al-Kayyālī, Sāmī, *Ma' Ṭāhā Ḥusain*, vol. I (Cairo 1952); vol. II (Cairo 1968).
Kilānī, Muḥammad Sayyid, *Ṭāhā Ḥusain al-shā'ir al-kātib* (Cairo 1963).
Langlois, Ch.V. and Seignobos, Ch., *Introduction to the study of history*, tr. G.G. Berry (London 1912).
Lanson, G., "La méthode de l'histoire littéraire", in idem, *Essais de méthode, de critique et d'histoire*, ed. Henri Peyre, Paris, 1965.
——, *Histoire de la littérature française* (Paris 1951).
——, *Méthodes de l'histoire littéraire & Hommes et livres* (Geneva 1979).
Louca, Anouar, "Taha Hussein et l'Occident", *Cultures*, II (1975), pp. 118–142.
——, "Taha Hussein ou la continuité de deux rives", *Qantara*, July-August 1992, dossier spécial.
Louca, Leïla, "Le discours autobiographique de Ṭāhā Ḥusayn selon la clôture du *Livre des Jours*", *Arabica*, vol. XXXIV (1992), pp. 346–357.
Lukes, Steven, *Emile Durkheim. His Life and work* (Harmondsworth 1975).
Lutfi al-Sayyid, Afaf, *Egypt and Cromer. A Study in Anglo-Egyptian relations* (London 1986).
Luṭfī al-Sayyid, Aḥmad, *Ta'ammulāt*, ed. Ismā'īl Maẓhar (Cairo 1946).
——, *Ṣafaḥāt maṭwiyya min tārīkh al-ḥaraka al-istiqlāliyya fī Miṣr*, ed. Ismā'īl Maẓhar (Cairo 1946).
——, "Mā li'l-siyāsa wa'l-'ilm" in ibid., pp. 170–172.
——, *Al-Muntakhabāt* I, ed. Ismā'īl Maẓhar (Cairo 1937).
——, *Al-Muntakhabāt* II, ed. Ismā'īl Maẓhar (Cairo 1945).
Mahmoudi, Abdelrashid, "Ṭāhā Ḥusain wa-Descartes", *Fuṣūl*, vol. III (July/August/September 1983), pp. 104–113.
Malti-Douglas, Fedwa, *Blindness and autobiography. Al-Ayyām of Ṭāhā Ḥusayn* (Princeton 1988).
Manḍūr, Muḥammad, *Fī 'l-mīzān al-jadīd* (Cairo 1977).
Margoliouth, D.S., "The Origins of Arabic poetry", *JRAS*, 1925, pp. 417–449.
——, Notice on *Fi'l-adab al-jāhilī*, *JRAS*, 1927, pp. 902–904.
Martin, Germain, 'L'Université Egyptienne', *Revue du Monde Musulman*, XIII (1911), pp. 1–19.
Massignon, Louis, "L'Histoire des doctrines philosophiques arabes à l'université du Caire", *La Revue du Monde Musulman*, XXI (1912), pp. 149–157.

——, "Rapport: Mission d'études sur le mouvement des idées, philosophiques dans le pays de langue arabe" (manuscript, 1913).
——, *La Passion de Hallāj, martyr mystique de l'Islam*, 4 vols. (Paris 1975). 1st edn. (Paris 1922).
Mubārak, Zakī, *al-Badā'i'* (Cairo 1935).
Muḥammad, Aḥmad al-Sāwī, "al-Duktūr Ṭāhā Ḥusain fī Baris", *al-Hilāl*, 1928, pp. 1181–1183.
Nallino, Carlo, *'Ilm al-falak, tārīkhuh 'ind al-'Arab fī'l-qurūn al-wusṭā* (Rome 1911).
——, *Tārikh al-ādāb al-'Acabiyya min al-jāhiliyya ḥatta 'aṣh Banī Umayya*, ed. Maria Nallino (Cairo 1970)
Nallino, Maria, "Taha Hussein e l'Italia" in *Taha Hussein, Omaggio degli arabisti Italiani a Taha Hussein in occassion del settantancinquesimo compleanno*, L'Instituto Universitario Orientale (Naples 1964), pp. 53–65.
Nicholson, Reynold Alleyne, *Studies in Islamic poetry*, reprint (Cambridge 1969).
Al-Qabbāni, 'Abd al-'Alīm, *Ṭāhā Ḥusain fī al-ḍuḥā min shabābih 1908–1913* (Cairo 1976)
Qulta, Kamāl, *Ṭāhā Ḥusain wa-athar al-thaqāfa al-Faransiyya fī adabih* (Cairo 1973).
Renan, Ernst, "Maḥomet et les origines de l'Islamisme", *Oeuvres complètes*, ed. Henriette Psichary (Paris 1947–1961), vol. VII, pp. 168–220.
——, *L'histoire du peuple d'Israel*, *Oeuvres complètes*, vol. VI.
——, *La vie de Jésus*, *Oeuvres complètes*, vol. IV.
Ringer, Fritz, *Fields of Knowledge. French academic culture in comparative perspective, 1890–1920* (Cambridge 1992).
Riḍā, Muḥammad Rashīd, *Tārīkh al-Ustādh al-Imām al-Shaykh Muḥammad 'Abduh*, 2 vols. (Cairo 1931).
Rizq, Yunān Labīb, *al-Aḥzāb al-siyāsiyya fī Miṣr* (Cairo 1984).
Robson, J., *EI*^{2} art. "al-Djarḥ wa'l-Ta'dīl".
Sa'fān, Kāmil, *Amīn al-Khūlī fī manāhij tajdīdih* (Cairo 1982).
Said, Edward W., "Islam, the philological vocation, and French culture: Renan and Massignon" in Malcolm H. Kerr (ed.), *Islamic studies: A tradition and its problems* (California 1980), pp. 53–72.
Al-Ṣa'īdī, 'Abd al-Muta'āl, *Tārikh al-iṣlāḥ fi'l-Azhar wa-ṣafaḥāt min al-jihād fi'l-iṣlāḥ* (Cairo n.d.).
Saint-Simon, Henri, *Selected writings on science, industry and social organization*, tr. and ed. Keith Taylor (London 1975).
Al-Sakkūt, Ḥamdī and Jones, Marsden, *A'lām al-adab al-mu'āṣir fī Miṣr*, I, *Ṭāhā Ḥusain*, 2nd edn. (Cairo-Beirut 1982).
Salama, Ibrahim, *L'Enseignement Islamique en Egypte* (Cairo 1939).
Santillana, David, *al-Madhāhib al-Yūnāniyya al-falsafiyya fi'l-'ālam al-Islāmī*, ed. Muḥammad Jalāl Sharaf (Beiruit 1981).
Schacht, J., *EI*^{2} art. "Muḥammad 'Abduh".
Al-Shāyib, Aḥmad, *Adab al-lugha al-'Arabiyya bi-Miṣr fī al-nisf al-awwal min al-qarn al-'ishrīn*, 2nd edn. (Cairo 1966).
Seignobos, Ch., *La méthode historique appliquée aux sciences sociales* (Paris 1901).
Semah, David, *Four Egyptian literary critics* (Leiden 1974).

Shumayyil, Shiblī, *Kitāb Falsafat al-nushū' wa'l-irtiqā'*, in *Majmu'at al-Ductūr Shiblī Shumayyil* (Cairo 1910), vol. I.
Tadié, Arlette, "Le troisième *Livre des Jours*", *La Nouvelle Revue du Caire*, vol. I (1975), pp. 49–58.
Ṭāhā Ḥusain, Suzanne, *Ma'ak*, tr. Badr al-Dīn 'Arawdakī (Cairo 1979).
——, "*Le Progrès* écoute : Suzanne Taha Hussein", *Le Progrès Egyptien*, 18 May 1980.
Tahar, Miftah, *Ṭāhā Ḥusain, sa critique littéraire et ses sources françaises* (Tunis 1976).
Ṭāhir, Bahā', *Abnā' Rifā'a* (Cairo 1993).
Al-Ṭahṭāwī, Rifā'a Rāfi', *Takhlīṣ al-ibrīz fī talkhīṣ Bārīz*, ed. Maḥmūd Fahmī Ḥijāzī, (Cairo 1974).
Taine, H.A., *History of English literature*, tr. H. Van Laun, 2 vols. (Edinburgh 1871).
——, *Philosophie de l'art* (Paris 1985).
Al-Ṭalkhāwī, Sayf al-Naṣr, *Shaykh udabā' Miṣr Sayyid Ibn 'Alī al-Marṣafī* (Cairo 1984).
Tharwat, 'Abd al-Khāliq, speech at the inauguration ceremony of the Egyptian University, *al-Muqtaṭaf*, vol. xxxiv (1909), pp. 138–140.
'Ulbī, Aḥmad, *Ṭāhā Ḥusain, rajul wa-fikr wa-'aṣr* (Beirut 1985).
——, *Ṭāhā Ḥusain, qiṣṣat mukāfiḥ 'anīd* (Beirut 1990).
'Uṣfūr, Jābir, *al-Marāyā al-mutajāwira. Dirāsa fī naqd Ṭāhā Ḥusain* (Cairo 1983).
Vatikiotis, P.J., *EI*[2] art. "Ḳawmiyya".
——, *The History of modern Egypt from Muhammad Ali to Mubarak* (London 1991).
Watt, W.M., *Islamic philosophy and theology* (Edinburgh 1979).
Weisz, George, "The republican ideology and the social sciences; the Durkheimians and the history of social economy at the Sorbonne" in Philippe Besnard (ed.), *The Sociological domain* . . . , pp. 90–119.
Wellek, René, *A History of modern criticism 1750–1950* (Cambridge 1983).
Wendell, Charles, *EI*[2] art. "Luṭfī al-Sayyid".
——, *The Evolution of the Egyptian national image from its origins to Aḥmad Luṭfī al-Sayyid* (Berkeley, Los Angeles, London 1972).
Wilson, Edmund, *To the Finland station. A Study in the writing and acting of history* (New York 1947).
Zakī, Aḥmad, speech at the inauguration ceremony of the Egyptian University, *al-Muqtaṭaf*, vol. xxxiv (1909), pp. 141–145.
Zaydān, Jurjī, *Tārīkh ādāb al-lugha al-'Arabiyya*, with a preface by Shawqī Ḍayf, 4 vols. (Cairo, n.d.).
——, "Radd 'alā intiqād", *H*, August-September 1911, pp. 624–631.

Index